MINORITIES, INC.

"A story of civic chicanery involving just about everybody"

REVEREND JUSSIE S. JACKSON II

ISBN 978-1-961227-35-4 (paperback)
ISBN 978-1-961227-36-1 (digital)

Rev. date: 07/20/2023

Rushmore Press LLC
1 800 460 9188
www.rushmorepress.com

Printed in the United States of America

For Chief Wilburn Chandler Hamilton
and probably
P.F. Kluge

TABLE OF CONTENTS

1

SCREW EVERYBODY'S CIVIL RIGHTS!

The year was 1978, and after being subjected to a bipolarized upbringing fostered by radically different Irish and Italian parental theatrics, which was occasionally enhanced by some rowdy Negro and Mexican neighbors in a dysfunctional Southern California town called Pacoima, Paddy Aloysius Puzo suffered from perpetual anxiety and had developed a philosophical sense of denial for nearly everybody's self-serving and ethnically-driven civil rights. In fact, the year before he had flatly refused to watch the very popular and very politically-correct televised mini-series called "Roots," which was about black slavery in the early American South and showcased the most diabolical living creatures on earth—-white people! When later asked about his rejection of "Roots," he said he considered it a mass media lecture on "How to Make All White People in America a Guilty Party to the Past, Present and Future Problems of All Black People in the Entire Universe."

At the time of his ongoing state of personal angst about his life in general, Puzo was an unmarried thirty year-old with a variety of nagging social issues. He was also living alone in a seedy, low-income apartment in crowded West Hollywood, and trying his best to pay off a student loan for a useless degree in sociology with a minor in Ladonia art appreciation. Furthermore, his latest career choices for the better paydays and better furniture were somehow getting sabotaged by America's Affirmative Action Programs that apparently favored people of all colors except white. Consequently, he ended up barely surviving by driving a taxicab six days a week and all night long in the least desirable parts of the mentally perverted City of Angels, Los Angeles.

And to further agitate his plight as just another white college graduate getting nowhere, Puzo's fellow white cabbies swore to him that "The Civil Rights Act of 1964" had some hidden payback language that mandated that black people should overnight become the masters of the universe and get all the best white peoples' jobs. As a result, the whites would now have to pick up all the garbage, clean restrooms and/or drive taxis all night long.

But Puzo really didn't have too much time to dwell on the continuing vagaries of this federally-inspired and race-reversed social pecking order, because he was mostly involved in a grueling, low-paying job that kept him occupied for a majority of his waking hours. Although at times, while being stuck in his cab waiting at a taxi stand in the cold early morning hours of December, he would idly escape into a delusional world of thinking he could write successful short stories about adventurous space travel. These rambling short stories were supposedly geared towards the completion of his "Great American Novel," which was about whites and near whites having more control over their own destinies while traveling to other planets without any damn affirmative action programs in the way. Moreover, in this early morning schizoid-induced delirium, he also dreamed about bigger sumbitch paydays for the movie rights.

In spite of his amateurish spurts of manic creativity, which were made even more incoherent by sporadic shots of tequila from a bottle hidden under his front seat, he couldn't stop fantasizing that his surreal sojourns throughout L.A.'s chaotic street life might somehow be similar to how Ernest Hemingway and Ray Bradbury got their own inspired creative starts, and how writing their successful adventure stories later led to their big sumbitch paydays. Hell yes! If only he could write half as well as that sumbitch Ernie…

Following his long nightly work shifts, he would ruefully calculate his meager fares, and after deducting for the non-paying psycho passengers, he would just sigh and inevitably toss his scribbled paragraphs about being a bullfighter on Mars in the nearest trash can. Well, he could always look forward to driving his old truck home where he could commiserate with his recently deceased goldfish still floating in its bowl and sleep the rest of the day.

Since he didn't like to spend too much of his free time being awake at home, which would make him more cognizant of the fact that he lived in a squalid, one hundred and seventy-five dollars a month, semi-furnished, shithole of an apartment, Puzo would occupy his seldom conscious time by mainly drinking beer and staring at old classic movies on his cheap television set. His preoccupation with older movies was a by-product of his aversion to the more modern-day movies, which mostly seemed to masturbate on contrived civil rights themes. This aversion was a result of the newer politically-correct movies that continually featured super smart and super powerful blacks always getting the upper hand against the super stupid weeny white guys. Apparently, this was Hollywood's patronizing way of making up to the black folks for "Gone With The Wind," "Citizen Kane," "The Ten Commandments," "Superman," and a whole bunch of other "too whitey" movies. For reasons he couldn't quite grasp or care to challenge, his zombie-like existence adequately filled in most of his time off, before he anxiously went back to work again and continued his battle to avoid the occupational hazards of the L.A. inner city's asocial and mentally-challenging racial dystopia.

All things being considered, Puzo's life in L.A. really sucked. His taxi pay sucked, his living arrangements sucked, and so did his Hemingway and Bradbury attempts at writing sumbitchin' and great-paying stories. Because unlike Ernie and Ray, he had yet to confront any real epic challenges in his alcoholic stumbling through a government-sponsored payback era brought to America by "The Civil Rights Act and Fuck the White People Law of 1964, as amended."

For what it was worth, and to avoid continually contending with his bad timing in this historical shitgeist of racial comeuppance, he just wanted to survive in the utopian vagueness of quixotic Southern California Dreaming and not go prematurely bald.

However, his spectator outlook on life abruptly changed late one night at a taxi stand at the Los Angeles International Airport, when a trio of large, dangerous-looking Negro males, with shaved heads and wide-eyed expressions, quickly climbed into Puzo's cab. They had just returned from a federally-sponsored Black Power Convention held at the luxurious Regency Hotel in Detroit, and they were mighty hungry and loudly demanding that Puzo take them as soon as mother-fucking possible to Melba's Rib Palace, located in extremely dangerous south central L.A.

The three black brothers were all dressed in sequin-lined black tuxedos, with multiple gold chains and medallions draped around their necks, and they all sported large silver and diamond inlaid buttons on their lapels that read: "Be Black or Be Dead!"

Apparently, the prior triumph of "Roots" on television had inspired a more elaborate marketing plan in the Black Power's federally- supported struggle to "Get Even With Whitey." So, hundreds of the poor black brothers and sisters had eagerly attended the radically expensive convention in Detroit, in order to unanimously accuse all the white folks in America of being too damned rich and too damned stingy to donate to the United Negro Gold Chain Fund.

Consequently, after the convention had convened, the participants left for their homes with an extremely militant and passionately pissed-off outlook on all forms of Caucasian life. And unfortunately for a late-night, sleepy-eyed and stupefied Puzo, who normally avoided rough looking customers at any cost, he currently had three of the federally-sponsored militant black brothers sitting in his cab.

Puzo had been in such a nocturnal stupor that he had failed to lock his cab's doors, which would prevent unwanted customers from jumping into his cab. The locked-door routine would allow him enough time to drive away from any guaranteed maniacs by faking that he had another call from his dispatcher. But he was now trapped with three maniacal and very demanding customers of "color," who most probably would lead him into the ghetto world of racial Armageddon, and with Puzo as the main focal point of this possible end of his chaotic life.

He pulled away from the curb and for the first few miles the three brothers were all staring at him quietly with glazed eyes during a taxi ride that was overwhelmingly tense, but seemingly uneventful, until the ominous silence began escalating into menacing mumbles and gestures from his militant occupants.

While traveling east on Century Boulevard one of the mumbling brothers, who was sitting in the front seat, took notice of Puzo's company identification card that was pinned to the sun visor of the cab. The brother then grunted "shiiit," and angrily yanked it off the visor and threw it to his friends in the back seat, shouting in the close proximity of Puzo's ear, "Dis white boy gotta real bad-ass cracker name of Paddy, like in honkie-ass rice paddy!" The brother then got closer to Puzo's face and looked at him with a menacing expression on his face. The brother was just drooling for a racial confrontation as he continued with his next outburst: "You figger you gonna be da next white savior or somethin'?!"

After being fully awakened from his late night stupor, and then trying to equate his first name with some sort of controversial race issue, Puzo nervously grinned and started to explain about the origin of his unique first name and his mother's Irish father. Suddenly, one of the brothers in the back seat angrily interrupted him by kicking the back of Puzo's seat, yelling, "I think this white boy's parents thought he be so bad-ass dat someday he gonna send all us niggas back to Africa. Ain't that right, paddy ass?!"

It was definitely becoming a very anti-social event for Puzo, and he ruefully looked out his opened window for some kind of help. He soon sensed a chilling heat nurturing in the nape of his neck that was quickly drifting throughout his entire body. To compound the nasty situation, he felt that he was also emanating a pungent scent of growing fear, which he swore was causing all the intense growling in the back seat of his cab. All things being considered, he sincerely wished that he'd been home that night in bed with the bubonic plague, instead of verbally sparring with a group of gigantic, glassy-eyed, and pissed-off black radicals, who probably wanted to make up for two hundred years of racial bondage in one frigging night!

The taxi ride continued to escalate into a chaotic scene of further grunts, growling taunts, and the National-Association-for-the-Advancement-of-Colored-People-approved physical assaults, in which Puzo fully agreed that he was individually responsible for all the brothers' problems, including the unusually low number of black brain surgeons and the severe lack of astronauts named Tayrone.

A short while later, Puzo's cab was hastily maneuvering through sporadic traffic on Century Boulevard, which had other black drivers staring at this white fool driving his cab in this risky part of a L.A. ethnic battleground. The taxi ride was soon approaching their final destination, and the brothers became cognizant of this fact and, subsequently, they began interjecting into their tirade the fact that they could smell the great food cooking at Melba's. The trio then informed Puzo, in menacing shouts, that he'd better not miss the place because they were in a big hurry for both an important meeting of the "National Black Brothers For Killing White Suckers Society" and, more importantly, for some of Melba's outstanding barbequed ribs.

After a few more caustic remarks criticizing his rattled driving skills, Puzo tightly gripped the steering wheel, as he waited for a break in the oncoming traffic so he could pull into Melba's parking lot. Suddenly his body shuddered with a quick and violent nerve-jolting spasm, as his mind snapped and bolted from a selective indifference to one's ethnic upbringing, to an emotional state of racial fear and self-protective prejudice. He now realized that this one lousy taxi ride, on a fairly pleasant December night in L.A., could be the grand impetus of his own personal entry into the wonderful world of "Minorities, Inc.," which was dutifully sanctioned by all the crazed sociologists and even more crazed politicians who were all hell-bent on making just about everybody equally miserable. It also seemed ironic to Puzo that America had recently declared a global war on hijacking and terrorism around the world, except that the jerk-off politicians forgot about hijacked cabs being terrorized in America's own shit-raising inner cities.

In addition to his ongoing and terrorizing situation within the close quarters of his cab, Puzo had also entered into the roughest part of deep south-central Los Angeles in the middle of the night, where it had already been scientifically proven that the fastest vehicle on four wheels ever recorded on Earth was an outbound, Rambler station wagon that was full of white people from Iowa, who had unwittingly ventured into the area one night while looking for Disneyland.

Seconds later, Puzo finally pulled into the parking lot of Melba's Rib Palace, which was the last place a white guy wanted to be after midnight. Soon the brothers' shouts and taunts disappeared into maniacal stares and an uncomfortable silence as Puzo slowed the cab and fidgeted with the meter. Cabdrivers always hated it when they were about to announce the fare to guaranteed anti-social customers, who didn't have the slightest inclination to pay. "But what the hell," Puzo mumbled to himself, "even Malcolm X might have paid a nice white cabbie like himself once in a while."

So, after he had parked his cab near an old black man who had passed out on the asphalt, he gamely turned around and announced: "That'll be ten dollars and---"

"What da hell you mean ten dollas, chalk dick!" one of the brothers abruptly cut him off. "Ten slaps onna side of yo mama-fuckin' head is wha yo gonna get!"

7

All three brothers then jumped out of the cab and began shouting obscenities at Puzo and his wealthy, white-owned, oppressive cab company, and the loud shouting quickly drew the attention of more oppressed brothers at Melba's, who immediately joined in on the fracas.

Soon there was a whole crowd of angry would-be brain surgeons and astronauts yelling and screaming and urinating on and into a dilapidated taxicab and its beleaguered driver. It looked like another Black Power Convention had suddenly reconvened in Melba's parking lot, with Puzo and his cab company being the main topic of discussion--a discussion that was turning real ugly real fast for a frazzled and frantic white cabbie.

While the crowd became more and more unruly, Puzo began rolling up all the windows and hastily locked all the doors of his cab. He then shouted in the cab's radio mike for his dispatcher to send help pronto to Melba's before he became a highlight for Black History Month.

But before he could finish his urgent message, a large metal pipe shattered the front passenger window of the cab and a humongous black hand reached in and tore the mike right out of his grasp, and then it tore the mike right out of the radio box attached under the dashboard. Unfortunately for Puzo, part of his lip was still hanging to the mike that went sailing across the parking lot, and he completely freaked out as the other windows in his cab became loud explosions of flying glass.

At the height of the flying glass chaos, he covered his bulging eyeballs with one hand and prayed with the other that the present hour of his existence could somehow be mercifully erased. For he quickly acknowledged that he was entering into an even more dysfunctional and deranged ethnic lifestyle than Pacoima---and it was much more dangerous---with little chance of his escaping all this chaotic racial upheaval. And all this for being innocently caught in the middle of a socially convulsive civil-rights phenomenon called, "We shall overcome!"

The next scene was right out of destruction derby, as a few of the brothers jumped into their vehicles and began ramming their old Buicks and Cadillacs into the hapless, white-owned cab, convincing Puzo to quickly swing his legs towards the passenger door and shimmy to the floor underneath the steering column for protection. Meanwhile, during all the ramming, banging, and fender pulverizing, Puzo swore he heard a black lady yell over Melba's loudspeaker: "Hey, suckers! Who ordered deez five pounds of ribs?!"

As an inevitable consequence to the continued ramming attack and explosions of glass and metal, Puzo was convinced that he was definitely headed for an early and painful departing from this world. So, he hastily grabbed a fifth of Jose Cuervo, which was kept under his driver's seat for long miserable nights, and he wisely decided it was now a very miserable night and it would be a much less painful demise with a load of tequila sloshing around his nervous system. He clumsily opened the bottle as fast as he could, while wincing again at another loud ramming, and gulped down half the bottle and shuddered violently. He then took another large Cuervo gulp and anxiously grabbed his crotch with one of his trembling hands and fervently wished that the frigging cab would soon blow up and take everybody out, including himself.

After another loud explosion of commotion outside his cab, Puzo heard the sound of a police siren approaching fast, and this was followed by the gradual subsiding of the ramming, banging, and thumping sounds. Within seconds, the Los Angeles County Sheriff's Department was on the scene and the noise dissipated into an unusually eerie silence.

Then several of the brothers' voices filled the air with loud accusations that the bigoted white cabdriver refused to take one of the brothers to visit his sick mother at the L.A. County Hospital.

Inside the cab, after he had groggily listened to the incredible accusations against him, Puzo struggled to raise himself from the floor of the vehicle to join the debate. But his trembling, tequila-saturated state of being was making it difficult to coordinate his bodily movements, and he could only grope for the front door handle of the pulverized door on the driver's side, while being wedged on his back beneath the cab's steering column.

In the meantime, a nerdy Caucasian county sheriff was simultaneously prying open the jammed driver's side front door with an official L.A. County crowbar. After succeeding in opening the door, the young white sheriff leaned inside and closely peered in at Puzo, who was slurring to himself and still trying to free himself from his wedged position on the floor. The sheriff winced at the pungent smells emanating from the cab, shook his head in disgust, and firmly asked: "Is it true that you discriminated against one of these gentlemen out here and refused to take him to the hospital to see his sick mother?"

Puzo looked up from under the steering column, craning his neck to get close to the face of the uniformed idiot who had just made the previous statement, and finally blurted out in a spray of tequila droplets, "Are you fucking serious?"

The sheriff lurched backwards and angrily wiped the Cuervo spit his face, while cocking his eyebrows up a couple of notches, and tersely replied, "Pardon me, sir?!" The sheriff began thumping the steering wheel with his crowbar.

Looking at the sheriff's distinctly colored light-brown sheriff's uniform, Puzo loudly belched and asked sarcastically, "Where in the hell is the L. A. Police Department when you need them?"

The sheriff flinched at the rebuke of the Sheriff's Department and blasted Puzo with: "It's not their jurisdiction, mister!" The sheriff was beginning to really boil and added: "And I suggest you remove yourself from your vehicle immediately!" He then put his right hand on his gun holster, and held up the crowbar in his left.

Puzo carefully stared at the young wimp of a sheriff and decided he was in no condition to exchange sarcastic pleasantries with a well-groomed seething officer of the law, who had a loaded gun, a large crowbar, and the local government's permission to shoot his smartass, if necessary. He further wished that the L.A.P.D. was there to take care of his little predicament, because the county sheriffs had a bad reputation for screwing up even the easiest of assignments, like turning a simple I.D. check into a full scale race riot.

After reluctantly accepting the young sheriff's orders, Puzo painfully struggled and successfully kicked open the passenger front door that had been slightly ajar. While fighting a growing case of nausea he then wriggled out on his back towards the opening and eventually got outside of his cab. He somehow staggered to his feet, and ended up leaning against the battered passenger side of his vehicle, swaying slowly back and forth.

The young sheriff walked around the front of the cab and approached Puzo with his hand still on his gun, holding the crowbar across his chest in some type of official county ninja position.

Puzo studied the sheriff with blurred caution and finally asked with a more advanced drunken slur, "Well, offisher, now what?" Puzo was also observing the angry mob of brothers being barely held back by the sheriff's older, heavy set and befuddled white partner.

The younger sheriff angrily got into Puzo's face and demanded: "I want some company identification!" The sheriff then backed away from another potential shower of unsavory spittle.

"It's in the back seat…floor…or somewhere, I think." Puzo answered back pointing over his shoulder towards his cab.

"Get it!" screamed the sheriff in a high-pitched voice, and the sheriff began crazily prying the back passenger door open with his crowbar.

The sheriff's high frequency scream and crowbar attacks on the cab's back door made Puzo sober up a bit, and he was soon in the back seat area of his cab, gingerly sifting through trash, piss, and several icky materials that were on the floor and under the front seats. The sheriff aided Puzo search with a flashlight, but it made Puzo even more nauseous seeing some of the crap he was handling in the improved light provided by the L.A. County Sheriff's Department.

After a simultaneous sour juice belch and puke shower on the back seat and floor, Puzo found his crumpled I.D. card that was stuck under a piece of ripped floor mat. Slowly, he backed out of the rear of the cab and triumphantly handed over his official piss-covered and puke-smeared I.D. card to the disgusted sheriff. Puzo abruptly fell backwards against the rear fender and landed on his butt.

The sheriff held the card by a corner and gingery removed the piece of gum remnant from the vomit-laced, piss-splattered I.D., and glanced at the card. He then looked down and shook his head at the drunken heap leaning against the right rear tire of the cab.

"Obviously, you're quite intoxicated and you shamefully vomited all over yourself and in your cab, Mister Puza, and I plan to take you downtown for booking at the county jail." The sheriff took out a plastic baggy and carefully placed Puzo's I.D. in it and stuck it in his pants pocket while sternly continuing: "My partner will contact your company so you won't have to worry about your cab."

Puzo took a deep breath and exhaled with an accompanying painful and acid-filled belch. He then looked up at the sheriff and spoke slowly and deliberately: "It's Puzo, Mister Sheriff What's Your Face, and whadda you mean that I don't have to worry about my stinking pissed-on fucking cab!"

Puzo suddenly banged the side of his cab with a closed fist and awkwardly got to his feet as he began raising his voice in a loud crescendo: "Do you wanna know, Mister Crowbar Sheriff? Do you really want to know what I think about this shitty company-owned fuckin' cab, and you, and your fat-ass partner, and all the rest of these oppressed sons-a-bitches?!"

He then clumsily started climbing up on the cab's trunk and towards the roof of his battered cab, while both sheriffs were barely holding back some of the more irate brothers who yanked off the sheriffs' hats and threw them at Puzo.

Puzo reached the top of the cab and continued yelling: "And do you really want to know where the sick mother really is?!" He began pointing and jabbing his finger towards the battered sheriffs, as he continued his rant: "Well, she's here, you weeny sheriff assholes! You're surrounded with a whole bunch of sick mother fuckers!"

Both sheriffs went berserk and angrily pulled out their guns, while the incensed brothers began pushing and frantically shouting at the sheriffs: "Shoot da honkie racist! Shoot da sucka right in his fuckin' white ass, you honkie pigs!"

The whole affair was now getting completely out of hand for the beleaguered sheriffs. So the older sheriff took out his nightstick and he joined the younger sheriff with the crowbar as they both began beating on the roof of the cab near Puzo's feet while barely holding back the black brothers, and finally the sheriffs pointed their guns at Puzo and ordering him to get down.

But Puzo kept ignoring the sheriffs' orders and began dancing on the top of his cab and singing loudly:

"We shall re-overcome someday, someday,

Yeah, yeah, yeah, that's what I say!"

Needless to say, right after Puzo's sarcastic mimicry of Martin Luther King and singer Ray Charles, there was an instant shower of empty beer bottles and half-eaten ribs thrown at him. The sheriffs frantically ordered Puzo to immediately get down and surrender, before he agitated Melba's patrons into a full-scale race riot, which was the last thing the sheriffs wanted with only twenty minutes left on their shift.

Having ducked most of the beer bottles and ribs, Puzo finally stopped his singing and dancing and looked down at the sheriffs, who were in a crouched position with their guns pointed directly at the crotch of his pants.

Mumbling to himself, Puzo gingerly rubbed his head that had earlier made direct contact with an empty bottle of Schlitz. He then smiled and defiantly thumbed his nose at everyone while bellowing out towards the night sky, "I wish this was the Lincoln Memorial, but who cares, because now it's whitey's turn to fuckin' protest!!

He then pulled down his zipper of his pants, reached in, and triumphantly pulled out his penis and began urinating all over the pulverized taxicab, with a few spurts aimed at the sheriffs and the brothers.

In an instantaneous show of frenzied racial shock to Puzo's desecration of a substitute Lincoln Memorial, the place quickly erupted into surrealistic civil rights pandemonium, with the sheriffs being lifted up into the air, a battered cab and Puzo being lifted up into the air and, seemingly, the whole damned parking lot being lifted up into the air!

Meanwhile, the old black man, who had earlier passed out near the cab, and who had somehow escaped unscathed during the entire minority melee, staggered to his feet, shouting: "Hey, Melba! Where's my mother-fuckin' five pounds of ribs?!"

2

TRUTH, JUSTICE, AND THE
L.A. COUNTY JAIL

The next morning, following his first real and involuntary confrontation with the socially-oppressed, which hadn't gone over very well, Puzo woke up in the L.A. County Jail in very extreme pain.

He was closely surrounded by the "Who's Who of the L.A. County Zoo," and he felt like he had challenged the entire defensive line of the Dallas Cowboys to a maiming contest and somehow lived. He ached all over and vaguely remembered that prior to his finally being shoved into a squad car by two half-naked, riot-ravaged sheriffs, several of the Black Power membership had wreaked havoc upon his entire torso for an extended period of time.

Fortunately, he wasn't feeling the true effects of the one-sided beating, since a gargantuan Jose Cuervo hangover had mercifully taken his mind off the misery that afflicted every square inch of his entire anatomy.

After eventually sitting up in a foul-smelling cot, he slowly shook his throbbing head and then realized that he had somehow managed to share his narrow cot with an old, baggy-eyed Mexican drunk, who was looking at him with a big toothless smile.

The old drunk had slept with his head at the opposite end of the cot, leaving his odorous feet and filthy socks in the vicinity of Puzo's head and nose that had twitched all night. The old drunk winked and said to Puzo in a pleasant Chicano accent: "Thanks, amigo, for the comb and watch you gave me last night. I'll pick them up when I check out today."

The drunk grinned again, and he fell back to sleep in a fit of raspy noises and snores.

Puzo pulled back the sleeve of his light jacket and looked at his wrist, and sure enough his Timex was missing. What the hell happened? He must have been strip searched with the old drunk the night before and wanting to seek jailhouse compassion he probably told the sheriffs to let his toothless friend keep his watch and comb. But why did he give the old Mexican his comb? The guy was completely bald!

Actually, he couldn't remember much of anything after his South Central singing debut, and he didn't want to wake up the old snoring Chicano next to him to find out. Jesus, what a bad night.

So, while he continued to sit on the crowded bunk with nothing to do but glance back and forth at the assortment of drunks in his cell, which included a few conventioneers who had too much to drink at the "Thirtieth Annual L.A. Ball Bearing Convention," he knew without a doubt that he was a changed man.

But had this change totally shaken him out of the fake California dream world that had offered a devoted follower like himself a mellow refuge from the harsh reality of the true world? And if so, could he ever float back to his mixed-up California Dreaming ever again?

He began to shiver and murmured under his sour breath, "Jesus, what a bad night."

He was released from custody late that same evening, following his arraignment in an afternoon session of the Superior Court of

Los Angeles, with the Honorable Eliza T. Washington presiding. Judge Washington was an elderly and overweight black woman, who seemed to be in constant pain. Great, Puzo thought to himself, he's being tried for civil rights violations in front of an irritated descendant of white-owned slaves.

The courtroom's atmosphere was very tense that morning, since everyone was subjected to the judge's normal terrible mood, which was being exacerbated by a delayed hemorrhoid operation.

During his particular arraignment, Puzo was ordered to appear in court two weeks later in front of the very same Judge Washington in a morning session. Puzo almost received a contempt of court order because of a sudden attack of post-tequila hiccups while standing in front of the agitated judge, and to make matters worse, the other courtroom participants had difficulty suppressing their laughter when the charges were read aloud against Case Number 66778.

The charges were for public drunkenness, resisting arrest, denial of a black citizen's civil rights and refusal to transport a distraught brother to visit his sick mother at the hospital—-which made the judge shake her head in disgust---, littering in a public place, inciting a riot, indecent exposure in public, and the indecent urination on a taxicab while refusing to surrender to two of L.A.'s finest sheriffs.

Puzo appeared numb to the charges, but suddenly raised his right fist in defiance and prematurely pleaded not guilty to all charges. The judge then yelled, "Say what?! And put your damn arm down, you're not Elridge Cleaver!"

The courtroom laughter made the judge even more upset, and she slammed her gavel for order so hard that the vibrations rattled her chair and her pulsating hemorrhoids. As a result, she immediately screamed in excruciating pain and scheduled Puzo's hearing date in a seething rage. She then refused Puzo's request for a public defender and set his bail for one million dollars!

But soon after the court clerk waved the judicial rules book at the now standing judge, who was periodically bending over in agony, the judge begrudgingly lowered the bail to what Puzo could barely afford, and he was eventually allowed to go home after making arrangements with a sleazy bail bondsman.

Truth, justice and the American way would continue to prevail in the City of Angels!

But Jesus, what a bad night.

In the following two weeks, Puzo's cab company had naturally fired him under intense NAACP pressure, and the company immediately sued him for the reimbursement of one completely totaled and pissed-on ex-taxicab.

Furthermore, to add insult to both his multiple injuries and his expanding California nightmare, the National Association for the Advancement of Colored People, in conjunction with the American Civil Liberties Union, filed a multi-million-dollar lawsuit against him for numerous civil rights violations, including the failure to provide a taxi ride for one of the brothers, who needed to visit his sick mother. Puzo was socially, judicially, and economically dead meat.

Without a doubt, this was the lowest period in his life to date. For he was now out of a job, didn't qualify for unemployment benefits because his cab company said he had quit, and he would probably get ninety years in the slammer and additionally owe the NAACP a few million dollars. All things being considered and reconsidered, he frankly needed an escape to some kind of benevolent, anti-civil rights, isolated outpost, where he could retreat into an agreeable and non-threatening setting of social anonymity.

As the days rolled by until his upcoming court date, his diversionary escape plans, and the actual fear of not being able to escape, had been the main topics of his troubled thoughts.

Later on, as he was lying on the couch of his dingy apartment on the evening before his big day in court, his mind wandered aimlessly for any elusive break from his present turmoil.

A recurring part of his diversionary escape plan was a possible scenario involving San Diego State University, because he fondly remembered his earlier carefree days of college life. Yeah, maybe some old college friends might help him get "anonymous" in the cozy confines of San Diego.

However, this reminiscing about his college days was seriously inhibiting his concentration on the more pressing matters at hand, such as his present judicial despair and his probable jumping off his apartment building. But no matter how hard he tried, he just couldn't shake the momentary lapse into the past days of lazy collegiate euphoria, filled with sunny days at the beach, sailing around with bikini clad chicks for coed gym credits, and continuous social jerking off in a totally legal acceptable manner. Puzo also remembered the joy of being a part of a genuine California party school, where a guy like him could stretch his higher academic pursuits until he turned forty or even fifty years old. He had never wanted to become a real-life employee, and he never wanted to actually leave college.

For the most part, he had spent his college days nurturing a superior suntan and honing the other necessary traits needed for being a long-term disciple of the real California Dreaming, free of any real world problems and a legitimate excuse to not embrace a more mature outlook on life.

Ahhh, those wonderful college days…in those days did he really care about wearing a suit and making more than a minimum wage? Not really.

However, he did recall that he also had a more sensible white roommate at San Diego State, who reminded him periodically to get his head out of his non-suntanned ass and grow up. The roommate's name was Ralph Brubaker, and he had grown up in a rough part of New York and had bugged Puzo about what he planned to do if he accidentally did graduate from college.

Puzo shuddered at that last memory and suddenly looked at the broken clock with only a minute hand that was hanging on his living room wall and whined in a muffled whisper: "Oh, Lord, why did I ever graduate from college?"

He eventually began nodding off into a fitful sleep on his musty couch just twelve hours before his court appearance, and he wasn't thinking too much of jail sentences, or even a possible public hanging at Melba's. He just started to dream of a time some years before, when he found out that he was actually going to graduate from college.

During his troubling sleep that caused an unnerving, real life dream, which seemed to recreate his previous life in the spring of 1976, in which he was yelling at his roommate Brubaker: "I don't believe it! I just checked my records over in the administration office to see if I had too many gym credits this semester, and some freshman clerk with a thousand pimples had the nerve to tell me I'm going to graduate this fucking June!"

Puzo started pounding on the bathroom door of an off-campus apartment to get the attention of his younger roommate Brubaker, who was casually reading an old Newsweek while sitting on the toilet. Brubaker was a good-natured, street-wise guy from Brooklyn, who cared about most people and what happened to all of his friends, even Puzo.

"Hey, can you hear me in there?!" shouted Puzo.

After getting no response from Brubaker, Puzo continued: "I'm serious! What the hell am I going to do?"

Puzo then heard the flush of the toilet and impatiently waited for Brubaker to exit.

The bathroom door finally opened and Brubaker walked out, saying, "Sorry, I don't like carrying on a conversation while I'm on the crapper, but do you really want to know what you should do?"

Puzo nodded, so Brubaker continued, "Well, you're almost twenty-eight years old and I think you should seriously think about your future. That's what I think you should do."

Puzo followed Brubaker into the kitchen and continued talking in a rapid, staccato fashion. "Do you realize that this is it for me? No more college life! No more part-time jobs at McDonald's! No more eyeballing the young cashiers! No more sailing seminars for possible graduate credits! And no more saying that I'm studying to become a doctor someday!"

Brubaker butted in after getting a beer from the refrigerator, "Say, what ever happened to your application to that medical school in Mexico?"

Puzo grabbed Brubaker's beer and chugged it all, blurting out: "You know I wasn't serious about that."

Puzo re-opened the refrigerator and got two more beers and gave one to Brubaker. Puzo then added, "And if I went to Mexico I would have to learn Mexicano, and you know I have a hard enough time with English. Besides, the damn school questioned my overall abundance of sailing and art credits." Puzo chugged his second bottle of beer and put his hands up in the air, "I give up. I'm sunk. I'm not cut out for the real world."

Brubaker chuckled, "You California pussies never grow up," he then continued, "What you really need is a year in my old neighborhood in New York to toughen you up. As for me, I'm getting married to Shirley after graduating in June, and then it's off to Washington for a secure well-paying government job."

After finishing his beer, Brubaker eventually asked a dazed Puzo, "By the way, have you got any potential jobs lined up that will actually pay in your post collegiate life?"

Puzo sighed, "Who in the hell's going to hire a white person who can sail a ten-foot boat and believes in the apparent genius of Picasso? Besides, I have to contend with all this new affirmative action minority hiring bullshit, too?"

"You got a valid point there." Brubaker let out a belch.

"Thanks for the confidence builder, and why aren't you worried about affirmative action, white boy?" asked Puzo.

Brubaker replied, smiling, "I have certain Democratic Party connections on my wife's side of the family that transcends race hiring quotas, and I accept your thanks for my confidence building expertise."

"I wasn't thanking you." Puzo cocked an eyebrow.

"Someday you'll wish you had." Brubaker then belched again…

Puzo was suddenly awakened from his college dream after rolling over and falling off the couch. It was sometime in the middle of the night and he rubbed his face with his hands and vaguely remembered the final screwy part of the dream where he swore Brubaker was a black person who kept saying to him, "Someday you'll wish you had thanked me for being black."

He tried to grasp the entire significance of the dream, but ended up passing out in a stress induced sleep, sprawled on his living room floor.

Later, he startled himself awake again, and he eyeballed the early morning light that was gradually filtering into his apartment through the tattered curtains hanging in the room.

What time was it? He then shuddered. He looked at his wrist, but regretfully remembered the previous donation of his watch to a skid row derelict named Jose, who probably traded it for a cheap bottle of booze somewhere.

Still in a daze, he slowly crawled into the kitchen and stared at a clock that was working, and it said six o' clock, three hours away from his date in court.

He finally got up and began boiling water for a cup of coffee, but remembered that he hated the taste of coffee. Hell, he didn't even keep any coffee in his apartment. So why would he want to make coffee if he hated it? Maybe he was starting to really crack up, and maybe it was time to really take a leap off the roof.

Or maybe it was just the pressure of going to court and knowing that he would be facing the same old, civil-rights-embracing and mean black judge, who would soon sentence him to ninety years in the federal pen for the premeditated bothering of a fine upstanding member of the NAACP in a public place.

Yeah. That was it. Plus, the added pressure that he was denied a public defender and he hadn't even retained an attorney for his defense, since the bastardly vultures wanted everything he owned, and would own, for the next ten or twenty years in order to defend him for his wretched crimes against society. He had earlier solicited a few quotations from the legal guardians of truth, justice, and the American way, but soon realized that truth and justice were sometimes just not frigging worth it. Furthermore, none of them promised a not guilty verdict, due to his alleged civil rights' crimes and the fact that he would be in front of the hemorrhoid afflicted Judge Washington.

Various options raced through his mind while he fixed himself breakfast, which consisted of some old oatmeal topped with strawberry jam and some prunes. He could go before the court and gamble on the unlikely mercy of a judge who was probably a secretly crazed Black Panther militant, and a judge who also knew it would be the best decision to throw the judicial book at him and, subsequently, get a nice story about the trial in Ebony Magazine.

Puzo then contemplated about joining the FBI's most wanted list for the Ten Top Fugitives of the Week, by skipping his bail and fleeing to a small Tahitian island to become an island bum and half-assed writer. At least in Tahiti he would be a minority type person, and since he did have a legitimate adventure in L.A. terrorism under his belt, he could possibly write some good Hemingway shit and totally freak out with the wacky French Polynesians.

But this island scenario reminded him of his trauma after graduating from college, where he had a recurring premonition that the only way to return to being a "California Dreaming" beach bum would be to end up stranded on some small, disenchanted, and hostile tropical island. Moreover, while stuck on this hot and muggy tiny island, he wouldn't be able to escape the day-to-day isolation while being closely surrounded by strange natives, who would remind him that his escape from civilization and intrusion into their solitary island confinement would have a certain outsider price to pay.

Just thinking of being stranded on some strange, mosquito-infested, cockroach and rat colonized, claustrophobic island made him gag on his oatmeal and prunes, and he suddenly cried out: "Hell, why blame me for all the minority mayhem!! I didn't book passage for the Africans to America, or take California from the Mexicans!

23

And I didn't steal any land from the Indians! It's just the goddamned frigging history of America, Incorporated!!"

Now he was angry, and he impulsively began to formulate a definite plan of escape. He would simply bail out of L.A. and seek refuge somewhere else. A place that wasn't so screwed up with all this civil rights cockamamie.

Hmmmn. Where could that be? He would never be that desperate for any small and questionable tropical island, and a big modern island like Honolulu was too expensive for his current financial portfolio.

San Diego! Right! It's big and sprawling and near the beach, and the only racial problems they ever had was when the Mexicans in Tijuana overcrowded themselves across the border and then the U.S. immigration officials promptly escorted them back after the Mexicans visited their illegal relatives for a fiesta or two.

Yeah. He could move back to San Diego, enroll in some training courses for the employment-challenged at San Diego State, and also take advantage of the student housing and job opportunities around campus. And after a year or so of getting squared away in the security of his college alma mater, he might take Brubaker's previous advice and leave California for a few years and try to improve his survival skills in a more challenging place in the world.

Why, he might even try living in Mexico. The Mexicans weren't that bad, and he could maybe marry a pretty senorita with a bunch of land and a wealthy family. Yeah. He might become a rich landowner in Mexico and invite his old friend Brubaker down for a big fiesta. After college they had lost touch, but he still wanted to contact his friend someday and show him that he did make it out of college and survived.

Yeah!

The preparation for his impulsive retreat from L.A. didn't take very long. He immediately got up from the kitchen table and headed straight for his '64 Ford pickup, which he discreetly drove to the back of his apartment building before his landlord woke up. Then he quietly loaded the pickup with his clothes, assorted dishes, silverware, some old pots and pans, his toiletries and linen, a small radio, an old TV, some magazines and paperback books, an empty fishbowl that had its only occupant recently buried at sea in the toilet bowl and, finally, his college diploma that was glued to a piece of cardboard.

Following a last look around his apartment, he simply vanished from L.A. on an unusually cold and dreary day in December, only two days before Christmas. He didn't even call anyone, hoping that his parents and his few friends would understand, and he was soon headed south on the San Diego Freeway.

During the first few miles he was trying not to think, and nervously touched the only cash he had in his pocket that was his overdue rent money that he had kept. He figured that by sneaking out of his apartment and not paying his rent, and also skipping his bail, that he was a real outlaw now, even more despicable than the horrid character in Criminal Case No. 66778.

For all intense purposes, he was temporarily leaving the so-called civilized world and keeping his pilfered rent money and joining the sleazier side of criminal society.

Oh, what the hell, it was only temporary…he hoped.

3

REFUGE IN SAN DIEGO, SORT OF

It was the middle of June, and after spending nearly six months in a crowded, student-subsidized, off-campus apartment with two certifiably-insane college sophomores, Puzo had enough of his nostalgic slip back into the vacuous days of San Diego State collegiate life.

He was attending classes in a special studies program for the employment-challenged, and his classes had been filled with near brain-dead drug addicts and socio-economic slackers like himself.

At times, he wished he would have taken his chances in Los Angeles, with a likely jail sentence for the criminally perverted, rather than spend countless hours in class with asocial zombies. He was also tired of living with a pair of genuine pinball brains, who were still active members of the Mickey Mouse Club.

As a consequence, he was getting restless again for a new "escape" scenario elsewhere. There was also another reason for making Puzo restless for another change of landscape. It was the "Viva Mexico" effect caused by his newly-acquired second job that he had secured through the student placement center. His first job at the student bookstore was only part-time and paying him squat, and he needed another full-time job to better his survival stake. This second job threw him head first into the many challenges of being an all-night gas station attendant in a semi-rough part of southern San Diego, near the border with Mexico.

Puzo realized that the night job would be robbing him of sleep, and he knew that he had to stay alert for potential trouble in the barrio, but it wasn't that bad of a job pumping gas, and most of the Mexicans in the area seemed to be pretty pleasant, although Puzo also realized that he was a gringo whose ancestors probably stole California from them. He was also learning some interesting bits of Chicano culture during his swing and graveyard shifts, like how young, smiling beautiful Mexican women can make you dream of chasing them and living barefoot in Baja. Puzo seemed more content while thinking about exotic Mexico. Yes, it could be just the right place for him.

In late June, in order to alleviate the current chaos in his living arrangements, Puzo decided to move to another apartment, since he could afford a slightly better housing arrangement.

He had found a new place to stay, which would be partly subsidized by the college, in a 'Roommate Wanted' ad in the local newspaper, and his new roommate turned out to be a fairly decent guy who was recently divorced.

His name was Manny Schmidt, and he was another odd ethnic mixture of Mexican and German roots, which made Schmidt somewhat compatible for Puzo and his unique blend of an Italian and Irish ethnic background. Besides, this living arrangement with Schmidt could give Puzo some much needed inside information about Mexicans and how they lived, which would be used later for his brewing Mexican escape plan. But unfortunately, like himself, Schmidt wasn't that much of an expert on individual ethnic cultures either.

The new apartment arrangement, which was near the gas station where Puzo worked, did initially improve his disposition, and the anecdotes about his and Schmidt's radically different upbringings often made them both laugh at society in general.

However, with the costlier living expenses and his longer travel to attend his dreaded but necessary summer courses both taking bites out of his wallet, Puzo knew he urgently needed to make enough money for both his higher living expenses and for his important travel stake to escape to Mexico before he permanently cracked up.

This strong need for money created a chaotic schedule of grunting through morning classes, stocking shelves in the student bookstore in the afternoons and, finally, pumping gas and volunteering for extra hours at the all-night filling station in National City that was adjacent to the U.S. and Mexican border.

The most challenging activity for Puzo was the gas station job, which was robbing him of many hours of needed sleep. The schedule was very stressful but economically necessary, and he had symbolically hung his college diploma on the lube room wall to remind him of the reverse rewards of affirmative action. But, what the hell, he felt he was getting nearer to the fruition of his next escape plan.

Several weeks of this hectic schedule made his new roommate begin to worry about him, because Puzo appeared to be in a perpetual daze and some people figured he must be on drugs. It was terminal numbness for Puzo, and Schmidt finally asked him one early September morning, after Puzo finished his night shift, when he was going to quit at least one job for the sake of his emasculated health. Puzo answered Schmidt with, "What's emasculated mean?"

"It means to weaken or castrate," Schmidt replied.

"Well, on top of everything else--since I haven't had any time to date--I might as well be castrated." Puzo feebly laughed.

Schmidt added: "You want to know something else, because of your serious lack of dating, some of our neighbors want to know if you're queer on me or something?"

Puzo seemed bemused. "Well, tell them I like you, but I wouldn't marry a Mexican with a hairy white ass." He drank some orange juice from the refrigerator and then headed for bed.

"Yeah, I'll tell them." Schmidt called out as he followed Puzo to his bedroom door, then adding, "But seriously, I'm planning on moving to Arizona early next year to be close to my new girlfriend, so will you have enough money to take care of yourself by then?"

Puzo turned around and replied: "Soon after the Christmas holidays I should have enough money to head for Mexico. So I do hope you stay until then."

"No problem, amigo." Schmidt grinned.

Puzo smiled back. "You know, Manny, you half-Mexicans aren't that bad, and my luck should definitely change in friendly Mexico."

"Don't kid yourself. Those full-blooded Mexicans can be just as nasty as anyone else, especially when dealing with gringos who stole California from them."

"I didn't steal it." Puzo flopped on his bed and sighed.

"I know, Paddy. But sometimes we so-called white guys get blamed for everything just because we're white and it's politically convenient to pick on our albino asses." Schmidt turned and began to leave for his job selling used cars.

"I think I know what you mean." Puzo mumbled to himself. He then rolled over and tried to fall asleep. But it had taken two of his three hours of sleep time to fully fall asleep, because he was restlessly thinking about Mexico and what his roommate had just said.

It was now nearing the end of the year and Puzo was still pumping gas, but he was on break from school and getting more sleep. His biggest worry was hoping that nothing drastic would happen to disturb his final days in San Diego. Despite his concerns, everything seemed to be moving right along in a proper, southerly direction towards beautiful Baja.

One morning, just a few days before Christmas, he was writing holiday greeting cards to his folks and some friends. He figured that after heading for Mexico he might not be writing for some time, and he wanted to ensure his folks and few friends that he was basically okay. However, he purposely omitted the return address on his cards because he still didn't want his whereabouts known.

More and more he was beginning to finally forget about his previous trouble with the law in Los Angeles, but he still maintained a percolating paranoia about clandestine people who investigated mail and sent the law knocking on your door. His previously casual views on the growing era of "Big Brother" had been permanently changed by the recent events in his life and, furthermore, the infiltration of modem racial problems, which had finally reached the mellow shores of California, continued to seriously disturb his semi-sun-tanned persona.

As he finally sealed the last Christmas card to his folks, Schmidt walked in with the morning mail and newspaper. He handed Puzo a letter and said, "Here, Paddy, it looks like an important letter for you."

"Thanks." Puzo answered, and then he anxiously read the return address and let out a gasp. "Son of a ball-sucking bitch! They've got me!"

"What's the problem?" Schmidt asked as he sat down at the kitchen table.

Puzo yelled: "Did you see the return address?!"

Schmidt flinched at Puzo's outburst and replied: "I only noticed something about the F.B.I. office."

Puzo yelled again: "Yeah! And it's all the way from Washington, D.C.!"

"The feds after you?" Schmidt became more concerned about the letter.

"I fucking don't know." Puzo began biting his lower lip. "I had a little problem with the law in L.A. and I skipped bail and a court date..." He stopped talking and quickly ripped the envelope open and saw the FBI letterhead, and then he howled with laughter. "I'll kill that Brubaker when I see him!" He continued to read the letter.

"Now what?" Schmidt now seemed perplexed by his roommate's antics.

Puzo began speaking in a high-pitched fast manner: "My old college roommate, who now lives in Washington D.C. with a good federal job, just played a dirty dick trick on me." Puzo shook his head and continued: "He found out about the little escapade I had with the L.A. law through a mutual friend, so he decided to track down my address through a buddy at the Social Security office in Washington." Puzo continued after catching his breath, "He then borrowed official stationery from another guy at the F.B.I. office in D.C. and decided to screw with me." Puzo then laughed again and continued to read the rest of the letter to himself.

"Well, it looks like he screwed with you pretty good," Schmidt remarked.

"You bet your ass he did. And he says he's planning to come to San Diego for the Christmas holidays to visit his in-laws." Puzo returned to the letter and continued, "He wants to meet me at noon at the Hotel Del Coronado on New Year's Day for the Rose Bowl."

Puzo then looked at Schmidt. "We used to watch the football games in the bar there during our college days, and now he wants to have a little reunion."

"Sounds like a good friend." Schmidt finished reading the morning newspaper.

"You're right again, Manny. But I'm going to kill him for almost making me crap in my pants."

Schmidt began laughing at Puzo. "Hey, I'll see you later." He then put down the newspaper and got up to leave for work.

"Sure," Puzo grinned. "I'm just going to read this rotten letter one more time."

Puzo quietly read Brubaker's letter and eventually fell asleep with his head resting on the kitchen table, dreaming about Mexico and twitching about oddly working on Brubaker's Mexican ranch.

4

SAN DIEGO SURELY WASN'T THE ANSWER

Puzo was working overtime for extra money and it was the second straight holiday season that wasn't very merry for him. But at least New Year's Day promised to cheer him up with a visit from his old friend, and the timing was good, because it would be right before his departure to Mexico.

On New Year's Eve Puzo worked all night at the gas station in National City and contently watched his drunken customers set a new record for the number of times they ran into the gas pumps and trash cans in a single night.

He never saw so many drunks roaring around the streets and ricocheting off each other in alcoholic stupors. All night long National City was inundated with Mexicans celebrating with fireworks and gunshots, and the fortunate thing for most of the Mexicans and their crashed cars was that they all had brothers-in-law or cousins who did body and fender work for free.

After a long night of drunken and wild celebrations--and his replacement being late because of a brutal hangover--Puzo's shift finally came to an end at around eleven in the morning. Subsequently, one tired gas attendant quickly left for home to get ready for his Rose Bowl reunion.

He didn't have time for a nap prior to meeting with Brubaker, and he didn't even have enough time for a shower. So, he took a French bath with some cheap smelling cologne, and then drove to Coronado Island, arriving at the hotel bar just minutes before the start of the big football game.

After arriving, he anxiously glanced around looking for an absent Brubaker. The place was crowded and he squeezed in at the end of the bar and ordered a shot of tequila with a Coors chaser. The guy next to him slowly moved away as far as he could after having a sneezing fit due to Puzo's cheap cologne and camouflaged body odor.

The game began and Puzo kept waiting for Brubaker to make his appearance. He nervously tapped his fingers on the bar and ate enough free peanuts to gag an elephant.

About an hour and a half later, it was already near half-time of the game, and he was still waiting for Brubaker, but not anxiously.

Puzo was thoroughly inebriated on tequila and Coors, and he was also having serious doubts about true friendships, and even his ability to ever make it to Mexico. He tried to focus on the bartender, who was in front of him filling his peanut dish for the seventeenth time, and finally Puzo slurred out loud, "That bastard Brubaker!"

"Which team does he play for?" asked the annoyed bartender who had ducked a shower spray of Puzo's saliva.

"Neither," Puzo replied. "Are you sure a guy named Brubaker didn't call?"

"Positive. Do you need another beer or something, and what's that awful smell?" The bartender walked away coughing and didn't wait for an answer.

"I don't think I need another beer." Puzo said to himself while turning around to observe a bar full of animated customers who were pointing fingers and vigorously talking in his direction.

He stared at the other customers and in his current state of blurred vision and reactivated paranoia, he thought the customers were talking and gesturing at him.

Being completely unhinged due to his drunken stupor, he had forgotten that he was sitting right below the elevated television set at the end of the bar. Slowly, but surely, Puzo was beginning to really freak out.

He quickly turned around and tried to focus on his empty bottle of beer, and then got dizzy.

Suddenly, he attempted to get up to leave, but fell off his bar stool and landed square on his butt to the obvious delight of the other patrons.

The guy sitting on the bar stool next to him quickly yelled over to his friend, "Hey, Jimmy, there's an empty stool over here--some drunk just bailed out."

A roar of laughter followed the comment about his drunken mishap, and Puzo finally staggered to his feet and glared at the guy who made fun of him, spitting out, "Real funny. I almost break my butt in two, and you make jokes." Puzo then clumsily picked up the bar stool and began to carry it out of the bar.

The bartender quickly yelled, "Hey, buddy! Where're you going with my bar stool?"

"To Mexico!" yelled Puzo.

The bartender yelled back even louder, "Drop the stool now or I'm calling the police!"

Puzo had nervous visions of L.A. county sheriffs and jail again, and there was momentary silence in the bar as he looked around. He then dropped the bar stool and stumbled out of the bar to cheers of derision.

Once out of the bar, he headed for the serenity of the Coronado Island seashore where he passed out headfirst into the sand.

"Paddy? Hey, Puzo, wake up! It's me, Ralph."

Puzo thought he was dreaming and hearing Brubaker's voice. He rolled over in the sand on his back and squinted in the glaring sun, barely distinguishing a hazy silhouette of a person who was outlined by streaks of shimmering light. He heard the same voice again.

"C'mon, Paddy, it's me, Ralph. I'm sorry I'm late."

Puzo rolled back to a prone position and slowly pushed himself up to a kneeling situation. His head began to whirl and he returned to all fours, vomiting beer and peanut pudding several times. He then looked up, and sure enough, it was Brubaker.

After coughing up the final remnants of beer and peanuts and spitting it into the sand, he slowly said to Brubaker, "Remind me not to drink for a long time."

Brubaker inquired, "Are you okay?"

Puzo then stood up and put his hands on Brubaker's shoulders for stability, and began speaking between belches, "Sure, I'm okay… but I'm drunk…and what about you, Mister Fucking F.B.I.?"

Puzo's eyes rolled around and he fell backwards on the sand with a thump.

Brubaker got down on one knee next to Puzo, saying, "You liked my joke, huh? Hey, I'm sorry I was late to the game. My wife's parents had this big dinner, and you know how Shirley gets upset when I mention your name, and I lied to say I had to run to the store for something to get here, and by the way, U.S.C. beat Ohio State."

Puzo sat up with Brubaker's help and asked: "How'd you know I missed the end of the game?"

"Your friend, the bartender, explained your graceful exit from the bar at halftime." Brubaker sat down next to Puzo, continuing, "Well, how in the hell are you, anyway?"

Puzo gave a three-quarter smile. "Oh, great, just fine and dandy. I'm working steady and any day now I'll be heading for Mexico and the good life."

They were both silent for a while and Puzo finally mumbled, "It's been the shits, Ralph. I've been running from my problems for over a year, and coming back to San Diego hasn't solved anything. I guess you just can't go back to the past because things are never the same, if you know what I mean."

"Sort of," Brubaker replied, "but why are you headed for Mexico? I heard you've been having problems with the minority folks, and Mexico's got a whole bunch of minority-type people there."

Puzo nodded. "I know. But listen, I've had time to think about my future and I know it's time to leave my own backyard for a while, and Mexico and Mexicans seem okay. And as for America's other more privileged black minority, I'll try to give it to you straight about our messed-up civil rights system. Then we can drop it, okay?"

"Please make it short." Brubaker continued, "I realize that I just got here, but I need to talk to you about an offer I want to make to you. I'm also kind of late to get back to Shirley and her parents."

Puzo sighed and then spoke slowly, "I think we all are just jerking off until futurism arrives with all of its specialized Big Brothers, and they won't give a damn about race, creed, or color. Because the Big Brothers, and I'm not talking about the big brothers in the N.B.A., will just make decisions based on a person's competence, and not on the stupid racial theories of goofy sociologists."

He paused and then hurried up his speech after noticing Brubaker stifle a yawn. "And if a person fails to donate to our future society, then it's zap time, because there will be just too many people of all different colors to mess with. It will mean that Mister Afro, Mister Mexican, Mister Oriental, Mister White Boy and Mister Whoever won't be in the driver's seat anymore. It's going to be Mister Computer and Mister Big Brother in charge and the machines and robots won't give a damn about anybody's civil rights, even in south central L.A.!"

Brubaker looked at him pensively for a moment, saying nothing.

"Well?" Puzo finally asked. "What do you think?"

Brubaker grinned. "Paddy, my friend, I'm just glad you're not a real racist. Maybe a goofball philosopher, but not a genuine racist."

Brubaker then got serious and continued: "Which brings me to the real reason 1 came to see you. How would you like to stop running amok for a while and come work for me in Washington?"

"Are you serious?" Puzo coughed up a few more peanut parts.

"Serious as hell." Brubaker replied with an officious tone. He went on to say: "I'm Deputy Director for Technical Assistance Programs in the U.S. territories and other small island possessions, and I need to fill three slots for a federal program. I did some sweet talking, and I've wrangled one position for you if you want it. But you got to promise me that if you accept you'll give it your best shot."

Puzo just stared at Brubaker.

Brubaker finally snapped his fingers in front of Puzo, saying, "Well, it's a chance for you to start a new life. What do you say?"

"I don't know, Ralph, you seem pretty well suited for federal work in D.C..." Puzo paused... "By the way, how did you get promoted so fast to a deputy director?"

Brubaker retorted: "I'm just thankful for my good looks and some well-timed donations to my Director's Democratic Party."

"Oh, I guess that makes sense." Puzo looked up to the sky, slowly shaking his head. "You know, I got a weird nasty feeling about islands, and you did say small islands, right?"

Brubaker nodded his head, but clarified his earlier island statement: "We won't be actually going to any small islands, just monitoring reports from the island leaders. Anyway, here's the number at Shirley's parents' house. Call me if you're interested, and make your call by January fifth at the latest. I gotta go, Paddy. Good seeing you again."

Brubaker gave his business card to Puzo with the phone number of Shirley's parents on the back, and he started to stand up.

Puzo then stopped him from getting up. "Thanks, Ralph, for the offer, I'll try to call either way, but I think it's best that I head for Mexico for a decade or so."

"Suit yourself, Paddy, and adios, amigo." Brubaker emphasized the 'adios, amigo' with an exaggerated Spanish accent.

Brubaker departed, and Puzo continued to sit in the sand, pondering Brubaker's parting shot of sarcastic witticism, while unconsciously watching a great sunset slowly disappear into the creeping evening darkness.

5

MEXICO, HERE I COME

Three days later, Puzo was working at the gas station and waiting on his few customers in a goofy and aloof manner, knowing his final hours were numbered at the filling station. He just kept thinking about his upcoming decision to do the right thing, which in this case was his eminent departure for Mexico.

All through the night, his contact with customers was minimal and nothing was going to bother him. Well, nothing really did bother him until an impatient queer-looking guy in a yellow suit and purple tie got Puzo's complete attention while Puzo was under the hood, checking the guy's radiator.

With Puzo's body bent over and head stuck between the radiator and engine fan to check an old radiator hose, the customer honked his horn, which was three inches from Puzo's head. In a flash, Puzo's head flew up and banged the hood with a tremendous thump. Puzo then staggered back and angrily slammed the hood down and stormed over to the customer, shouting, "Your goddamn horn works just fine, you stupid jerk!"

The Asian-looking customer, a traveling lipstick salesman from San Francisco, looked at Puzo in disgust and said with a pronounced lisp: "I'm writing a letter to your company about your insulting behavior! What's your name?"

"Ralph Brubaker!" Puzo yelled back. "And make sure you include in your letter that I think you're the biggest fucking fruitcake I've ever waited on."

The customer quickly started his car and roared out of the station, ripping the gas nozzle from the pump. He kept driving down the street with the gas nozzle and hose flailing behind the car.

Puzo quickly turned off the emergency pump switch and inspected the damage. He slowly rubbed his throbbing head and realized that his current racial temperament was not likely suited for Brubaker's Washington job. He felt that his decision to leave for Mexico was probably correct all along, hopefully thinking that his unique rapport with Mexicans was pretty good and he wouldn't experience any real serious problems in Mexico.

After the customer had left, the gas station was deserted and he went into the office. He did a little paper work and deposited most of the money from the office cash register into the one-way slot of the night safe in the floor. He looked around outside through the office window and smiled at the empty station. It was so nice and quiet as he sat down and put his feet up on the desk.

It was approaching three-thirty in the early morning and he again felt that weird sense of escape exhilaration as he felt a beautiful bulge in his front pants pocket. It wasn't an erection, but the bulge was just as fulfilling as a result of his going to the bank the day before and withdrawing all of his savings---all twenty-eight hundred dollars.

Again, he felt the bulge of money once more and closed his eyes, thinking of pretty senoritas dancing around him.

His revelry stopped when he had the sudden need to relieve himself. So, he left the office to use the station's bathroom.

He arrived at the bathroom door and, as he fumbled with the key to unlock the men's toilet, he suddenly felt a hard object poke him in the back. He then heard a chilling voice that had a sinister Spanish accent.

"You make one stupeed move and you dead, meester."

"Oh, no!" Puzo gasped. A fucking robbery, and a goddamn armed robbery with a crazed Mexican sticking a fucking gun in his back.

Puzo was quickly led into the office by the robber and ordered not to turn around. The robber, who had previously worked at an all-night gas station, knew that Puzo wouldn't have a key to the safe. But he figured Puzo might have been lazy and hadn't taken the extra cash from the register to make a safe drop. So, he swiftly forced Puzo to open the cash register while the robber always kept behind him. The Mexican then groaned at the little amount of money.

After complaining about another low-paying robbery, the robber ordered Puzo to put his hands way up in the air and keep still. The robber then noticed Puzo's watch and hurriedly asked him to remove the cheap Timex watch---the second damn watch that Puzo had "donated" to a Mexican in a year.

With Puzo completely stretched out with his hands reaching for the ceiling, the robber also noticed a large bulge in Puzo's pocket and curiously felt the inside of the pocket. Puzo groaned in despair as the robber removed his twenty-eight hundred bucks.

"Holy sheeet!" rejoiced the robber. "Look at all dis money!"

Puzo's legs began to shake and the robber shouted, "I said don' move! I hate to shoot such a generous gringo."

The robber then laughed and told Puzo to not look around for maybe fifteen minutes.

Puzo's money was going to Mexico for sure now, but in someone else's goddamn Mexican pocket!

The silence was nerve racking after the robber had abruptly left the office, and after a few minutes Puzo desperately wanted to look around at the nearby sound of a sputtering engine.

Several seconds passed by but it seemed like forever.

Oh, what the hell, Puzo decided to turn around and found himself gawking at an old Chevrolet with primer spots and a multicolored paint job parked in front of the office. It was occupied by three laughing and shouting Mexicans, who were trying to start the car after it sputtered to a stop.

The Mexican in the front passenger seat quickly pointed a gun at Puzo and yelled, "I tol you not to look around!"

Puzo gasped at the sight of his earlier robber, who then fired two rounds in the upper part of the office window, shattering glass all over the office and showering a mortified, all-night gas attendant, who had hit the floor immediately at the flash of the gun barrel.

The robber laughed again and the Chevrolet finally started and lurched out of the station, leaving a trail of black smoke with the ebbing sound of derisive laughter and singing emanating from its open windows.

Puzo was still on the floor of the office, and after counting to about six hundred with his eyes tightly shut, he slowly got up and

looked around nervously at the deserted gas station.

After hyperventilating and checking for any wounds, he hastily called the police and was confident that this time he would be treated as a victim and not as a racist ogre, who had refused to drive a black brother to visit a sick mother in the hospital.

The police finally arrived in twenty minutes, along with the station manager, who had also been notified by Puzo.

Everyone then began asking Puzo a bunch of inane questions about if he was sure it was a Chevrolet. Was he sure they were Mexicans, because it was always easy to blame them for all the trouble in National City.

Puzo finally screamed. "Sure, they were Mexicans! And one had a gun, and the mother-fucking taco-sucker stole my life savings and then shot at me!"

After his outburst, the two police officers, one white and the other a black guy, figured that some racist remarks were probably made by Puzo and the Mexican gentleman fired in anger.

While shaking their heads at all the glass covering the contents of the office, the officers dutifully informed the manager that they would check back later after they did some cursory investigative work.

The officers then warned Puzo not to agitate the Mexican population anymore, since it could be dangerous. The police finally mentioned to each other that some hot coffee and donuts would sure hit the spot, so they said goodbye and quickly left for a Winchell's Donut House.

Puzo couldn't believe it. He just got shot at and lost his life's savings, and the police were more interested in hot coffee and fucking donuts. The cops also treated the robbery like it was a normal National City community activity.

Furthermore, Puzo's white manager was now worried that Puzo had said things that might anger the Hispanic neighborhood. The manager even complained that the Mexicans would probably file several civil rights complaints against him and the gas station.

"I warned you to be more careful," lectured the manager loudly. "You probably angered all of them earlier and they came back for revenge. Just look at the broken glass, and you told the cops that the station lost about twenty-one dollars from the cash register. Well, I hope you're satisfied, Mister Puzi, and you'd better hand me your keys right now. You're fired!"

Puzo stood staring at the manager dumbfounded, and as he handed over the keys he said, "You don't seem to realize I just lost my life's savings, and fuck your twenty-one dollars. I needed my goddamn money to go someplace where I can live in peace and quiet!"

"Goodbye, Mister Puzi!" the manager shouted, as he picked up broken glass and wished that he was a barber in Ohio, instead of a gas station manager in National City.

Puzo yelled as he left, "It's Puzo, asshole!"

Puzo now realized that his love affair with Mexico had been permanently strained and, while driving home, he reached inside his empty pocket and only felt the tingling sensation of tiny bits of broken glass, which made him cringe in disgust.

Only hours from quitting his job and leaving for beautiful Mexico, and he gets robbed and fired.

Only hours…goddamned Mexicans!

6

HELLO, RALPH?

"Hello? I want to speak to Ralph Brubaker. It's urgent, please!"

It was four-thirty in the morning, and after arriving at his apartment following the robbery, Puzo had aroused Shirley's father out of bed and asked him to wake up Brubaker.

He soon heard raised voices in the background on the other end of the line, asking who in the hell was bothering them at four-thirty in the morning.

"Yeah, this is Brubaker. Who is this?" Brubaker sounded irritated.

"Ralph? It's Puzo. Is the offer still good for Washington?"

"Paddy?! Couldn't this wait until later this morning?" Brubaker was less irritated and more surprised now.

"Sorry. I had the urgent need to call you now and let you know I want the job."

"What happened to your Mexican plans?" Brubaker quizzed.

"Screw Mexico! Is the job still available for me?" Puzo sounded flabbergasted.

"Sure, Paddy, relax. Just be in Washington by the fifteenth, and call me at the Department of the Interior when you get there. You can stay with Shirley and me, but only temporarily, until you get settled somewhere."

"Thanks, Ralph. Tell Shirley and your in-laws I'm sorry to wake them up." He could still hear muffled protests in the background about early phone calls, Puzo going to Washington, and staying temporarily at Ralph and Shirley's place.

"Don't worry. Just be in D.C. by the fifteenth." Brubaker asked for some quiet from a protesting Shirley, and he then asked Puzo: "Tell me something, what changed your mind?"

"Just too many damned Mexicans living in Mexico."

"I won't ask you to explain. See you in Washington."

After hanging up the phone, Puzo woke up his roommate, who was leaving for Arizona in a few weeks, and Puzo began rambling on that he was leaving for Washington soon, and he wished that someday the United States would nuke Mexico.

His roommate just nodded, and quickly fell back to sleep.

Following his last few days in San Diego and luckily selling all his scant worldly possessions to a generous and sympathetic roommate, Puzo prepared for his trip to Washington. He packed his aging pickup with his clothes, some toiletries and a few old Mad Magazines, and he then headed east on Interstate 8 in the early morning hours of January tenth.

Finally leaving the cock-sucking California ex-Dream World for a more radical East Coast lifestyle and a major change in his environment made him wonder…what life would have been like if he had been born in some simple small town in middle America, like somewhere in Kansas or Iowa? In middle America, he wouldn't have been nurtured into becoming a West Coast slacker or a soon to be East Coast maniac. In Iowa or Kansas, he could have just been a nose-picking farmer without a care in the world, except maybe an early frost or maybe a John Deere tractor with a flat tire. Whatever the case, he now wondered if his old pickup would make it across country in one piece.

Eventually, twenty miles outside of Tulsa, Oklahoma, his previously loyal truck finally deposited its transmission all over a highway in front of Floyd's Gas Station and Repair Shop.

Puzo ended up selling his truck to Floyd for three hundred bucks, and then hitch-hiked the remainder of his trip. He barely made it to Washington by the evening of the fourteenth.

It was a late freezing Sunday night when he did arrive in D.C., and he was finally dropped near the U.S. Capitol by a Marine who was on leave before reporting to a new duty station. The Marine had given him a ride from Louisville, Kentucky after returning from overseas security duty and he was in a hurry to get home in Virginia, just south of Washington, D.C. Puzo helped him with the driving to make good time, and the Marine made a detour to get Puzo to D.C. Puzo had tried to compare war stories with the Marine with his various terroristic confrontations in sunny California, but the Marine just smiled and didn't seem too interested.

After being dropped off in D.C. and walking in a numbing wind for a few blocks, Puzo checked into a not too expensive hotel somewhat near the U.S. Capitol. He later relaxed in his room that had a partial view of the Capitol building, which was bathed in floodlights in the distance. The illuminated Capitol building was very impressive and he felt somewhat important for the first time in a long while.

Following a long hot shower, he crawled into bed, thinking maybe, just maybe, things were going to turn around for him.

Who knows? The last fourteen months in chaotic California might have been preparing him for an important mission in Washington, a mission that would be dependent on his unique upbringing and later "diversified social interactions." Besides, this feeling of importance was starting to put to rest a nagging "stranded on an island somewhere" premonition that he had been occasionally experiencing for the last several days. Maybe it was possibly connected to his new job that Brubaker had explained to him that had indirect connections to remote islands that he was nervous about. He finally closed his eyes and fell soundly asleep. His first really good sleep in over a year.

7

WAKING UP IN D.C.

Sleeping in a very cold climate was a new experience for Puzo, and he snuggled himself under the covers in his hotel room and slept like a well-fed baby. It was already past noon on Monday, and he hadn't fully opened his eyes yet, and getting out of bed was still a distant proposition in his new life in Washington.

The drapes in his room had been tightly closed the night before, and during the times he did squint into the dimmed room light, it always looked like it was six or seven o'clock in the early morning.

Finally, at one o'clock in the afternoon a knock on the door made him open his eyes completely, and after twisting his head around and glancing at the clock that was built into the bed's headboard, he blinked his eyes and groaned out loud: "Jesus, it's one o'clock, and I was supposed to call Brubaker this morning."

He slowly struggled out of bed and answered the knocking at the door.

"Cleaning lady, are you checking out today?" A kindly old black woman asked.

Puzo winced at the sight of the black lady, but realized she wasn't a glassy-eyed or pissed-off militant. He politely responded, "Yes, ma'am, sorry I overslept. I'll be out in a half-hour, okay?"

"That will be fine. Just don't stay longer or they might charge you for another day."

"Thanks." Puzo closed the door and quickly made his way for a hot shower.

Following a scalding shower to get heat back into his body, he managed a careful shave over his boiled pink face. Next he dressed and packed his two battered suitcases that contained all that he currently owned, and then he scanned the phone directory for the Department of the Interior's phone number.

He soon sighed at the list of several hundred numbers and shrugged his shoulders. He began dialing the various Interior numbers, hoping he wouldn't have to pay for another day in his hotel room while dialing a multitude of federal phone numbers all afternoon.

It took him awhile, but he eventually heard a familiar voice asking his whereabouts.

"Where in the hell are you, Paddy? I wish you would have called me this morning." Brubaker was irritated at first, but then sounded happy to hear his voice.

"Sorry, Ralph, I'm staying at a hotel near the Capitol and I overslept."

"Never mind. I just wanted to show you around before you begin work tomorrow."

Puzo cringed, "Tomorrow! Well, I can be there in thirty minutes…"

Brubaker cut in: "We have to forget about today. I'm real busy this afternoon. Just call Shirley and let her know you're in town and she'll give you directions to our place."

"Are you sure she'll do that?" asked a doubtful Puzo.

"I think so," Brubaker laughed. "I told her you'll be staying for only a week at the very most. But remember, you've always been pretty high on her shit list, so be cool and coherent."

"Sounds like you made a temporary Puzo peace treaty with her. Well, give me your phone number and I'll call her and try to be cool and coherent."

"The number is four-five-six, one-four-one-four, and don't skimp on the coherent."

"Got it, Ralph. Thanks, and I'll see you later." He hung up the phone and dialed Brubaker's home phone number.

The phone rang several times with no answer, so he decided he'd better check out of his room before being charged another day, which would put a big dent into his paltry savings. He figured to call later after a much-needed late lunch. He was starving and really didn't want to talk to Shirley on an empty stomach.

Soon after a tasty lunch of two chili cheeseburgers, two orders of onion rings and a banana milkshake in a much cheaper restaurant next to the hotel, he called Shirley again, but still got no answer. He waited a few minutes, dialed again, and still no luck. So he decided to leave his bags back at the hotel's baggage storeroom, saying he might stay another night, and go for a short walk.

It was now twenty minutes past two, and after an abbreviated stroll in below freezing weather, he called Shirley again in the hotel lobby and was actually relieved to hear her charming, Washingtonian socialite voice.

"Yes, this is the Brubaker's residence. May I ask who's calling please?" Shirley didn't recognize Puzo's voice that was getting raspy from the cold weather.

"It's Paddy, Shirley. Ralph asked me to call and let you know I'm in town." There was a long, silent pause. "Hello? Is the phone dead?" Puzo finally asked.

A chilly voice eventually inquired: "When did you arrive?"

"Last night. Ralph said I could come over if it's convenient for you right now."

'Sorry, I'll be gone the rest of the day." Shirley coolly replied. "You can call back after seven tonight when Ralph's home." Her voice could have discouraged Attila the Hun from pillaging a cheerleaders' convention.

"Uh, sure. I'll call you later, Shirley. Nice talking...," the line went dead as he continued into the phone, "Yeah, nice talking with you too, Shirley Ass-Hole!" He slammed down the phone and mumbled a few more obscenities.

What was it with that woman? Just because at the Brubaker's wedding reception he got drunk and threw up all over the cake and Shirley---big deal. He then remembered that the cake was a pretty gross sight and Shirley was extremely pissed off.

He also realized that it must have taken a long debate to allow him to stay at the Brubaker's for even just a week, knowing Shirley's serious dislike for any friend of Ralph's with the last name of Puzo.

Well, he now had four and one-half hours to kill, so he left the hotel for some more frigid sightseeing. He took his bags with him this time and eventually hailed a cab to drive him over to the National Mall area where most of the federal museums and buildings were located.

Two hours later, after he had visited some aviation exhibits at the Smithsonian National Aeronautics and Space Museum, he was idly sitting on a warm indoor bench in the museum, looking at the various historical displays of American flight achievements hanging from the ceiling. He looked down at his new souvenir NASA watch and sighed.

He sat alone on the bench, still shivering from the thought of the cold weather that was playing havoc with his light California clothes. The combination of his casual summer clothes and looking out the museum window at the freezing ice and snow everywhere made him feel like a hairless ape in a North Pole zoo. Buying some winter clothes real soon was very high on his Washington list of priorities.

Finally, he stopped shaking and felt relaxed on the bench. But it didn't take long before his head dropped to his chest and he slowly nodded off for a nap. His nap made him mostly oblivious to the visitor noise and the taped messages that were being broadcasted from the nearby NASA exhibits, although the NASA messages were subliminally encouraging him to get off his butt and do something in the adventures of space.

Ironically, the NASA messages were being interfaced with his other mind travels, which in turn were all combined into a weird dream about being chased all over Saturn by two shouting, machine-gun totting Mexicans, who were traveling in a multicolored, Chevrolet rocket ship.

His goofy dream was abruptly ended by a femail security guard, who nudged him on the arm and asked him to please leave the museum because it was closing time. Puzo shook his head to wake up and then tried to stand, but his legs had fallen to sleep and he collapsed back on the bench.

The guard frowned and curiously asked, "Have you been drinking, sir?"

"Not a drop, "Puzo replied, "I'm just getting over jet lag."

"In that case, sir, could I help you out the door to get some fresh air, so we can close." The guard was friendly but getting a little impatient.

Puzo nodded and stood up again, testing the stability of his legs. After getting some feeling in his wobbly legs, he slowly took a few steps, smiled at the guard who was helping him, and then meandered towards the exit door on his own, knowing that a blast of Arctic fresh air was waiting to greet him square in the face.

Later in the evening, he glanced at his wristwatch from the space museum, which had a picture of an orbiting NASA space capsule and Mickey Mouse in a space suit depicted on its face. He observed with immense gratitude that the time was slightly past seven o'clock, and as soon as he found a pay phone he would be calling Brubaker.

He finally found an outdoor pay phone near the White House, and couldn't believe the weather could get as cold as it was, while a freezing wind unmercifully whistled through his light jacket and thin shirt.

He fumbled in his pocket for some change and placed his call, hoping to make a more successful attempt in securing shelter at Brubaker's place.

"Hello?" Puzo rasped in the phone.

"Yes, who's calling please?" Brubaker inquired, not recognizing Puzo's hoarse voice.

"It's me, Paddy, and I think I'm dying of pneumonia." He coughed and sneezed loudly.

"Why didn't you come over earlier? Shirley's been home since two o'clock."

"What the...oh, yeah, Shirley said...never mind, Ralph. I...I decided to see the sights." Puzo didn't let on about Shirley's cold reception for him earlier. Matter of fact, her reception reminded him again how really cold it was and he began to shake violently.

"You sound frost bitten, but how do you like Washington so far?" Brubaker cheerfully asked.

"Fine, fine. But can you get over here and pick me up before my butt turns to solid ice."

"Sure. Where are you?"

"I'm near the White House, on the corner of Seventeenth and Pennsylvania Avenue." Puzo could hear Shirley complaining in the background.

"Right. That's Pennsylvania and--" Brubaker was interrupted and spoke away from the phone to Shirley, "I know cabs are running at this hour, but give the guy a break, okay?" He returned to his conversation with Puzo. "Okay." It's Pennsylvania and Seventeenth. I'll be there in about twenty minutes."

"If it's any bother I can take a cab, Ralph."

"No need, Paddy," replied Brubaker, adding, "Just promise not to later throw up on our couch or any wedding cakes you see around our place."

"I promise." Puzo tried to laugh and began coughing. "Hope to see you before I freeze to death." He then hung up the phone.

No matter what he did, Puzo couldn't escape from the freezing cold. He tried walking briskly back and forth along Seventeenth Street, and even stepped inside a Chinese restaurant and bar momentarily to warm himself.

However, as soon as he stepped back outside of the bar and into the cold it got worse. He almost went back into the bar to order several drinks to keep himself warm, but he had promised not to drink and show Ralph his good intentions upon his arrival in D.C. Furthermore, he just wanted to start the Washington chapter in his life on the right sober foot, without any drunken miscues.

He eventually headed back towards the corner of Pennsylvania and Seventeenth and sat huddled on his two suitcases. He had taken out two extra shirts and another pair of pants from one of his suitcases and put them on over his existing outfit, trying desperately to provide himself more insulation.

While he added the extra clothes, he ignored the occasional stares of pedestrians who watched him dress on the sidewalk.

Thirty minutes later, he watched a 1978 Volkswagen Rabbit finally pulled up along the curb where he was sitting. Brubaker was driving the car and eagerly waved for him to get inside.

Puzo slowly stood up and he could barely move his body.

Brubaker finally got out of his car with the motor still running and went over to help him.

"You're slowing down in your old age, Paddy?" Brubaker kidded.

"Please, Ralph," Puzo moaned, "my freezing is not a funny subject right now. What took you so long? Did Shirley figure I'd be dead in an hour?"

"Now Paddy, why would you think that," Brubaker replied sarcastically, and then added: "I made a quick stop to buy you a present. C'mon, let's get in the car before I freeze, too."

They placed Puzo's suitcases in the back seat of the car and they both climbed in. Brubaker then looked over to his friend trembling in the passenger seat and chuckled, "You are a sight for sore eyes. How many shirts do you have on, anyway?"

"Not enough," Puzo chattering his teeth. "Is your heater working?"

"Full blast. And against my better judgment I think you need my little present right away. Reach in the glove box and get the brown sack." Brubaker pulled away from the curb and headed his car for Alexandria, Virginia, which was just across the Potomac River.

After opening his present, Puzo stared at a pint of Jose Cuervo gold tequila. He shook his head at the irony of not buying a bunch of drinks at the Chinese bar and said, "Thanks,' Ralph. I always knew you had good timing." He slowly removed the bottle's cap with his numb fingers and took a long and body-shaking drink of the tequila.

"That's enough, Paddy, remember work tomorrow and Shirley's temper." Brubaker had cautioned him while driving across the Potomac River.

Puzo shook his head. He then took a deep breath and drank a little more tequila, shivered, and then slowly sighed, "I think I might live now."

"That's good to hear." Brubaker reached over and patted him on the shoulder. "Hey, look, isn't the Potomac beautiful?" Brubaker kept being optimistic.

Puzo looked at the Potomac River as they crossed the George Mason Memorial Bridge and scoffed, "It just looks frozen to me."

"You know what your problem is, Paddy? You're too cynical. Look on the bright side of being here in D.C. This is where all the feds run America. And now's your chance to correct any problems the country has that really bother you." Brubaker then smiled as he drove southeast on the Henry G. Shirley Memorial Highway.

Puzo gazed out the side window of the car, winced at a road sign that had the name "Shirley" on it, and asked: "Where in the hell do you live, Ralph? From one of the signs back there it looks like we're in Virginia."

"You're right. We live in Lincoln Heights, a suburb of Alexandria, Virginia. It's not that far from work and it's a safer area than Washington."

"I did notice an excessive number of severely tanned minority folks living in downtown D.C.," Puzo commented. "Is the F.B.I. aware of the situation?" he wryly asked.

"I'm sure they are. It's just a matter of lower income blacks migrating to Washington for menial jobs over the years. Washington even has a black mayor now."

"How close is that to the U.S. Presidency?"

"Hey, I thought you weren't a racist?" Brubaker then made a turn and entered into a residential area.

Puzo looked at Ralph and said: "I'm not a racist...unless I get robbed or shot at again."

"Is that what changed your mind about Mexico?"

"You got it," Puzo responded, "some out-of-work, taco-bending bastard stole my life savings and had fun taking pot shots at me."

Brubaker frowned. "I know that's serious, Paddy. But try to do your best here even though you had a bad experience. It's not just for my sake in recommending you for a job, but for your own good."

"Yeah, I know. I plan to give Washington my best shot. But please don't send me to any oppressed areas in the world to solve their problems, because I've got enough of my own." He drank some more tequila and offered Ralph the bottle.

"No thanks, I'm driving. And don't overdo it, you got an important interview tomorrow."

"With Shirley?!"

"No, with my boss."

"Great, now you tell me."

Later, at half-past eight, they stopped in front of an old, quaint-looking townhouse near Lincoln Heights. Brubaker explained that the house was divided into two rentals and that he and Shirley rented the top floor. A person working for the Central Intelligence Agency lived alone on the bottom floor. Brubaker continued to explain that he had only seen the guy a few times early in the morning, when the poor bastard nervously checked his car for explosives while carefully surveying the neighborhood with his binoculars.

They quietly entered the dimly lit house and tried not to disturb Shirley, who had gone to bed unusually early and consequently missed seeing her bosom buddy from San Diego.

Brubaker showed Puzo his "very temporary" bedroom and the location of the bathroom, and then asked him if he needed anything before he went to bed. Both agreed that Puzo only needed sleep, and they further agreed that they also wanted to avoid a possible Shirley showdown, especially since Puzo had enough tequila floating through his veins to say something tremendously stupid.

A few minutes later, after taking a handful of Contac capsules for his horrendous head cold, Puzo, with all of his clothes still on, was fast asleep under three blankets and two quilts.

The following morning it took a long and loud ringing from the alarm clock to finally revive Puzo from his Contac overdose. He somehow stumbled to the bathroom and struggled to finish his morning shower and shave. He then dressed for his first day at work in the nation's capital, and finally, took a good look into a mirror, thinking what in the hell had he gotten himself into. He looked again and realized he had actually gotten into an old pinstripe suit that Ralph had given him to wear. He moaned at the sight of the somewhat tight fit, and sighed that he hadn't worn any suit since his grade school graduation. But he was committed now and he eventually joined Ralph in the kitchen.

"Where's Shirley?" Puzo asked as he sat down at the kitchen table.

"She's sleeping in this morning...said she had a terrible headache or something." Brubaker wryly smiled at Puzo, then poured his friend some orange juice.

"I know, I know. Will I ever convince her I'm not a complete ogre?" Puzo then drank the whole glass of orange juice and loudly belched and farted at the same time.

"At least you still got classy table manners," Brubaker quipped, "but class won't make Shirley happy if you stay longer than a week."

"Fair enough, Ralph. Let's get down the road and greet my future in Washington. Somebody has big plans for me and I want to find out as soon as possible if I can live with them."

Brubaker finished his coffee and they then left for the notorious United States Department of Interior.

8

THE DEPARTMENT OF
INTERIOR, ET. AL.

The United States Department of Interior (DOI) is mainly located in a humongous old building on an entire city block in downtown D.C., adjacent to the General Services Administration (GSA).

Brubaker worked for one of the many different agencies that comprised the DOI, and his agency's official title was the Department of Technical Assistance Programs, or "D-TAP," which was in the Office of Territorial and Insular Affairs (OTIA).

The OTIA kept a shaky federal eyeball on infamously corrupt places like the Virgin Islands and Puerto Rico. Furthermore, it also monitored American Samoa, Guam, Northern Mariana Islands, and the Trust Territory of the Pacific Islands, which were all located in the Pacific Ocean region and Micronesia.

The feds loved acronyms like DOI, OTIA, and D-TAP, especially ones that ironically hinted at the truth of the matter, like how "dee-islanders" love to "dee-tap" into the federal money train.

During their slow drive through traffic to the downtown DOI Building, Brubaker kept busy telling stories about the hectic history of the DOI and OTIA.

Meanwhile, Puzo continued nodding during Brubaker's conversation and looking at a brochure of the layout of Washington. He finally spied the Lincoln Memorial to his right and rolled down his window to get a clearer view of the memorial that was dedicated to the 16th U.S. president and his emancipation views. But he quickly rolled his window back up after getting a blast of winter morning air in the face. As he rolled up the window though he simultaneously mumbled under his breath, "Someday, I'm going to piss on your nice memorial, Mister Lincoln, for that miserable night at Melba's"

"What was that?" asked Brubaker.

"Uh, I just said I don't want to miss visiting the Lincoln Memorial for some emancipated friends I met in L.A. a while ago."

Brubaker raised his eyebrows and then frowned at him. "Remember Paddy, you're outnumbered here by emancipated folks, and before I forget, if you're asked about your ethnic background during your interview this morning, make sure you mention that you're part Apache Indian. It was part of the racial requirements for the job."

"Apache?!" Puzo muttered. "Well, whatever makes you guys happy at Interior. Anything else I should know?"

"Yeah, don't disagree with anything that my boss, Oliver Johnson, has to say about the entire universe and its only decent inhabitants, who, according to him, are loyal Democrats. Okay?"

Puzo smiled. "I think I know what you're getting at." They eventually pulled into the DOI parking lot and headed for the OTIA section of the building.

For Puzo, he was about to have his first real encounter with the unique federal way of life, and he seemed uncomfortable with this oncoming federal feeling that sent tingles throughout his entire body.

An hour later, Puzo was sitting at a short conference table in a small meeting room with three other people. One member of the group was Mrs. Imogene Buttmeyer, an assistant in the DOI personnel office, who was helping Puzo and the other new employees fill in their federal application forms and questionnaires. Buttmeyer was white and quite pretty.

The other two aspiring workers, who were joining Puzo to form a small and insignificant federal program analysis team, were ironically two vivid reminders of Puzo's most recent and less rosy past. One was a Mexican with the name Angel Martinez, and the other was a black guy named Leroyo Hamilton.

However, no matter what the seriousness of these two reminders of his recent racial escapades, Puzo tried to remain calm and kept remembering his promise to Brubaker about starting a new life of open mindedness. So while silently chanting some of the parts of a mostly forgotten Buddhist prayer, he diligently filled out his federal paperwork, without making any sarcastic comments about the screwed-up federal policies for hiring too many of the pampered under-privileged and underqualified jerk-offs in America.

The numerous federal forms that Puzo was filling in could have wall-papered the entire insides of the gigantic DOI building, and if it wasn't for the mellow Contac hangover he was currently experiencing, he would have probably reconsidered his previous plan to flee to Mexico, Chevrolets and all!

Later, as he was busy writing down that he was part-Apache Indian on a "volunteer" ethnic questionnaire that was a mandatory submittal, he noticed Martinez checking out his new NASA souvenir watch. Martinez kept nodding and finally commented, "Funny looking watch you got there, man. You gonna be a spaceman someday?"

Puzo bit his lip, replying with a touch of sarcasm: "Maybe. At least in space my watch would be safe from banditos in red Chevrolets."

Martinez laughed, "You get robbed or something?"

"Yeah, something like that," Puzo tried to smile, "but I promised to forget about it and not let it bother me."

"That's a good way to think, man." Martinez bobbed his head a few more times. "In the barrio, you know, it's problems every day, and you can go crazy worrying about what's happening to you."

Hamilton looked over to Martinez and gruffly said, "Where I come from the only thing that's crazy is making friendships with white people.

Martinez just snickered at Hamilton and then Mrs. Buttmeyer scolded everyone, saying "Now gentlemen, we can't be wasting time here. You're on federal time and the Department of Interior can't afford lollygagging.

Martinez made a strange face and asked, "What's lollygaggin' mean? I never heard that word before."

"Never mind, just complete your forms." Buttmeyer instructed. "You all have interviews soon with Mister Oliver Johnson, the Director of the Department of Technical Assistant Programs, and he's a very busy man."

They finally completed all their forms and were then led to Oliver Johnson's office to be interviewed one at a time.

Johnson was a genuine, long-standing, professional bureaucrat, who knew no limits to his condescending demagoguery, or his overwhelming sense of self-importance to the future of the world. He was a very fat, sixty-year-old white man, who was bald, bombastic, and a genuine liberalized idiot from Georgia. He was also married to an Atlanta socialite and the father of two grown children. His son was a homosexual hairdresser in New York, and his daughter was in the Peace Corps somewhere in Micronesia. He tried his best to get along with his decent but flighty son, but he detested his daughter for blabbing to his wife about his long junkets and reported sexual escapades in Micronesia, which was a part of his D-TAP domain.

It seemed that Johnson's field trips to the U.S. Trust Territory in Micronesia were sprinkled with several generous payoffs, in order to keep young and pregnant native girls from going public about his affairs. And God only knew the number of times that U.S. policy in Micronesia was compromised because of a sexually perverted DOI director in charge of island technical assistance.

Martinez was first to be interviewed by Johnson and he came out smiling after about twenty minutes.

Martinez was followed by Hamilton, who quickly finished his interview in a record amount of time of just under two minutes, as a direct result of Johnson getting extremely nervous about Hamilton's very intimidating militant stares.

Next was Puzo's turn, and he was beginning to feel nauseous. He had already learned from Brubaker what the federal objective was for everyone's hiring, but he was afraid he might blurt out his true feelings about the racially oppressed and even blow his Apache cover.

The main objective for their hiring was to form a Program Management Analysis Team (PMAT) within D-TAP, comprised of three minority types from around the United States. President Jimmy Carter was up for re-election later in the year, and the push was on for minority hiring.

This Democratic strategy, which was specially created for Carter, was hastily arranged to upstage the likely Republican candidate for the U.S. Presidency in November of that year. The Republican candidate was a staunch conservative from California by the name of Ronald Reagan.

But no matter who would later run the United States of America, or the universe for that matter, Puzo just wanted to walk into Johnson's office right before lunch and hopefully get a job to salvage his unraveling life.

So after a deep breath and a few nervous coughs, Puzo anxiously walked into Johnson's office and quietly sat down in a chair in front of a big cluttered desk.

Johnson was closely perusing Puzo's ethnic questionnaire and asked. "How much Apache you got in you, son?" Johnson's eyes glanced up with a sly smile on his face.

"About one third, on my mother's side, I think," Puzo replied, adding, "and her mother was almost full Apache and married an Irishman who was a half-breed...I mean a part-Indian from Oklahoma." Puzo coughed again, "And my other grandparents were from Italy, and..."

Johnson kept smiling and interrupted. "Interesting, well, you're here mainly because Brubaker says you've had good experience in the field of minority activities. Do you have anything to say about that?"

Puzo gritted his teeth. "Oh, sure. I believe in equal opportunity at all costs, and President Carter is doing a fine job of equalizing everybody."

Johnson cringed at the double talk, but he liked it, adding, "Sounds like the President could use a boy like you in his social programs."

Puzo sighed. "Well, thank you, sir."

"As they say in Georgia, don't thank me, because it's no fuzz off my peaches, only President Carter's!" He laughed at his own goofy humor and then abruptly asked, "You serve in the military?"

Puzo replied, "No."

Johnson seemed serious. "Why not?"

Puzo hesitated and answered: "I had a very long college deferment."

Johnson shrugged, "Never mind, your lack of military preferential points is made up by your being part A-pa-chee." Johnson then inquired as he kept mangling the word Apache: "Excuse me, son, I've never heard any A-pa-chee language before. Can you say something for me in Indian before you go?"

"Ah, yeah, let's see. Well, my mother didn't teach me much because, did I tell you she was raised in Ireland and..."

Puzo was again interrupted by an impatient Johnson who said: "I already know about your mother and it's getting late for my lunch, so just say something quick like, okay?"

"Okay...here goes, uh, mawoppy kunta kinte." Puzo nervously grinned.

Johnson furled his eyebrows. "What the hell does that mean?"

"Short mother mean long life." Puzo then waited for a response from Johnson.

Johnson unfurled his eyebrows and chuckled, "You A-pa-chees are just as interesting as all hell." Johnson then leaned forward and officiously announced: "I tell you what. I'm going to put you on excepted service status for a year, and if everything works out, you'll get permanent civil service status later. One more thing before you leave, what do you think about a Democratic lesbian black woman for vice president of the United States next election?"

"Just wonderful" Puzo grinned even more.

Johnson seemed pleased as hell, saying, "Good. Report to Brubaker before he leaves for lunch."

Twenty minutes later, after getting lost twice in the large DOI building, Puzo flopped down in a chair outside Brubaker's office, still feeling a rush of rising self-esteem after his successful interview. A pretty young Latina lady of twenty was typing at her reception desk and notified Brubaker that he had a visitor. Brubaker then poked his head out of his door and asked Puzo to wait a bit, after which they would go to the basement cafeteria for lunch.

So while sitting and waiting for Brubaker, Puzo smiled at the secretary and asked what her name was.

"My name's Maria Lopez," she rapidly answered, and then she continued her typing. She was also new at the DOI and appeared anxious and serious about her work.

"Kind of a beautiful Spanish name you have there," Puzo remarked confidently, as he thumbed through an old magazine.

She looked up momentarily with a cool stare, and resumed her typing again.

Puzo lowered his eyes and mumbled to himself about his lame attempt at socializing, adding, "You look busy and so I won't bother you."

He continued to scan the magazine, and then caught the secretary giving him a quick glance.

He smiled at her again, and decided to try again, "Say, it's lunch time, and Ralph and I are going to the cafeteria. Care to join us?"

She looked up again and silently pointed at her left hand. It had a large engagement ring securely in place on the ring finger and it seemingly flashed: "Not available, loco gringo."

Puzo then stared at the ceiling and pondered his inept social skills and any female's innate ability to further expose his lack of social graces.

Brubaker, who was watching from the doorway of his office, broke the awkward silence with: "I can see you plan to go far here, Paddy. By the way, you did get hired, didn't you?"

Puzo looked over at Brubaker, semi-boasting, "You're right on that account. Johnson and me are real good buddies. And if you ever try to fire me, son," he bragged with a Southern accent, "I'm going to tell Oliver. At least he thinks I have a future here."

Brubaker shook his head and laughed. "I'm starved. Let's go eat. And be careful about your future around this place."

Puzo momentarily stared at Brubaker's wry remark and felt a sudden chill.

Following lunch, Brubaker and his new PMAT group met in a cramped cubicle, which was situated within a large maze of other similar cubicles. It basically resembled a DOI-approved working lab experiment for two-legged rats with GS ratings.

Hamilton, Martinez and Puzo each had their own small desk, and Brubaker was giving them a fast orientation speech on the reasons for their being there.

"You three gentlemen will be our Program Management Analysis Team, which will be called P-MAT around here, and you're all under the D-TAP section. We love acronyms in the federal government, so get used to them. You'll be analyzing federal programs in the U.S.

Territories and will report on the management or the mismanagement of federal funds in these territorial areas."

Brubaker paused and waved some reports in his hand, continuing, "We don't expect you to be experts on the financial matters in the territories, but as you read the reports from the various island groups you should be able to make simple judgments on the efficiency of their planning, spending and the implementation of certain federally-funded projects. It's a challenge for new people to quickly learn the federal way of doing things, but I have every confidence in your abilities. Are there any questions?"

"Yeah, where's the nearest toilet around here?" Hamilton asked.

Brubaker nodded with a smile. "Down the hall three corridors, turn left for one corridor, then right one corridor until you see it on the left next to a water cooler."

"Can you draw a map?" Martinez asked. "By the time any of us find the place we won't need it anymore."

Brubaker sighed. "My secretary can help you with that. She'll be here in a minute with information pouches for each of you. Also, if you haven't been there already, there's a cafeteria in the basement for those who don't bring a lunch to work. And try not to order any pizzas from the outside restaurants, because the last three delivery boys got lost and finally left the cold pizzas with our hungry security guards."

As Brubaker finished his pizza story his secretary walked in, shoving a large cart into the small cubicle with three monstrous pouches on it. "If you haven't met already," said Brubaker, "this is Maria Lopez." He then pointed to each of the PMAT group as he introduced them individually to Lopez.

After the introductions had been made, Brubaker departed and Lopez took over and pointed to the cart, saying: "On this cart are three large pouches marked with your names and different places you'll be studying. Mister Hamilton will have the Virgin Islands, Mister Martinez will have American Samoa, and Mister Puzu will have Guam, the Northern Mariana Islands and the Trust Territory of the Pacific Islands."

"That's Puzo."

"Oh, yes, Puzo. Anyway, there's an introductory message in each pouch from the Assistant Secretary for O.T.I.A., Mister Herbert T. Sinclair, and there's also an explanation guideline to help you in your reports. Any questions?"

"Could you draw a map for us to the nearest bathroom?" Martinez asked with a grin.

Lopez firmly replied: "There's an office map in the pouch. I believe all of you can read a map. If that's all, I'll be leaving now." Without hesitating, she started to leave.

Martinez quickly called out with a pleasant Mexican accent, "Please don' get mad at me, Meester Brubaker said you would help us find the restroom."

She slowly turned and said, mimicking Martinez, "Adios, Meester Martinez, and good luck finding the restroom."

Hamilton and Puzo looked at Martinez, a handsome and happy- go-lucky Chicano who was flashing a big smile at Lopez. Then they all watched her slowly break into a smile, too. She then got slightly embarrassed and hastily left the cubicle.

After she departed, Martinez grinned at Hamilton and Puzo, stating, "I bet five dollars I'll be kissing those tender lips in two weeks."

"She's engaged," Puzo advised.

"Then make that ten dollars!" Martinez confidently bragged.

Hamilton just shook his head, since he was mostly sullen and acted distant with the trivial social activity that was going on. He was wearing a button proclaiming "Black Power" on his African styled smock and thought he should maintain a certain aloofness. He didn't seem to be a real militant radical, but at times he acted like he was as big a racist as most members of the Klu Klux Klan.

Eventually, all three had their desks completely engulfed in stacks of federal reports, and the burning question was where would they all begin?

Well, Martinez began his federal stint by going to the toilet and walking around the building for a long time. Hamilton pulled out a copy of Ebony Magazine from a pocket in his black trench coat and began reading, and Puzo finally started reading the reports and just stared at the pages with a bewildered daze.

An hour later, Martinez leaned back at his desk and sighed, "No wonder those browns in the islands are going crazy. These white boy feds are driving them crazy with all these reports. I've seen three different reports on why young Samoans like football."

Hamilton casually remarked, "It's just another case of underdeveloped areas being oppressed by the white mentality of America."

"Wait a minute, Hamilton," Puzo was suddenly jostled to life, "I think you're wrong. You can't blame whites for everything. I know it's the national pastime nowadays, but it's getting to be an old excuse for all the problems of every minority."

Martinez laughed at Puzo. "Hey, amigo, it sounds like you got more white blood than Indian blood in you."

"Just stupid white talk," Hamilton then scoffed.

Brubaker then popped his head in the door and asked, "Everything okay in here?"

They all looked at each other and finally Martinez gave a thumbs-up sign and said, "Everything's fine, except Puzo wants to order a pizza."

Brubaker waved his hand towards them saying, "I don't care, the security guard is probably hungry anyway. I'll see you guys later.

"Everyone returned to their reading, except Puzo. He wanted a sign that his move to D.C. was the right move, and that most federal employees were highly conscientious, dedicated patriots.

After a few minutes, he saw Hamilton resting his head on his one hand and giving him the finger with the other hand, and then he observed Martinez continuing combing his hair and singing to himself.

Yes, Puzo acknowledged, these signs were genuine federal alerts that his D.C. mission to find some stable meaning in his life was in definite jeopardy.

9

SHIRLEY DOESN'T WANT
TO BATHE ANYMORE

The next two weeks were very traumatic for most of the world in general as reported by various sources: 1) several American hostages were being terrorized and held captive in Iran by a jovial guy called the Ayatollah something or other; 2) a beleaguered Poland was being assaulted by the boys from Moscow again; 3) Ireland was blowing itself apart with religious rioting; 4) El Salvador was keeping the reputation of chaotic Central America alive and well with its civil turmoil; 5) Afghanistan became another casualty to Russia's siege on the planet; 6) the entire Middle East was boiling over with regional warfare between the Arabs and U.S. backed Israel that was dragging the rest of the world into further chaos; 7) super world powers like the U.S. and Russia were becoming dangerously involved in inane political disputes between petty places all over the globe; and 8) on top of it all in Washington, D.C., capitol of one of the biggest super powers of all times, an intense struggle was taking place between Shirley Brubaker and a very unwanted guest, who had just finished his second week of a planned one-week stay.

Shirley was fit to be tied and threatened to gain tremendous amounts of weight if her husband didn't do something about Puzo moving out very fast. Brubaker understood her position, but he also felt sympathetic towards a guy who was essentially broke until his first government payday, which normally took four weeks. The sympathy ran real short, however, when Shirley refused to bathe until Puzo was gone.

The very next day Brubaker loaned Puzo two hundred dollars and personally drove him to his new housing arrangement that Brubaker had found himself during an extended "emergency" break from the office.

Puzo's new home was in a large, low-income residential area near R.F.K. Stadium, a block off Constitution Avenue and near the Emancipation Monument, which Puzo had promised Brubaker that he wouldn't deface or urinate all over it. The rickety old house had been previously converted into a boarding house and it handled from six to sixteen guests. The number of boarders usually fluctuated with the amount of Pakistani and Bangladeshi cabdrivers who crowded into the various cramped bedrooms.

The atmosphere in the crowded house was similar to a United Nations' refugee camp, and Puzo would be stuck in this raucous camp for some time due to his low-paying, government service rating at Interior. The problem of low pay resulted from the fact that he had been initially rated a lowly G.S. Nine, because of his probationary and excepted service status. He was told that he needed to put in a good year to achieve permanent status and a higher rating.

Reluctantly accepting his struggling situation, Puzo had pledged to himself that he would accomplish this one-year challenge, although he was thoroughly dismayed by the federal system.

Compounding this challenge now, he was living in a converted, dilapidated attic, just above a bunch of strange lower level inhabitants. Furthermore, he was constantly gagging on all the weird foreign smells that drifted up from the Pakistani-Bangladeshi-United Nations kitchen and into his tiny quarters. The only good thing about the attic was that he was the sole beneficiary of the rising heat in the house. If not, he would have seriously considered living in Florida and commuting to work by Greyhound bus.

Following his move out of Brubaker's place, he noticed that Ralph appeared much happier and less tense around the office. Brubaker even volunteered to help him with his written reports by giving him important inside tips that would guarantee complimentary comments from the administrative higher-ups.

Brubaker carefully instructed Puzo not to use insensitive terms like gross mismanagement, or blatant corruption in any of his reports, which would invariably offend sensitive political leaders in the usually corrupt U.S. possessions and territories. Brubaker told him that the proper term for "gross mismanagement" was actually "managerial fluctuations in a maturing U.S. territory," and the term for "blatant corruption" was "traditional island monetary disbursement activities."

It seemed that these innocent sounding terms were more pleasing to the federal ear, and they also prevented touchy territorial leaders from screaming to the press that the United States was an oppressive and insensitive nation that always misunderstood their innocent island ways.

Whatever it took, Puzo didn't care. He was going to climb the freaking G.S. ladder to D.C. stardom. He also had a mission to overcome his prejudices and be worldly successful. As it turned out, his new roommates were thoughtful and instructive people, who enlighten Puzo on international affairs and how to handle bigotry that had faced them in their homelands and even in America.

Puzo was a changed man from his California days, and even Brubaker wondered what kind of federal career creature had he now created.

But getting back to his initial low payday situation, if Puzo had only known that Hamilton and Martinez had already been given more lucrative G.S. Ten ratings--because of their higher ethnic status with the feds--, he would have probably joined the American Indian Movement to protest this outrage and, most probably, get thoroughly skinned and scalped after the real Apaches discovered that he had about as much Indian blood in him as General Custer.

A month later, after spending a busy day inserting Brubaker-approved euphemisms into critical reports of the U.S. possessions in the Western Pacific, Puzo decided it was high time for some night-time rest and relaxation. So, he decided to meet Martinez at "Spats", which was a fairly casual nightclub in Georgetown that catered to rising G.S. stars in Washington.

The place was packed and they stood at the bar until they found a small table by the front door. They were having a pretty good time until a lady G.S. Twelve from the State Department stopped by their table and scoffed at the mention of Puzo's rookie G.S. Nine rating.

She soon left their table, looking for a good-looking Thirteen or Fourteen. After she had left their table Puzo asked Martinez: "What's wrong with a Nine rating?"

Martinez looked at him with a broad grin and said, "I don't know about you, but I'm already a Ten, and I didn't even finish college. And I think Hamilton was given an Eleven rating yesterday because the black reps in Congress have been pushing for higher salaries for all their brothers."

"Are you shitting me?!" Puzo exclaimed.

"No, man. You better check with your Apache people and have them get the Indians a higher rating with Congress. We brown and the black brothers are doing okay, but if you Indians don't be careful, those Eskimos and Pacific Islanders are going to pass you guys soon." Martinez continued to down his drink and smiled at a passing girl.

"What about half-breed Indians and Italians? Aren't they considered brown like you." Puzo said.

"Half-breed Italians?! Forget it, man. Columbus had his chance to claim this place for the wops and blew it. You know, Paddy, this America is a great place for most minorities, except for all you minorities with semi-white skin!" Martinez laughed out loud and suddenly spied an encouraging young lady and quickly excused himself.

Puzo just remained at the table, idly stirring his drink with his finger and seriously thinking of changing his name to Gomez, or even Jesse Jackson. This was definitely a setback to his road to racial recovery. But he told himself to maintain and let time heal his lousy, goddamned, fucking, son-¬of-a-bitching, horse shit G.S. Nine rating!

The next three months went by rather quickly and Puzo counted every DOI day as an asset that was securely banked away towards his more permanent security in Washington. And as an added federal pastime, he became interested in NASA through inter-agency information memos.

Traveling safely to the moon sounded like more fun than a week at Disneyland, and he occasionally thought of working at NASA in Florida and becoming a space agency adventurer in the future. But for now he was quite satisfied living in Washington and he had no plans for any trips, anywhere.

He actually enjoyed the current stability in his life and society's inequities didn't really bother him too much anymore, except for maybe the excessive monetary waste caused by the Western Pacific Islands that he was reading about in his federal reports.

It was his daily duty to read about case after continuous case of waste and more waste in the Western Pacific region, and it became a broken record of "Traditional Island Monetary Disbursement Activities."

Over time, he had reviewed a myriad of cases of blatant island chicanery with the U.S. taxpayers' money, and he privately wished he had only one percent of all the money that he knew was flushed down the tropical toilet. Then he wouldn't have to worry about his lowly G.S. rating ever again.

After weeks of reviews, he began to get more and more cynical about the situation, and even went to the extremes of making his first serious statements in public about U.S. politics. He realized that he might upset Brubaker and his big boss Oliver, but he impulsively began to support a conservative Republican for president in an overwhelming environment of Democratic liberals.

After a while, his occasional vocal support for the Republican presidential candidate Ronald Reagan was dismissed as the harmless ravings of another Californian, who knew more about suntans and surfing than what it actually took to run U.S.A. Minorities, Inc.

But could this be his true mission in D.C.? Could it be that he was to become a loyal Republican and support the "Gipper" to the top in the upcoming election?!

Anyway, for what it was worth, it was a part-time diversion for Puzo that kept his mind occasionally free from a returning, nagging premonition about his eminent future.

One day in early June of 1980, he and Brubaker went over to Constitution Gardens, across the street from where they worked, and had lunch. It was a rather warm day, and they ordered sandwiches and cold beer at an outdoor food stand. They sat on a wooden table by a pond full of quacking ducks and begging squirrels, and then started eating their lunch.

Soon, Puzo was devouring a pastrami and cheese sandwich with mustard oozing all over his face and it was making Puzo sigh with delight. He had kicked off his shoes and drinking the cold beer was a pleasant addition on a warm day for a struggling G.S. Nine, who could already envision the next six months being successfully logged in the books. Before he knew it, he would be initiated into the higher order of G.S. Tens, or maybe even the Elevens, if maybe the American Indian Movement would ever get out of their condo wigwams in Washington and demand that all Apache-Italians working in D.C. deserved a better deal.

Puzo's momentary mental revelry was finally interrupted by Brubaker, who threw a remaining piece of his sandwich to a horde of squawking ducks, inches away from Puzo's shoeless feet.

Puzo had to quickly move his feet to the side, preventing his toes from becoming the main course for a bunch of famished, feather-bearing maniacs, who had no qualms about going through his sweaty socks to their next meal.

He was still shuffling his feet back and forth when Brubaker quipped: "Guess what, Paddy?" as he threw another piece of his bread to the ducks next to Puzo's dancing feet.

"What?!" Puzo shot back, while moving his feet away from his hungry guests. "And stop encouraging these damned ducks!"

"We're going native for the next six months!" Brubaker happily announced.

"What da hell you talking about, boy?!" Puzo talked in a voice like Oliver Johnson. He then gulped his remaining beer.

Brubaker swallowed some of his beer and said, "I've been assigned to travel to Guam by the first of July to establish a temporary technical assistance center for the Pacific region." He took another swallow of beer as Puzo just stared at him. Brubaker continued: "I will oversee Guam, American Samoa, the Trust Territory of the Pacific Islands, and the newly-formed, U.S. Commonwealth of the Northern Mariana Islands, which had been a part of the Trust Territory. Martinez will be stationed on American Samoa to assist me there, and you, my friend, will be helping me with the Trust Territory and living and assisting me on Saipan, the largest populated island in the Northern Mariana Islands, where the Trust Territory Headquarters is located.

Brubaker paused again to finish his beer, and added: "Hamilton is being sent to the Virgin Islands and will report directly to Johnson. So, what do you think of those coconuts and paradise, boy?"

Puzo had been continuously staring at Brubaker with beer and mustard running down his paralyzed lips and lowered jaw. He couldn't believe what he had just heard.

Brubaker waved his hand in front of Puzo's face. "I said, what do you think of those coconuts, boy? We're headed for paradise!"

"Oh, my God, it's happening!" Puzo finally blurted out. "I'm just getting my shit together here in D.C. and now it's happening. You're actually talking about ripping me out of my federal security blanket and sending me to some remote island with real jungle-type natives, who like federal guys like us about as much as they like killer hurricanes!"

"They're called typhoons where we're going, and the natives are called islanders and are mostly friendly," Brubaker corrected him with a big grin.

"Okay, okay, typhoons and islanders, but you keep saying 'we'. Don't I have a choice in this matter?" Puzo finally asked.

"Not really." Brubaker replied, adding, "Unless you want to quit your job altogether. The P-MAT group has been assigned to the territories to add visibility to President Carter's campaign for more social programs both here and abroad. Besides, I thought a trip to paradise was everyone's dream."

Puzo threw the rest of his unfinished sandwich to some patrolling squirrels. "I just don't need to go to paradise. I grew up in a so-called paradise called California and got screwed."

He then shook his head with disbelief, adding: "Hey, a weekend in the Caribbean sounds okay, but not six frigging months on a remote island with a whole bunch of island guys, who like jerking off the few white men there who carry big stupid federal reports around all day in the hot jungle sun."

"Look on the bright side," Brubaker quickly offered, "you'll be moving out of your Pakistani Palace, as you call it. Then we'll be back next January and you'll get your permanent status, and you can spend the rest of your life in Washington in a nice heated townhouse."

Puzo lamented, "What if Reagan beats Carter in the election this November? Then we P-MATs and all the other Mickey Mouse positions that Carter created will get thrown right out into the unemployment bin."

"Reagan won't win, believe me." Brubaker sounded assured. "There are too many deadbeats in the voting majority who always let the minority groups sway the elections."

"You always say look on the bright side. Well, Ralph, it's bright as hell in the tropics, and I've been having this nagging feeling that something strange was going to happen to me concerning a permanent island living arrangement. Are you sure we'll be back in six months?"

"Guaranteed. Six months, tops." Brubaker grinned.

"Are you sure?" Puzo implored again.

"Guaranteed, Paddy, with whip cream and nuts on top, and as an added bonus, you'll be a minority person for a change." Brubaker stood to leave.

"Okay, okay!' Puzo began to put on his shoes. "I don't understand it. Why was I hired to study the financial waste in a place where I'm now being sent on a costly trip that's going to waste even more taxpayers' money?"

"Carter and his boys believe in plenty of taxpayers' financial fertilizer to make his public policies grow!" Brubaker laughed.

"Well, my daddy always said that too much manure is just too much damn manure." Puzo sighed and ordered two more beers to go.

10

SENTENCED TO PARADISE

The next two weeks were a blur of trip preparations for Brubaker and his PMAT troops, who were now headed for the tropical hinterlands.

Initially, Shirley didn't really care for the idea of a long trip to the Western Pacific Islands, but Ralph had promised her that Guam had actual shopping centers, and that Puzo would be living over a hundred miles away on a small, remote island. So, she reluctantly changed her mind after Ralph promised it would be only six months, and she secretly prayed that Puzo's island would be situated on an active volcano.

Everything was eventually ready for the big departure to the islands, and the last major obstacle to clear for everyone in PMAT was their successfully attending an OTIA going away party for them, sponsored, of course, by the other pissed-off OTIA employees, who had to grudgingly donate to the party.

The party was held on the PMAT group's last Friday night in Washington, at the Assistant Secretary Sinclair's plush townhouse near the DuPont Circle. As a rule, to make it successful for one's own good, everyone did their best not to get too drunk and throw up on the Assistant Secretary's new carpet, which would definitely guarantee occupational oblivion at the OTIA.

Sinclair had slyly used employee parties to eyeball any new girls working at OTIA, since his bored wife was always traveling in Europe and furthermore, he liked to get his underlings drunk and gain political information from his spies who would wander about the party. Everyone at OTIA dreaded going to the party, knowing alcoholic slips of the tongue could mean quick transfers to Point Frozen, Alaska.

However, it was an invitation that no one at OTIA could turn down. As priorities went at the OTIA, one could turn down an invitation to the White House if it fell on his or her bowling night, but no way could one snub a party of the Assistant Secretary of OTIA, not even if one's house was set on fire and his or her spouse was held hostage by a radical group of crazed Puerto Ricans, who wanted either a million dollars or ten used Chevy Impalas.

Later, at about ten o'clock on the night of the party, Brubaker, Puzo and Martinez were officially surrounded in the living room by three white OTIA Desk Officers, who were asked to brief the PMAT guys.

The Desk Officers or D.O.'s, who were stationed in D.C., represented the various destinations of the PMAT's upcoming trip to the Pacific region. There was a D.O. for Guam, for American Samoa, and one for the Trust Territory of the Pacific Islands (T.T.P.I.), which also included the new U.S. Commonwealth of the Northern Mariana Islands.

Each D.O. was trying to dominate the conversation with their special "white" expertise of the U.S. Pacific possessions and their brown inhabitants.

"You must realize," the Guam D.O. said with a condescending tone, "that the islanders have a very unique culture on Guam and their wonderful traditions must be experienced to the fullest. It behooves us to acknowledge all the island practices at any cost, while we of course bring all the benefits of our United States government to their quaint little villages."

"Yes, yes. That's so true in the Trust Territories, too." chirped in the petite lady D.O. for the T.T.P.I. She then added: "The island districts in the Trust Territories are all so different and so distinct that each government entity must be treated with utmost respect and convivial perspicacity."

Meanwhile, the American Samoan D.O. would always start to say something and then get interrupted. He resigned himself to mainly nodding his head and picking his nose. Martinez was also bobbing his head in comical synchronization with the guy, and then started combing his hair again.

Puzo finally looked at Brubaker and discreetly winked. "Uh, Ralph, I think Oliver wants to see us over by the bar."

"That's right," agreed Brubaker. "Please excuse us." He then spoke to Martinez. "Angel, please hang around and take notes for us, especially about the Trust Territories."

Martinez caught the hint about the good-looking T.T.P.I. Desk Officer and smiled. "Sure, boss, I'll do my best."

On the way to the bar Puzo asked Brubaker, "Have any of those D.O.'s ever seen a Micronesian island, or been in the Pacific jungles before? From what I read about the islanders, they don't want "tradition" in the islands anymore, all they want are their Sony twenty-one-inch TV sets and air conditioners in their "traditional" little huts, with brand new cars parked outside under their coconut trees."

Brubaker cautioned Puzo with a whisper: "Shh, don't let one of the Assistant Secretary's spies overhear you." Brubaker then continued with a low voice. "I heard the Guam D.O. has been on Guam for only a day and a half, which damn near qualifies him as a federal expert on the place. The Trust Territory lady is new and has never been west of New Mexico, and the American Samoan expert got beaten up by a drunken Samoan on his first night in Pago Pago and was medically evacuated to Hawaii on a stretcher. So, in a nutshell, we're better off waiting till we get there ourselves before we make any official judgments."

They reached the bar and ordered their drinks. Puzo had been drinking beer and tequila all night long and Brubaker noticed his increased loss of sobriety. "I hope you realize we have a six o'clock flight tomorrow, and it's in the A.M., not P.M."

"Gimme a break," Puzo said. "It's my last night in civilization for six months, and I want my transition to the island jungles to be an incoherent experience."

Puzo had another shot of tequila and asked Brubaker, "Say, what the hell does perspas, perspiss, perspissidy mean, anyway?"

Brubaker responded: "You mean perspicacity. It means good judgment, like not drinking a whole bottle of tequila and puking on Sinclair's rug."

Brubaker put his arm around Puzo and continued: "Listen, I hear there's one advantage in Micronesia for you. Nobody ever uses any words longer than two syllables." Brubaker laughed, adding: "Hey, I'm going to see some friends, Paddy. If the police come and throw you in jail, just make sure you're at the airport and on time tomorrow."

"And if I do get thrown in jail," Puzo replied, "please don't send Shirley with the bail money, okay? By the way, where is she, Ralph. I haven't seen her all night."

"Her last night in civilization is being spent at the ballet with her more civilized friends," he replied with a wry smile. "See you later."

After Brubaker walked away, Puzo ordered another shooter of tequila and tossed it down. He then got a cold bottle of beer and started to wander aimlessly around. The bartender had told him that the Assistant Secretary had been called away for an emergency meeting with President Carter's campaign coordinator, so Puzo felt more relaxed walking among the various OTIA people with a big goofy grin on his intoxicated face. If they only knew his true feelings about his pending departure to a tropical sauna with millions of flies and cockroaches, they would mercifully kidnap him and make him miss his flight.

He finally wandered all the way up to the sacrosanct third floor of the Assistant Secretary's townhouse, which most OTIA employees knew was off limits. He hadn't been fully informed about the third floor restriction and inquisitively poked his nose into the Assistant Secretary's unlocked home office. The room had been accidentally left unlocked and he decided to take a quick inspection of the big guy's office.

He went in and locked the door behind him. After turning on the light he saw that it was a very unusual, politically-decorated office, with photographs of President Carter, Vice President Mondale, and the Assistant Secretary shaking hands with various Democratic VIPs on the right wall. On the left wall were strange-looking wooden carvings, and in the back of the office were different governmental flags on wood staffs that stood behind a huge mahogany desk. Most of the flags were unfamiliar to him, other than the U.S. flag.

Then it dawned on him that these flags must be from various U.S. island possessions. He had remembered seeing a few of the flags in his reports, and their also being displayed during the previous month around the OTIA section, when he managed a glimpse of some visiting island leaders. The island leaders had come on expensive trips to Washington for their emotionally-packed, big-budget-beg-a-thons, which included quick visits to the Atlantic City gambling casinos for "recreational studies."

After perusing the flags, he gulped down the last of his beer and stuck the empty bottle in his pocket to prevent any evidence of his unauthorized visit.

Suddenly, he heard a thump from above and quickly looked up. A panel in the ceiling had swung open and the head of a good-looking young woman hung out.

"Whoops," she said in a surprised voice, "I thought it was someone else."

Puzo smiled and quickly caught on. "The bartender says he'll be gone for quite a bit."

"Is that so?" She returned his smile.

"That's so, ma'am." He just stood there with a big dumb grin on his face.

"Well, since you know who won't be here for maybe an hour or so, would you care to come up here for a friendly visit, cowboy?" She appeared very intoxicated on something other than tequila and beer.

Puzo slowly nodded yes several times with his mouth wide open. Then he realized his odd behavior was delaying a possible trip to true paradise, and it was right in the middle of Washington, D.C.!

After looking around for a ladder, he urgently asked, "How do I get up there?"

She pointed down at the wall, explaining: "See those weird, wooden pictures of coconut trees and islanders on the wall? Well, they're nailed in such a way to make a ladder." She then giggled.

Puzo walked over to the wall and inspected the heavy, wooden carvings, saying out loud to himself, "I'll be damned."

He continued shaking his head and made a clumsy ascent into the semi-dark attic, hoping to God that he didn't fall and break his neck.

The attic was a typical haven for naughty people, with a nearly wall-to-wall water bed mattress, mirrors on the low ceiling, tons of pillows, and a miniature wet bar hanging in the corner. The young lady had propped herself against one of the walls and was smoking one of her funny-smelling cigarettes. This was definitely not Marlboro Country.

"Do you smoke?" she asked, holding out a self-rolled joint of marijuana.

"Not really." Puzo replied, then he lied to cover up his apprehension of never having smoke marijuana: "I'm part-time with the C.I.A. at Interior, and the policy manual says it's dangerous to smoke in bed." He awkwardly sat down on the rolling mattress.

"So, what do you do for the C.I.A. over at Interior?" She took a big hit of her joint, held her breath, and exhaled.

"Well, since the D.O.I. has screwed up more projects in the last hundred years than anyone can imagine, the C.I.A. wants me to keep an eye on the place. By the way, what's your name?"

"Never mind my name. So, you think Interior's full of idiots---excluding yourself, of course." She began to get more interested in his cynical remarks.

"I didn't say that." A drunken Puzo suddenly felt nauseous on the swaying water bed and said without thinking: "I just think Reagan should get a chance to change things around a little."

"So, you're a Reagan supporter, too?" she coolly asked.

"Did I say that? I was only kidding. Carter's my main man. Excuse me, do you have a bathroom up here, I feel seasick and need to puke or pee pretty soon."

"You better go back to the party before Sinclair gets back." She took another puff and closed her eyes.

He took the hint and barely made it down the makeshift ladder to return to the party. He wanted to make a meaningful move on the lady, but his latest attempt to score just passed out in a pungent cloud of Democratic smoke.

At a quarter past midnight the party wound down to a quick halt, due to the fact that the Assistant Secretary had arrived back from his meeting and was busily counting drunk and obnoxious heads who were now destined for Alaska.

Martinez had earlier rescued Puzo out of Sinclair's den, where he was watching live television for the last time for the next six months, and after they had picked up their luggage from their respective homes, they were now driving towards Spats for a D.C. drinking finale.

Martinez was driving and talking to Puzo: "You know, Brubaker says that if we don't show up at the airport on time, he's goin' to throw us off the nearest bridge and into the Potomac River, with our island information pouches tied to our dicks!"

"Sure, Angel, I know already." Puzo was holding his throbbing head, adding, "Hey, did you see Hamilton tonight?"

"No, man. He left yesterday morning for the Virgin Islands. He said he'd rather party with the brothers in V.I., and not with a bunch of dumb whiteys from O.T.I.A."

"What did Johnson say about Hamilton's skipping Sinclair's party?"

"He got him excused." Martinez replied. "Johnson made up a story about the importance of Hamilton going to the islands to get an early start on the public relations. You know how Johnson agrees with everything Hamilton wants, especially when Hamilton glares at him with those 'Malcolm X eyes."

"I think I'll change my name to Hamilton instead of Gomez," Puzo slurred.

"Whatta you mean, gringo? You might pass for a Gomez, but no way as a brother!" Martinez laughed and honked his car horn several times.

They eventually made it to Spats without Martinez putting his rented car into the Potomac, and they stayed until the place closed down.

After leaving Spats, they retrieved a spare bottle of tequila from Puzo's luggage and drove over to the Constitution Gardens for a last toast of Washington, deciding it was best not to sleep and surely miss their flight.

At approximately five o'clock in the morning they were sitting drunk on the steps of the Lincoln Memorial.

"You know something?" Puzo broke the silence. "When I first got here I swore I was going to urinate on Mister Lincoln's shoes."

"What for?" Martinez asked.

"For emancipating some black terrorists who almost killed me one night in Los Angeles."

"How do you feel now, amigo?"

He looked at the bottle of tequila in his hand and winced with a throbbing headache that was pounding downwards throughout his entire body.

"Well, after drinking this Mexican loco water all night, I now feel like urinating on the Poncho Villa Memorial instead, if he has one."

"Hey, man, he's a relative of mine!"

"Sorry, Angel. I was only kidding. Both the Lincoln Memorial and Poncho Villa are beautiful. I wouldn't want to put a hex on my return to civilization anyway."

Puzo got up to his feet and wobbled back and forth. "We'd better head for the airport before the cops nail us for puking in front of Lincoln." He then suddenly recalled: "Hey, you ever score with Brubaker's secretary?"

Martinez shook his head and smiled. "No way. She was too smart for me, and I think we'd better be careful, Paddy, while the black brothers and we amigos hassle one another, the women are taking over."

Puzo nodded in agreement and they slowly walked back to their parked car. They then proceeded to the Washington National Airport, without the benefit of showering, shaving, or even changing their smelly party clothes.

Brubaker silently sat in an aisle seat of the six o'clock flight to Los Angeles, with his wife Shirley at his side. They sat way up in the front of the plane.

Earlier, Martinez and Puzo had barely made their flight on time, and an anxious Brubaker was breathing a little easier when he greeted them at the door of the plane with only minutes to spare.

However, with Brubaker's next inhalation, in which he had sucked in the aroma of his two foul-smelling friends, he had fully agreed with Shirley's demands that Martinez and Puzo sit in the rear of the plane for their entire trip to the Pacific islands.

Brubaker's only complaint about the seating arrangement was not being able to converse with his PMAT friends about the details of their upcoming Pacific project. Although from the looks of both of them sprawled out later in their seats with air sickness bags taped to their mouths, his alternative plan for a meeting in Los Angeles or Hawaii seemed to be a wiser decision.

As it turned out, they did have a twelve-hour delay in Los Angeles, and Brubaker got a satisfactory amount of coherent grunts from both of them, which would take care of most of the initial details of their assignments. The twelve-hour delay also compounded the tequila-drenched hangover for both Martinez and Puzo, and after another three and one-half hour flight to Hawaii, Martinez was almost loaded as non-human cargo for his final flight to American Samoa.

Puzo had missed seeing Martinez leave, since he had taken several Tylenol and Contac capsules and passed out in the waiting lounge.

Following another twelve-hour delay in Hawaii, the Brubakers and Puzo finally arrived on Guam at ten o'clock on Monday night, June 30, 1980. They had gained a day passing the International Date Line, which was fifteen hundred miles west of Hawaii, and everyone hoped that the time zone jump would somehow help heal their individually rotten conditions. They also made it to Guam by some miracle before July first.

After waiting for their delayed luggage, the Brubakers finally left the Guam International Airport in a new air conditioned shuttle bus for the Hilton Hotel, while Puzo had to wait another two hours for an old and air conditioned-less shuttle bus to a cheap, cockroach-infested hotel near lower Tumon Bay.

He had previously agreed to stay at a different hotel to make Shirley's trip a complete success. Puzo also promised Brubaker to catch the early flight the next day to Saipan. It had already been scheduled that a T.T.P.I. government driver would be waiting for

Puzo on Saipan, and he was expected to be there on the first flight in the morning.

While Puzo rode in the bus to the cheap hotel in a near coma, he vaguely remembered telling Brubaker that he would probably call from Saipan upon arrival and asked, "What in the hell am I supposed to do now?!"

Nearly three hours following his arrival in the steaming tropics of Guam it was well past midnight, and he had painfully crawled into a musty bed in a dark and muggy hotel room after repeatedly advising the front desk to please wake him up at five o'clock in the morning. He had pulled a partially-ripped sheet across his sweaty body and was listening to a faulty air conditioner shuddered to power fluctuations as it loudly rattled in the background. He hadn't even showered because the water pressure was nonexistent in his third-floor room. He didn't even care about the deteriorating level of his body hygiene. He was going to try to sleep for as long as he could in this hot and humid room in paradise, dreaming of majestic pine trees and cool mountain breezes blowing on his naked torso…

RRRING!!! RRRING!!! RRRING!!!

11

OH, GOD, I'M ON GUAM

"Hey, you! It's five o'clock!" a loud, Spanish-sounding female voice shrilled over the phone in a most irritating manner.

The early morning wake-up call caused a sleep-deprived Puzo to flinch at the ear-thumping announcement, and he stuffed the phone under his sweat soaked pillow. He still heard muffled shouts emanating from the phone and decided to carefully hold the hotel phone near to his ear again, but he painfully flinched at yet another revolting announcement that ricocheted off his throbbing eardrum and prevailing hangover.

"Hey, you, don't you hear me no good? It's five o'clock! You said wake you at five!" screamed the front desk operator.

"Yeah, yeah, I heard you already," Puzo hoarsely replied, and he added in a loud whisper, "What's a crazy Mexican doing on this jungle island?"

"I heard that!" the hotel operator angrily shot back. "I'm no crazy Mexican! I'm Guamanian, stupid!!"

Puzo then heard a burst of one of the strangest languages that he had ever heard, and he implored in a raised voice: "Okay, don't get so excited, alright?! And whoever you are, can you speak English so I can understand you?"

There was a short pause, and then the operator shouted, "I get you, you smartass statesider! You on my island now, my family get a big bullet for you. You understand that English good, mister white stupid?!" The operator then quickly disconnected the line.

Puzo closed his eyes and barely held the phone next to his ringing ear, and recollected from previous DOI conversations that the indigenous American islanders referred to their white counterparts from the U.S. mainland as statesiders, mostly in a derogatory manner. Following a short pause to collect his shattered thoughts, he unconsciously dropped the phone to the floor and pushed back his musty blanket, which smelled like it was made out of sticky two-thirds mildew. He then slowly shook his head in the early morning darkness. It felt like he was lying in a wet, foul-smelling sponge, as he stared into the darkness and ruefully listened to a faulty air conditioner that occasionally sprayed a watery mist onto his bed. He slowly began to comprehend the reason why his bed was so wet from the spraying air conditioner, but he still couldn't fully comprehend his current situation in life.

Puzo suddenly cringed as his wet boxer shorts became wedged further up in the crack of his ass, as he further groveled in self-pity and realized that his nagging premonition had finally decided to come true and trap him, a reasonably innocent young man of thirty-two, in a shabby, rundown tourist trap of a hotel on a semi-sleazy island called Guam.

So far, he didn't like anything about Guam, which was a two hundred and twelve square mile volcanic lump in the middle of nowhere. It was situated approximately thirty-six hundred miles west of the Hawaiian Islands, and about eight hundred miles north of the equator, in an area called Micronesia.

The United States had picked up Guam in a spoils-of-war grab bag after its Spanish owner quickly surrendered in the Spanish-American War of 1898. The rest of the Spanish-held Mariana Islands north of Guam, including Saipan, became the Northern Mariana Islands that Spain later dumped on Germany. After the

U.S. acquisition of Guam, it had continued as a shipping outpost for America in the Western Pacific, and supplied fresh water and coconuts for strung-out sailors on early twentieth century cargo ships.

Guam's major claim to historical prominence could be classified as having the dubious distinction of being the only American possession ever to be subjected to enemy occupation. It was attacked and captured by the Japanese in December of 1941, shortly after Pearl Harbor got caught with its military pants down and, subsequently, it was recaptured by the American forces in July of 1944.

Guam eventually became an official U.S. territory by virtue of the Guam Organic Act of 1950, and then became an important U.S. military naval installation and later air base for B-52's. With the military presence, it also became an important source of booze-laced revenue for the local bars. But by the 1980's, after thirty years of being a genuine American territory and after having the Fourth of July and George Washington's Birthday regularly observed, the semi-indigenous Guamanian-American residents, who were ethnic Chamorros and comprised about forty percent of the population, and who had earlier migrated from Malaysia and the Spanish held Philippines, still mostly acted as if Guam was their very own private little country.

And as for Puzo's current predicament, he was receiving his very first dose of dysfunctional Guamanian hospitality from a crazed hotel operator, and he had been on the island for less than a day.

He finally sat up in his hotel bed, took off his sweaty t-shirt, and started to wonder if the operator's threat of "getting him a big bullet" was only a bluff, or what he thought it meant. Anyway, he was glad that he would be soon leaving Guam for his new assignment on the nearby island of Saipan, where it was rumored to be slightly cooler, and a little more hospitable.

Still drowsy, he continued to contemplate the hotel operator's threat until he fell asleep again in a sitting position on his bed.

A moment later a loud thud was accompanied with a flash of pain to the back of his head, and then a queasy feeling of things scurry all over his body had brought him back to consciousness. He had fallen backwards and struck his head cleanly on the headboard shelf which, consequently, panicked a whole bunch of non-paying guests.

Cockroaches! Oh, God! He hated cockroaches, and these were the tropical kind: large, ugly and fearless.

The cockroaches were fleeing across his bed and onto his naked upper body. He was instantly airborne and out of bed, screaming and crushing the disgusting creatures that were clinging to his hairy frame. He then retreated hastily towards the bathroom, and on the way he stumbled over the phone that he had earlier dropped to the floor. He subsequently kicked an immovable table leg with this previously healthy big toe and let out another agonizing scream.

Finally, he limped into the darkened bathroom and immediately began flipping on all the light switches. The instant combination of overhead lights, make-up lights and a blazing sunlamp made him recoil in even more pain, and when he finally did focus his bloodshot eyes on the several remains of squashed cockroaches stuck to his quivering body, he quickly leaned over and puked his entire insides into the bathroom sink.

After a few last dry heaves, he slowly tried to wash up, but the water pressure was too low and he gave himself a wet rag wash with rusty water. He then looked up into the bathroom's broken mirror as he brushed his teeth and tried to recognize the face of a doomed adventurer, who was now peering strangely back at him.

Puzo then closed his eyes and began slowly lamenting out loud, "Gimme a little slack, Lord? First, Carter and Brubaker invite me to tropical oblivion and now you're starting to really rub it in!"

Incredibly, it seemed like only a little while ago that Brubaker had bailed him out of a chaotic lifestyle in California, and now he was stuck in island chaos, and later to be sent to tiny Saipan island, where seven thousand island folks ambivalently lived with a few dozen white folks like himself. And according to his federal reports, these island brown guys definitely belonged to "Minorities, Incorporated."

After a short period of personal lamenting, Puzo shook himself and realized he was getting behind in his departure for Saipan. The only good thing about this trip so far was that he had been paid a nice travel advance from the feds, which would allow him extra alcohol and therapy.

So, while nursing a very sore toe, he dressed and repacked his luggage that was supposedly airing out in the dank room. Finally, he was ready to depart his room, and he did so with a knot in his stomach and a strange feeling about his need to proceed.

Upon paying his hotel bill with a crisp hundred-dollar bill to impress the pretty cashier from the Philippines, he noticed an extremely obese Guamanian woman with a PBX headset in her hand, who was lurking in a dimly lit hallway behind the hotel's dingy front desk. The gargantuan Guamanian woman, who was obviously his morning operator, gave him a real dirty look and then ran her finger across her enormous neck to pantomime a long and slow throat-slashing.

Puzo sighed, and vaguely remembered reading the U.S. government publication entitled, "Department of Interior's Orientation Handbook for Occupational and Inhabitational Personnel in the U.S. Pacific Possessions." The pamphlet had described the native Guamanians as "friendly" Chamorros who were always very kind to outsiders.

Sure, very kind and friendly with big bullets. He should have read instead: "Jungle Survival of Dumb White Statesiders in Micronesia!"

After paying his bill, he asked the young and friendly hotel cashier what would be the quickest way to the airport. The cashier directed him to stand in front of the hotel and wait for a limousine service that would take him to the airport for a ten-dollar fee.

Puzo said okay, and then he painfully limped outside with a badly-stubbed toe until he eventually found an old concrete bench to sit down. He sat down and began to patiently wait for his ride, trying not to think about his pulsating big toe.

Several minutes passed by, and he anxiously went back inside the hotel lobby to ask the Filipina cashier about the nonexistent limousine service. He explained to her about his flight at six-thirty that morning, and that it was near six o'clock already.

The smiling cashier responded, "Don't worry, Mister Puzo, our hotel operator finally contacted a taxi driver, and it's only a short ride to the airport. We're sorry, but our limousine driver was jailed for drunk driving last night and isn't available this morning."

"Oh, okay, and thank you for getting my name right." Puzo thought why does it take a foreigner to get his name correct? He gave the cashier a return smile, and thought about making a move on the sweet-looking Filipina. But he felt pretty rotten and only said, "I'll just wait outside, and tell the operator thanks for the taxi call. We had a misunderstanding earlier, and I don't want any bad feelings between us."

She smiled again, and Puzo had a quick change of heart and asked the cashier with a sly smile, "By the way, are you planning to visit Saipan someday?"

"I don't think so," the cashier answered, "I'm married to our operator's older brother."

"Is that a fact?!" Puzo quickly subdued his wandering libido and backed away. "Well, it was nice meeting you. Bye." He cringed at the thought of the size of the fat operator's brother and wisely decided to limp outside for his taxi. He didn't need any further delays, and he also didn't need to flirt with a pretty young lady who for practical purposes and a U.S. citizenship had married an apparently much older member of a hot-tempered Guamanian family.

Once outside, he again sat on the old concrete bench. It was now six o'clock and he stared at his wristwatch intently.

Suddenly, he jumped up at the piercing sound of screeching tires. An old dilapidated, rust-eaten taxi cab had arrived out of nowhere and squealed to a stop right in front of him. A very mean-looking Guamanian guy was quietly sitting behind the wheel. The big hulking driver angrily flipped a switch inside his taxi that opened the trunk, and then glared at Puzo.

Puzo took the hint and picked up his suitcases and placed them in the trunk and accidentally slammed the lid closed, as a chunk of rust fell off the bumper.

The driver quickly yelled, "You take it easy on my car!"

Puzo nodded and he carefully climbed into the back seat. But before he could close his door the angry driver roared out of the hotel. Puzo vaguely remembered that he and his fellow taxi drivers in L.A. were a tad more courteous than his current diabolical driver.

"I'm going to the airport and I'm in a hurry," Puzo shouted above the racket of the beat-up old taxi and loud music from the radio, as he finally managed to close his door.

"You don't yell at me, and you don't tell me nothing and what to do. I know where to go. Where else would you statesider go with a suitcase? I'm no dumb Guamanian!" The driver sounded unusually angry, and continued shouting: "You owe me twenty dollars," while he drove erratically down an empty back road to the airport.

Puzo gulped, and after a short interval, asked, "Aren't you supposed to turn on the meter? I mean twenty dollars for such a short---" He was abruptly cut off.

"You shaddup, you stupid! You give my mother bad time at the hotel, and she said you smile at my Filipina wife!" the Guamanian yelled.

The very mean and large driver now became even meaner and larger to Puzo, and he knew he was presently in serious trouble because the crazed hotel operator had fixed him up with her psychotic son.

It's unbelievable, he thought, the whole freaking family is now after him. He just sat back, anxiously watching the road and wondering, what's next?!

"You never give my mother or any my relatives a bad time, you understand?" the driver suddenly shouted. He then grabbed an old .38 caliber pistol from under his seat and stuck it in a holster-type hole in the dashboard for Puzo's benefit.

"Sure, sure! Never again!" Puzo quickly replied in a conciliatory burst. He couldn't believe this was really happening, and he added, "To make sure I don't bother any of your family again, you please sure give me your family's name, okay?" Confused speech patterns were always a sign to Puzo that he was in serious, serious trouble.

"Never mind my family's name, statesider," the driver laughed with a menacing tone. "We Guamanians are all one family to you stupid white stateside fuckers."

Abruptly, the taxi ride was almost over, to Puzo's sudden realization and relief, as the driver sped over some speed bumps at the entrance to the airport. And hitting the bumps at a fast speed made Puzo's head slam against the roof of the taxi, and he didn't realize it at the time, but a long-time medical maxim came into play as the pain in one part of his body increased, a pain in another part proportionately decreased. In other words, his mangled toe and frayed nerves seemed to feel better at the onset of a cracked skull.

The taxi finally came to a rapid halt in front of the airport and the driver flipped open the trunk and loudly said: "Get you bags and give me thirty dollars!"

Puzo climbed out of the taxi and retrieved his suitcases from the taxi's trunk. He cautiously approached the terrorist taxi driver and meekly inquired, "Wasn't that twenty dollars?"

The driver slowly placed his hand on the pistol that was still stuck in the hole in the dashboard.

Puzo nodded, and said, "Sure, it was thirty dollars, how stupid of me...I hit my head...and made a mistake." He hastily gave the driver a fifty-dollar bill and was emotionally caught between waiting for his change or the urge to back away from the cab, for this was one cabbie that really didn't deserve a damn tip unless you figured in the driver's fucking gun.

The driver suddenly grabbed the pistol and pointed it at Puzo and clicked off an empty chamber.

Puzo gasped.

The driver laughed and sped off.

Puzo gasped again. He was dumbfounded. He looked around the front of the airport for someone who might have witnessed this possible attempt on his life and theft of his change…anyone! But he only saw a few islander people, who might have weapons, too! He then looked at his watch. It was now six-fifteen. He thought about notifying the police, but he had noticed the few police officers that he had seen on Guam were all Guamanians, too, and it seemed futile to pit "family" against one another.

He quickly felt a painful shiver run down his spine. He was becoming convulsive with hot and cold flashes as he looked at his watch again and gasped: "Six-seventeen…my flight!"

Without further worry about his physical or mental state of being, or the failure to get his damn change, he jerked and hobbled into the terminal as fast as his racked body could move, trying to forget the last half-hour of his new life in paradise.

His flight to Saipan was fortunately delayed thirty minutes and he was safely checked in, and when he finally did get settled in his seat on the plane, he leaned back and tried to relax.

He had picked a seat in the rear of the mostly empty small commuter plane and had placed on his chest a "Do Not Disturb" sign that he found in the in the seat pouch in front of him. He was in shambles, physically and mentally a living wreck.

In an attempt to numb himself for the flight that was destined for adventure due to high winds in the area, he sneaked out a pint of tequila from his briefcase and started to get the attention of an airline hostess for a cup, but decided to drink his tequila straight out of the bottle. He needed it in a hurry and didn't want the cup to delay the unique experience of an "I don't give a damn" tequila stupor.

After a couple of large swallows of tequila, he closed his eyes and contemplated his first full day in Micronesia. It was a complete disaster, and he really didn't want to dwell on it too much. He did, however, have a short chuckle at the old office joke about DOI personnel who travel to Micronesia. The joke was: if anyone had visited a Micronesian island for even just a few hours, like he had done on Guam, then the person would get a notation in their personnel file, reading, "Potential expert on whatever island he or she had once visited for more than one hour."

However, island familiarity breeds contempt, and if the visit lasted much longer and you became overly familiar with the island you were visiting, then your expert status was immediately dropped to non-expert status. This was due to the fact that Interior's shaky reputation couldn't afford any contemptible employees floating around their culturally sensitive U.S. Trust Territory of the Pacific Islands.

Puzo couldn't sleep on his flight to Saipan, even though he was essentially zombied out on tequila, so he decided to try and study the section of Interior's orientation handbook on Micronesia, especially the part about Saipan, which was rumored to be friendlier than Guam. That would be nice.

He kept reading and made a serious mental note that the Saipanese being the same Chamorro types as his Guamanian friends, although the Guamanian Chamorros had some earlier bad blood between their counterparts on Saipan. This was a result of the Saipanese Chamorros being in cahoots with the Japanese on Saipan island during World War II.

At the time of the outbreak of WWII, Saipan was the capitol for Japanese controlled Micronesia, except for America's Guam island, and when Japan invaded and captured Guam simultaneously with the bombing of Pearl Harbor, the Japanese military used some Saipanese Chamorros to translate, spy, and harass their Guamanian Chamorro cousins.

This social anomaly was getting somewhat confusing for Puzo, along with the fact that Carolinians had also migrated to Saipan from the Caroline islands, and the Carolinians were a whole different story.

Wow, this trip was beginning to seriously affect Puzo's vexing sense of adventurism, and he was already planning his rapid departure from Saipan immediately after, if not before, his temporary assignment was finished.

For the most part, he would humbly survive his ongoing tropical trauma, and then humbly get the hell back to the U.S. mainland and civilization very, very fast.

The Micronesian handbook that he was studying highlighted the history of Micronesia after World War II, when the Marshall Islands, the Caroline Islands of Yap, Truk (to be named Chuuk later), Ponape (to be named Pohnpei later) and Kosrae (formerly Kusaie), the Palau Islands, and the Northern Mariana Islands had all become a part of a United Nations Trusteeship administered by the United States of America. These islands had been captured from the Japanese by the U.S. military during World War II on a bloody trip across the Western Pacific, and Saipan, the main island of the Northern Mariana Islands, eventually became the headquarters for the T.T.P.I. administration and later the main island of the U.S. Commonwealth of the Northern Mariana Islands.

The T.T.P.I., or T.T. for short, covered an immense, three million square mile patch of the Western Pacific. The T.T. had being administered in a hapless manner by the United States government after the war, and it was now being supervised by the DOI and monitored by the nitpicking United Nations Security Council.

Puzo further read that Japan, before their defeat in WWII, had administered the Micronesian islands, excluding Guam, from 1914 to 1944. The Japanese mainly used Saipan and nearby islands for agricultural purposes of sending processed sugar cane as sugar and synthetic fuel to Japan, and later used Saipan for its civilian/military headquarters and the other Micronesian islands for military outposts in the Pacific region. Puzo pondered about the Amelia Earhart WWII alleged spying connection to Saipan and wished he could find some evidence, either authentic or manufactured, and gain instant fame and a quick ticket to Hollywood.

Puzo sighed and returned to reality and continued reading that prior to the Japanese administration of the Northern Mariana Islands, Germany had control over the islands from 1899 to 1914 after buying them cheaply from the Spanish. And prior to the time that the Germans had a chance to liven up the island with beer barrel polkas, Spain had sovereignty over the area during the lucrative trading days of the 19th century.

Consequently, each of these conquering countries had left its own peculiar trademarks on the islanders, who were mixed together with an erratic sprinkling of foreign leftovers who had resettled in the Northern Mariana Islands and other islands in Micronesia.

It suddenly appeared to Puzo that he was embarking on a journey into an island asylum of intrusive international bastards and pirates, who had joined a mixed menagerie of schizoid and overly xenophobic islanders, imported U.S. federal "experts," burned out Peace Corps defectors, and well-meaning, but commercially inspired missionaries. Moreover, the whole conglomeration of brown-skinned islanders and white-skinned bureaucrats was being daftly administered by that cracked outfit from Washington, the infamous Department of Interior.

From the vast pages of American history books and Puzo's own experiences so far, Interior had already showed its historical incompetence by screwing up the affairs of the American Indians and almost the entire Wild West of the United States. And now Interior was in the process of repeating history in the last Wild, Wild West---Micronesia.

12

WELCOME TO THE ISLANDS OF THIEVES

The plane finally touched down at Saipan Airport on a clear sunny morning at the very southern-most part of the island, and as Puzo peered out the aircraft window he took a deep breath and cautiously looked forward to his new adventure in life. He couldn't resist thinking about the explorer Magellan and the uncomplimentary name that Magellan gave the unique Mariana Islands, including Guam, in 1521. Puzo already experienced the unsavory uniqueness of Guam, and now he would be living on another unique Marianas island for the next six months. Magellan had named the whole infamous place "Islas de Los Ladrones," which translated to English means, "Islands of Thieves."

Upon disembarking on Saipan it did feel cooler than Guam, and the small island gave him a strange sensation that he couldn't quite put his finger on, although he did know that it still had to do with his nagging premonition of island doom and gloom that would come to fruition because of this thirteen-mile-long rock near the middle of nowhere.

He eventually made his way through an unorganized immigration and customs facility, and finally rested his weary body, cracked skull, and throbbing toe on a bench outside the terminal in the arrival area.

There had been only a few passengers on his flight, and they were all Saipanese locals who had relatives picking them up. He watched everyone depart and wondered where in the world was his scheduled ride. It was already past seven-thirty in the morning, and that was the time he was supposed to begin work at the Trust Territory Headquarters.

After a twenty-minute wait, he grew apprehensive over the delay of his ride and began looking for another way to T.T. Headquarters. He didn't see any local taxicabs, to his partial relief, so he checked the rent-a-car booths.

There he discovered that the local girls who ran the booths had quickly closed their operations just five minutes after his flight. He was rapidly learning a few quirks about island service, like don't expect it to compare with U.S. mainland standards. He then realized that he had left his suitcases unattended in the arrival area, so he quickly limped back to check, remembering again about Magellan's dubious label for the island. However, what he did find in the arrival area was a uniquely dressed security guard, carrying his luggage away. Puzo yelled, "Hey, wait! That's my luggage!"

"No problem," said the guard, who had turned around and was now facing him. The guard curiously looked at a bedraggled Puzo and then asked, "Can you prove this your luggage?" The guard was wearing a non-matching uniform, rubber sandals called zories, and he looked like a relative of the maniacal cab driver on Guam.

Puzo quickly noticed that the guard had an ancient gun stuck into his homemade holster, which also reminded him of the pistol episode he had on Guam. So, he spoke with cautious respect. "Yes, I can prove it."

"How? These bags have no name tags. Do you have baggage checks?" the guard asked.

Puzo looked in the shirt pocket of his recently acquired Hawaiian shirt for his passport where his boarding pass and missing baggage checks were once crumpled and stuck between the pages, and said: "Sorry, they must have fallen out after customs."

"Now we have problem, okay?" The guard continued walking towards his office and went inside with the bags, with Puzo dejectedly following him.

It took Puzo nearly fifteen minutes to finally convince the guard that he had legal claim to his two bags, because they were the only bags remaining and he was the only passenger left in the terminal. He also didn't get the bags until after he guessed that the guard was having a little island fun at an outsider's expense.

After taking inventory of his life's possessions, he then asked the guard, "Are there any buses or taxis on this island? I need a ride to Trust Territory Headquarters, and I'm in a hurry."

"Sorry, taxis all at the hotel now," the guard answered, adding: "No bus, too. But don't worry. You no need to hurry on Saipan. I call my brother to give you a ride to T. T. office."

The guard smiled with a mouth full of red-stained teeth from chewing too much local betel nut, and then he began dialing the phone.

Puzo quickly stopped the guard from dialing and said, "Never mind bothering your brother. I'll walk...it can't be that far. Where's the T.T. office, anyway?"

"You see that big road out there, just go north, maybe ten or twelve miles, almost to other end of island." He smiled again at Puzo with his big red teeth.

Puzo frowned. "Wait a minute. You're telling me that some idiot of a local planner put the stupid T.T. building on the other end of the island!"

He didn't wait for an answer and started out the doors with his reclaimed luggage. Then he suddenly stopped. He had done it again. He acted like a smartass statesider to a Chamorro islander again, and another one with a gun, too. He twirled around, expecting something to happen like on Guam. But the smiling guard was just sitting at his desk, busy eating a green mango and salt.

"Maybe nine miles," said the guard, while still eating his mango. He added, "You keep walking funny on maybe sore foot, I call my brother."

Puzo sighed, "No thanks, it's just nine miles." He turned around and started limping towards the main road.

As he was walking along the main road, he felt slightly embarrassed, since the guard did act nice enough. But then again the guard's ancestors on Guam were also nice to Magellan in 1521 when they invited him and his crew ashore for some barbequed coconuts, and then during mango-papaya dessert, some of the gracious hosts swam out to Magellan's unguarded ship and stole everything they could swim with. Hence, the name "Islands of Thieves" was historically dubbed on the Mariana Islands forever.

Puzo kept on trudging along the hot and dusty road, knowing that he just hadn't been on Saipan long enough to fully experience the history of Magellan's misfortunes yet. Guam, for sure, with the deranged cab driver. But on Saipan the armed airport security guard wearing rubber sandals didn't steal his luggage or even point a gun at him like his crazy Guamanian 'cousin.' So maybe Saipan was nicer to statesiders according to some earlier DOI gossip. Well, he hoped and prayed that this nicer hospitality lasted for at least another six months.

He just continued walking in the mid-morning tropical heat and oppressive humidity, hoping his ride would come and spot him soon before he sweated to death, or died of a throbbing big toe and sunstroke along a deserted roadside in freaking island paradise.

13

THE INFAMOUS T.T.P.I.

After hobbling along on an isolated road for nearly a mile, Puzo finally observed a car with a white stateside driver who was slowly driving up to where he was standing.

After the T.T.P.I.-labeled government car had finally stopped alongside of him, Puzo looked at the driver and implored, "You are my ride, aren't you?"

"Yeah," replied the driver indifferently. "You must be Puzi."

"It's Puzo." Puzo corrected the driver who was checking a personnel file with Puzo's picture on it.

The driver looked up. "Oh, yes, it's Puzo. I'm sorry about being late to pick you up, we had a miscommunication problem at the office. My name's Trevor Webber, Assistant A.G. in the T.T. Attorney General's Office."

Webber was over-dressed in a white silk shirt and purple tie, and looked extremely aloof and bored with paradise. He gave Puzo the car keys and started combing his perfectly coifed hair, while idly waited for Puzo to put his luggage in the car's trunk.

After putting his bags in the trunk, Puzo carefully shimmied into the car, avoiding any contact with his ailing big toe. Webber was still combing his hair until Puzo was settled in his seat, and then Webber got the keys back and started to drive away towards T.T. Headquarters. Puzo just leaned back in his seat and temporarily closed his eyes in relief.

Webber eventually noticed his shaky condition and coolly inquired, "Rough trip?"

"How'd you guess?" was Puzo's blunt reply. He wasn't too concerned about Webber's feelings at the time. He was just relieved to see the T.T. car had air conditioning, but he also noticed Webber was slowly rolling down his window and sniffing the fresh air blowing into the car.

Puzo asked, "Do I smell that bad?"

Webber mockingly replied, "Don't worry, you aren't the first to arrive here smelling badly after a long trip from the mainland."

"Thanks for being honest," Puzo mumbled back, then he asked: "So when can I check into a hotel for a needed shower?"

"Later," Webber said, "We're already late for your eight-thirty appointment with the T.T.'s High Commissioner."

"You mean the High Commissioner wants to see me already?" Puzo quickly answered.

"Relax, it's just a courtesy call to see if everything was okay with your trip to Saipan."

Webber then made a turn at a forked intersection and proceeded to drive onwards to T.T. Headquarters, as he arrogantly continued: "The Hicom will probably ask you why you're out here, and how you're going to help the great island nations of glorious Micronesia."

"I don't think the High Commissioner wants to hear about my chaotic trip," Puzo quipped. "And I'm not much help to anyone right now, if you know what I mean." Puzo then yawned. "Would you excuse me while I sightsee for the rest of the trip?"

"Go ahead." Webber seemed relieved at the curtailing of the conversation and began humming Beethoven's Fifth to himself.

Puzo leaned back and spent the rest of the trip half asleep, and as far as he could determine through half-opened eyes, Saipan was just a simple tropical island with the ordinary growth of coconut trees, breadfruit, mango trees, and an overabundance of skinny trees called tangan-tangan. Small villages were also scattered along the main road, which ran mostly north and south, and their final destination of Capitol Hill, home of the T.T. Headquarters, was located in the northern part of the island.

Capitol Hill was previously the hilltop home of the U.S. military during its occupation days after World War II. It also served as a secret outpost for CIA activities during Taiwan's nationalistic days of 1949, the Korean conflict in the 1950's, and some Vietnam activity in the 60's.

The U.S. military and CIA strategically picked the hilltop location for the following reasons, and these reasons were usually listed backwards in the proper order of importance to the people who had to serve there: Fourth, it was a good site for radio communications; Third, it was near the island's only power generator; Second, it was far enough away from the main village of Chalan Kanoa and all its island local people, chickens, pigs and noisy kids; and, first, it had the greatest frigging view and the best bar on the entire island!

Webber soon pulled into the parking lot of the T.T. Headquarters main building area, and Puzo gaped at the large grey structure which architecturally reminded him of a gigantic elephant with its butt serving as the main entrance to the building. Webber parked the car near the main door and told Puzo to leave his luggage in the trunk until later.

They then proceeded to enter the main building and went up to the second floor, and down a long corridor towards the Hicom's office at the rear of the building. As they walked along, Puzo noticed that the vast majority of folks in the building were white people.

They finally approached a receptionist's desk, and a slightly past forty and very sexy white secretary originally from Texas noticed them approaching. She asked Webber with a sweet-sounding, southern accent, "Where did you find him, Trevor?"

"Oh, along the main road. Is the Hicom upset that we're late?" Webber sounded irritated at his chauffeur and baby-sitting assignment.

The secretary took notice of Puzo's dislike of Webber's demeanor and acted diplomatically as a referee. "Don't worry you two, the High Commissioner understands the problem of late arrivals. He's busy right now, but please have a seat, Mister Puzo. You are Mister Puzo, aren't you?" She was looking coyly at Webber while Puzo sat down in an exhausted heap of pain.

"Oh, pardon me." Webber replied with feigned embarrassment. He then made a quick introduction: "Miss Betty Jo Hunter, this is Mister Paddy Puzo."

Everyone nodded, and Webber then told Puzo that he was supposed to take him to his hotel during lunch hour, and that he expected to see him in his office promptly at eleven-thirty sharp. He then abruptly left.

"Don't mind him, Mister Puzo, he's been acting upset ever since his stateside wife left him for a handsome and younger islander." Betty Jo continued, noticing the painful movements as Puzo tried to comfort his sore foot: "And please relax, it looks like you've hurt your foot recently?"

"Yes, I did." Puzo answered, and then he tried to vainly cover up his misfortune. "Just before I left for Saipan I got hurt in a ski race in Vermont."

"Oh, I see. Does it really snow in the summertime in Vermont?" Betty Jo asked with a big smile.

"Okay, I lied." Puzo put his hands up, signaling a plea for sympathy. "I stubbed my big toe this morning while fighting off a bunch of killer cockroaches in my hotel room on Guam."

"I'm sorry to hear that. How many casualties on the other side?" Betty Jo was now teasing him into a better mood.

"Tens, maybe hundreds." Puzo caught a friendly glint in Betty Jo's eyes as she answered her telephone. It was a little past ten in the morning, and with all the running around and tropical heat, Puzo unconsciously closed his eyes and fell fast asleep in his chair.

"Excuse me, excuse me, Mister Puzo," Betty Jo was nudging him on his shoulder, "the High Commissioner will see you now."

Puzo shook his head and tried to focus on Betty Jo's face but kept looking down at her cleavage as she leaned over and expose some of her great anatomical assets.

He was still in a trance when he replied, "Sorry, didn't mean to doze off, and, you know, thanks for getting your tits, I mean your…I mean my name straight."

He suddenly felt foolish after his sexual gaffe and very self-conscious of his need for a shower when Betty Jo was close to him. "Do you think I could get a quick shower before I meet the High Commissioner? I mean, I could really use one."

"Don't worry, Mister Puzo, about showering or making a silly comment about my boobs." Betty Jo was smiling and continued: "We're used to arriving officials and visitors who are feeling pretty numb from the long trips out here and aren't as fresh as little old daisies. Besides, the High Commissioner has sinus trouble anyway and he won't smell a thing."

Puzo then inquired: "By the way, what's the High Commissioner's name?"

"He doesn't have a name; we only call him the High Commissioner or HiCom for short."

"Oh, really?" Puzo frowned.

"Only kidding," Hunter teased, "his name is Rodney Finkel." She then led him into a paneled office with Micronesian handicrafts hanging all over the place. It looked like an island bargain shop for tourists, and behind a large executive desk with his body half turned, stood a cantankerous old man with a bulbous, scotch-on-the-rocks nose. He was watering his prized plants with a watering can and whispering sweet nothings to his little green friends.

Betty Jo got the High Commissioner's attention with: "Excuse me, Mister Finkel, this is Mister Paddy Puzo. He's the person Interior sent here to help the island districts with their technical assistance needs."

The High Commissioner nodded his head in recognition without looking their way.

She then motioned for Puzo to sit down and pointed towards the plants that the High Commissioner was still tending. Puzo understood her meaning and took a seat near the Hicom's desk. He then waited and watched Finkel watering his plants.

After a few minutes, Finkel turned around and said in a booming voice, "Good to have you here, Pozo." He was all business now and instructed Betty Jo to call in his two staff assistants, Max Buford and Frank Rose, to join the meeting.

Finkel then sat down and asked, "Now Mister Pozo, how can you help us here in the Trust Territory, and what can we do to make your stay more pleasant in Micronesia?"

Puzo was still partially comatose from his quick nap outside the Hicom's office, but he cleared his throat and sounding like a robot as he repeated the blurb that was written in his technical assistant packet for the Trust Territory. "It is the objective of the Department of Interior to assist the territories of the United States to their fullest, thus enabling self-sufficiency and a stronger relationship between the U.S. federal government and its possessions. And my name's Puzo, sir."

"Very interesting." Finkel had barely concealed his boredom with the standard federal reply.

Two middle-aged white statesiders then walked into his office and Finkel waved them over to his desk. "Ah, good. We have everyone here." He then looked at Puzo and asked: "Uh, what's your name again?"

"It's Paddy Puzo."

"Yes, well, Mister Paddy Puzo, this is my special assistant, Mister Max Buford, and the gentleman in the bow tie is my public affairs officer, Mister Frank Rose." Finkel continued hurriedly: "I don't have much time, since Mister Puzo was late getting here, so I want Mr. Buford to take Mister Puzo over to his temporary office, and Mr. Rose, you chat with Mister Puzo and distribute a press release about his arrival here. So, gentlemen…" the Hicom began sniffing the air. "Does anyone smell something peculiarly bad? My sinuses are starting to twitch and uh, never mind, as I was saying, I have a luncheon engagement with the local governor, so excuse me." Finkel got up and then abruptly left.

Buford and Rose got up to leave and were holding their noses, smiling at each other. They were waiting for Puzo who was still sitting. Puzo was unprepared for the quick ending to the meeting and was now feeling real self-conscious about his body odor now.

Rose abruptly spoke to Puzo in an officious nasal voice, while holding his nose, "Mister Puzo, can we go now?"

Puzo got up to leave, and as he left the office with Buford and Rose he smelled his armpits and began to gag.

They passed Betty Jo on their way out and Puzo gave her a smile, saying, "Hope to see you later, Miss Betty Jo." The group then continued walking down the hallway and out of the building across a grassy field towards a one-story, concrete building that contained the Office of Planning and Statistics (OPS), which would be Puzo's future place of work.

On the way over to his new office, Puzo was asked some inane questions by Rose for an upcoming press release. Puzo was very reticent and kept insisting that Rose hold off the press release until later. Buford was also telling him that his government housing would not be available for another two weeks and that he would be staying at the old Royal Palms Hotel in the main village of Chalan Kanoa. Buford further explained that the T.T. personnel office was sorry, but the better hotel was booked solid for the next three weeks. Buford then suddenly excused himself and asked Rose to show Puzo his new office.

Rose and Puzo finally entered the OPS building, which had an immense, open interior with work cubicles partitioned off by six-foot high walls. There were also individual closed offices near the front for program directors and their staffs. Puzo again noticed that almost all the people in the building were white, except for a few islander secretaries and assistants thrown in for some tropical color.

Puzo's new work location was all the way in the rear of the building, where he would share a large cubicle with the chief engineer for the Trust Territory water and sewer projects. The guy's name was Al Jennings, and he was currently home sick with the tropical flu, or more commonly called an island hangover.

Rose told him to make himself at home at an empty desk in one corner of the cubicle. Puzo again reminded Rose to hold off on any press releases until later. Rose just grunted and then departed, leaving Puzo alone and mostly bewildered.

He quietly sat down at his new desk and shoved his briefcase between the desk and the filing cabinet. His head was swirling around with a sense of being totally out of control.

After some time, he began to settle down a little and started thinking about what that fruitcake of a public affairs officer would later release to the public after he had been around for at least a few weeks. He didn't want any special attention about his federal assignment in the T.T.P.I., especially since he didn't really know what was expected of him. He just wished Brubaker was there explaining everything for him while he just stayed incognito for the next six months.

However, the problem was that Brubaker wasn't coming to Saipan until the following month, and Puzo was supposed to fake it until then as much as possible. Fake what? He already knew he was in seriously deep tropical shit.

Besides, the Hicom, Webber, Hunter, Buford and Rose all knew that he was just another federal jerk-off sent to Micronesia by Interior. But what they didn't know is that he actually didn't have a clue about how to handle his assignment to keep the islanders happy and off everyone's backs, including his Eminence, the Hicom.

It was nearing lunchtime and he couldn't hang on any longer. Furthermore, the different time zone was claiming another newly-arrived, long distance traveler. So, he laid his head down on his desk and promptly fell asleep.

It wasn't until way after lunch that Puzo was awakened by Al Jennings, who had finally recovered from his hangover and showed up late for work.

"Hey, wake up, time to look like were're working." Jennings tugged on Puzo's shirt.

"Huh, what time is it?" asked a drowsy Puzo.

"About two-thirty. Did you have a rough night, too?" Jennings asked.

Jennings was a gruff-looking man in his early fifties, but his hard drinking made him look much older. His entire wardrobe consisted of heavily stained Bermuda shorts, a tattered tank top with permanent body odor, and one pair of old zories.

"No…uh, yes." Puzo seemed confused. "I mean, I just flew in from the mainland to work here and…uh, oh, I slept through lunch and didn't check Webber!" He picked up the phone that was on his desk and hurriedly asked Jennings, "What's the number for the Attorney General's office?"

"Never mind the number," Jennings scoffed, "you're better off walking over to the A.G.'s office. The phone system doesn't work too well around here."

Puzo dropped the phone, and quickly left for the A.G.'s office.

He stopped at the parking lot on his way over to the main T.T. building and discovered that the staff car used for his trip from the airport was missing with his luggage presumably still in the trunk.

He then rushed into the main building and up the stairs to the A.G.'s office, where he eventually found Webber's office. He poked his head into the opened doorway and saw Webber dictating a letter to his secretary. He impatiently interrupted the dictation. "Excuse me, Mister Webber, I missed seeing you at lunch, and now the staff car's gone with my luggage still inside."

Webber held up one finger, indicating to Puzo to wait a minute, and he continued dictating, "...furthermore, our position is, notwithstanding the fact that the total damages against your company now exceeds one hundred thousand dollars, that we move ahead, nevertheless, towards a fair and reasonable settlement for both parties. The Trust Territory Government is willing to waive the monetary damages on these conditions based upon: one) you hold no more press conferences attacking the High Commissioner for racism against your Micronesian-owned construction company; two) you return all the T.T. construction materials that you have offered for sale in your brother's new lumberyard; and three) you instruct your relatives to refrain from shooting at our field inspectors when they are checking on the progress of the T.T. project while on Palau Island. Sincerely yours, Rodney J. Finkel, High Commissioner. Extra copies to the President of Palau, the F.B.I., C.I.A., and the State Department."

After he finished dictating, Webber looked at Puzo and said, "I have no idea where the car is now. I waited for you at lunchtime but you never came. You'd better check with the High Commissioner's secretary."

Puzo had left even before Webber was finished. He headed straight for Betty Jo Hunter.

He soon discovered from Betty Jo that the staff car containing his luggage was being used by someone in personnel for some personal errands, and Betty Jo started checking around to locate the car. She quickly assured him that the car would return before quitting time. She also volunteered to help him get checked into his hotel after work. Puzo felt relieved, and thanked Betty Jo.

He then returned to his office cubicle, where he resigned himself to sitting at his desk in a quiet stupor for the rest of the afternoon. Besides, Jennings didn't mind skipping the small talk with a new arrival since his lingering hangover made him want to just sit in a stupor, too.

A little later, he peered over at Jennings who was fast asleep and loudly snoring. He now understood why Jennings was assigned an isolated workplace in the back of the building. What he couldn't understand was, "Why me, Lord!"

After work, he met Betty Jo in the parking lot. She had already retrieved his suitcases and had placed them safely in the trunk of her car. They both got in Betty Jo's car and headed for the Royal Palms Hotel.

Puzo remained quiet most of the trip, while Betty Jo pointed out some places of interest on the island.

There weren't many interesting sites, except for the remaining signs of the World War II battles that had left their dramatic marks among the swaying coconut trees. Betty Jo also mentioned to him that he would later get the use of a T.T. staff car while he was there on assignment.

So, things were now slowly looking up for him, until they pulled into the front of a shabby excuse for a hotel called the Royal Palms. It should have been called the Royal Pits.

According to Betty Jo, some Koreans had bought the hotel the previous year, and they had let it go to hell while waiting to sell it for a quick profit.

Puzo got out of the car and fetched his luggage from the trunk. He then apologized for being so quiet during the ride to the hotel, saying he felt like sleeping for a day or two.

"Then get a good rest," Betty Jo said just before leaving, "and I want you to know that I've seen a lot of so-called federal experts come here, and I think you're way over your head on this technical assistance project of yours. But don't hesitate to call me, if you need a good lifeguard."

Puzo curiously watched her pull away, then shrugged his shoulders and entered the open-air lobby of the Royal Palms Hotel.

The only redeeming features the Royal Palms had were its location next to a beautiful lagoon and an outdoor bar. It was so peaceful outside by the lagoon that a person could have a nervous breakdown, and not even know it. He quickly checked in, however, and immediately headed for his room, deciding to have a shower and his nervous breakdown there instead.

The next morning, he hitched a ride to work from a vacationing Japanese tourist who stopped every few minutes to take pictures.

By the time he arrived late at his office cubicle, Jennings was already busy making flow charts of sewage disposal. Jennings used colored pens to vividly illustrate the different types of wastes, and the huge charts were usually works of unusual abstract art.

Puzo wanted this day to be uneventful. It was going to be the first of a whole bunch of uneventful days, say around a hundred and eighty, then adios, Saipan, and welcome back to Civilization.

For the time being he decided he would lie extremely low, and let Brubaker implement the overall project next month. Like Betty Jo said, he was way over his head, and he knew it.

He didn't realize, however, what Rose had already done in his public affairs office that very same morning.

14

ROSE REALLY FUCKED ME

FOR IMMEDIATE RELEASE
WEDNESDAY, JULY 2, 1980
SAIPAN, NORTHERN MARIANA ISLANDS
TRUST TERRITORY HEADQUARTERS
UNCLASSIFIED
TO ALL TTPI GOVTS., GUAM, CNMI
PLS. PASS TO ALL NEWS MEDIA

(INTERIOR SENDS TECHNICAL ASSISTANCE EXPERT TO
THE TTPI)

HIGH COMMISSIONER RODNEY J. FINKEL OFFICIALLY
ANNOUNCED TODAY THE ARRIVAL OF PADDY A. PUSO,
TECHNICAL ASSISTANCE PLANNER FROM THE U.S.
DEPARTMENT OF INTERIOR, WASHINGTON, D.C. PUSO
WILL ASSIST THE ENTIRE TRUST TERRITORY WITH HIS
TECHNICAL EXPERTISE, AND HE WILL ALSO ADVISE
THE TTPI DISTRICTS ON ALL THE VARIOUS SOURCES
OF FEDERAL MONEY AVAILABLE TO THEM. PUSO WILL
REMAIN AT TTPI HQ ON SAIPAN FOR SIX MONTHS

AND PLANS TO MEET WITH ALL THE ISLAND LEADERS FROM THE TTPI DISTRICTS DURING A DOI POLITICAL LEADERSHIP CONFERENCE TO BE HELD ON SAIPAN ISLAND NEXT WEEK. (END OF RELEASE) ... BT #00412

"Holy shit!" Puzo blurted out, along with his morning hot chocolate, after he frantically read a copy of Rose's release that was just handed to him by a local T.T. assistant. "That jerk-off in public affairs has just done me in!"

"What's up?" asked Jennings, who was touching up some of his sewer charts.

"That crazy Rose wrote an immediate press release making me out to be some kind of federal expert, and that I'm going to dump a large load of money on all these freaking islands. Well, he's dead wrong on both counts, and he's got my goddamn name wrong again!"

Jennings shrugged, "Oh, yeah, Rose does like to joke around a little. Hmmm, I'm going to the toilet. If there are any calls, tell them I'm out in the field."

Jennings left for the restroom, and Puzo felt an anxiety attack creeping up on him. The phone suddenly rang and he jumped, thinking a big shot islander was calling him for some of that free federal money already. He slowly picked up the phone and a voice on the other end casually asked, "Are you Mister Puso?"

Puzo cautiously answered, "It's Puzo, with a "z", and who's this?"

"This is Jim Morrison from the Marianas Daily News, and I'm doing a story on that technical assistance news release from T.T. public affairs. Anything you want to add, Mister Puzo?"

Puzo froze. He had never talked to the press before. He was temporary speechless. He just breathed heavily into the phone.

"Anything wrong, Mister Puzo? I mean, is there something we don't know about your visit?" The reporter's voice seemed to swoop in like a vulture taking a pass at a piece of dead meat.

Puzo mumbled, "No, nothing wrong, just that it's my first interview and I…, how about 'no comment' for now?"

"It's your choice, Mister Puzo. Talk to you later. Bye."

Puzo looked at the phone and imagined a little flag would pop out saying, "Great interview, Dumbo!"

He quickly called the T.T. main receptionist and asked for long distance to Guam. He gave the receptionist Brubaker's number and waited for the connection. The receptionist soon told him that Brubaker was not in his office, and she would dial Puzo back when she had contacted him.

He waited all day for Brubaker's return call, but apparently Brubaker had taken the day off. He finally left an urgent message for Brubaker to call him IMMEDIATELY and also ASAP and MAYDAY-MAYDAY!

That night he sat at the outside bar of his hotel, cringing at the thought of what that reporter was going to do with his 'no comment' reply, which means in journalism circles that you're either hiding something, or you're just too stupid to answer. It was a statement that he later regretted making, especially after reading the next day's newspaper and its front page banner headline.

"INTERIOR EXPERT FIZZLES"

The story read in part: "…and when asked about the federal monetary assistance to the Micronesian islands, Puzo replied, 'No comment,' which again shows an apparent disinterest to the welfare of the underdeveloped islands of the Trust Territory. However, comments were made by various island leaders when contacted yesterday. Polybark Rammarungo, a Palauan senator who is on Saipan negotiating his multi-million-dollar hotel deal on his home island of Koror, blasted Puzo, saying, 'It's just like the United States to send another so-called federal expert to our poor islands without any concerns for our welfare and without any solutions to get more money!'"

Puzo sat at his desk later that same morning in a daze, again reading the news account of his alleged disinterest for the "poor" islanders, who were all building luxurious hotels with the Japanese in Micronesia. He unconsciously called Betty Jo for some sympathy.

Luckily, he got through on the first try. "Hello, Betty Jo? This is Paddy. Did you read the story in the paper about me?"

"Yes, I did. We're getting a big kick out of it over here."

"I'm sunk. The Hicom probably wants me transferred to Alaska."

"You're not sunk, Paddy, but maybe sinking fast," Betty Jo chuckled.

"This is serious, Betty Jo. I really am in over my head, and I'm scheduled to meet all the island chiefs next week!"

"I told you about the danger of drowning out here in the islands, honey. I've seen it out here plenty of times with stateside rookies. Just hang in there."

Puzo asked: "How pissed is the Hicom, really?"

Betty Jo replied, "The Hicom isn't angry as much as disappointed, but try to have a good showing next week at the T.T. leadership conference. It may take a few years, but before you know it, you'll soon realize how clueless we all are."

"I really hate being a rookie, Betty Jo."

"I'll tell you what, Paddy, I'm having a few drinks with some friends tonight at the Continental Hotel. You know, the better hotel here. Meet me there at eight."

"Yeah, why not, I'll see you then. Bye for now."

He hung up the phone and felt slightly better after talking to Betty Jo. He began daydreaming about how great she must have looked fifteen years before. Hell, she still looked great. He closed his eyes and continued daydreaming about Betty Jo's big beautiful bosom and someday being a G-Fourteen.

The phone rang and it was Brubaker calling from Guam. "Hey, Paddy, how'd you manage to make page one in the newspaper already? A guy in our office arrived here from Saipan early this morning with a copy of the Marianas Daily News. It even managed to get read on our Guam morning TV news. Can I have your autograph someday?"

"Very funny, Ralph. But seriously, how do I handle this mess you've got me into?"

Brubaker replied, "Just be on your toes when those island leaders visit you next week."

"That's the problem, Ralph. What should I say to those island leaders, because it's been already reported that I don't care about them, and I also don't have a billion dollars to give each of them either."

"Well, Paddy, you'll probably have a long meeting with all the island leaders asking you a whole lot of questions, mostly about federal funding." Brubaker was trying to be helpful, and continued: "Just listen attentively to all their wishes and demands, and make sure you write everything down, like it will be hand carried to the President of the United States himself the very next day. And remember, agree with everything, even when the say you're a dumb American with no comment." Ralph ended on an unusually cheerful tone of voice, which compounded Puzo's anxiety.

Puzo responded: "You're beginning to sound a little too wacky, Ralph. Are you on drugs or something?"

"No drugs…yet, but this island living is doing something good to me. Even Shirley thinks I'm going 'island happy'. Hey, listen, I'll see you the first week in August. Until then, lay some of that Puzo brilliance on them, okay?"

"Yeah, right. See you later." Puzo hung up as Jennings returned from another long morning visit to the toilet to read old Playboy magazines.

"Was that call for me?" Jennings asked.

"Yeah, it was the HiCom." Puzo replied. "He wants a full report from you when I go right in the toilet."

"No kidding. I hate doing reports, so I'm leaving." Jennings promptly left and didn't return all day. It really didn't take much of an excuse for Jennings to leave early anyway, since the bars on Saipan were normally open all day long.

Puzo spent the rest of the day preparing for the following week's onslaught of island leaders, who were probably planning to offer him up as a burning sacrifice to the island gods for failing to comment in the news about any incoming Yankee dollars. Paradise, what a pain in the ass.

Later that night, in the bar at the Continental Hotel, Betty Jo Hunter was sitting at a table with two of her close friends, and they were talking about life after Saipan.

One of Hunter's friends at the table, a white computer programmer for the T.T. by the name of Linda Brown, was leaving Saipan soon to go back to the U.S. mainland. She was just completing her two-year contract with the T.T. and she had enough of Micronesia. She wanted to leave before she became terminally burned-out on tropical islands and too many Pina Coladas.

"You know, Saipan's nice and everything," Brown was saying to Betty Jo and their other friend at the table, a black guy named Laymarcus Davor, who was also a T.T. computer programmer, "but after two years, it, it--"

"Sucks!" Davor interjected.

"Yes, that's the right word." Brown responded with a Pina Colada giggle. "It's just too boring most of the time, you know? If you don't like sweating and getting sunburned all the time, what else can you do on an island?"

"Drink!" exclaimed Davor, who had turned into a transvestite after a year on Saipan. "I just wished Saipan had a better selection of ladies' lingerie. It's so primitive here!"

Betty Jo was laughing at Davor's continuing assault on Saipan when she spied Puzo walking towards their table. Puzo quietly walked up and stood behind Davor, who was wearing a beautiful blond female wig and slinky dress, and asked: "May I buy you lovely ladies a drink?"

Davor turned around and sensuously replied, "Sure, big boy, I'll take a papaya daiquiri," he then spoke to Hunter and Brown, "and besides drinking and sweating, there's of course screwing around in the boonies."

Puzo stared at Davor with his long blond wig and full beard for an awkward moment and slowly backed away.

"C'mon over here, big boy," Betty Jo teased. "I don't think you're the right type for Laymarcus." Puzo walked around the table and sat next to Hunter.

"So this is our latest expert from Washington with no comment," Brown piped in. "How long do you figure it'll take you to save these crazy islands out here? Two, or maybe three days?"

"Don't mind Linda," Betty Jo said to Puzo. "She's on her seventh Pina Colada." She then made introductions. "This is my friend, Paddy Puzo, who works in the OPS building. Over there is Laymarcus Davor, and this is Linda Brown, they both work in the computer and finance building on the other side of administration building."

Puzo then volunteered, "Well, now that we all know each other, let me buy a round of drinks," while starring at Betty Jo intently.

"Great idea," Brown slurred, and she subsequently fell face first into her plate of half-eaten shrimp appetizers.

Davor slowly lifted Brown's head up, shook his head, placed a several napkins on the plate, and then gently lowered Brown's face back onto the plate. Davor then turned towards Puzo and coyly said: "All right, Mister Paddy Puzo, I know you'd rather be alone with Betty Jo tonight and cry on her shoulder about that awful story about you in the newspaper, but go ahead and spill out your problems to us girls."

Puzo nodded at Davor's bluntness, and he loudly called over to a waitress, "Excuse me, Miss, we need a bunch of drinks over here right away." He then looked over at Davor and said, "You're right about the story in the paper, I don't know what I'm doing here. So, I want you to visit the High Commissioner for me, kiss him on the lips, and tell him what a wonderful guy I am. Also, tell him from what I've seen so far out here, it would probably take my entire lifetime to figure out this tropical funny farm. However, I plan to spend only six months here, then it's adios and back to U.S. civilization."

"Well said, for a new guy on island." Betty Jo laughed, then continuing, "That's what it takes to survive on this rock. Honesty and craziness!"

They all laughed, except a passed-out Brown, and they continued drinking into the wee hours.

Later, after everyone had departed for home, Puzo realized Betty Jo was right about his needing to relax a little. He had drunk with Betty Jo and Davor until way after midnight, and after he helped Davor wedge a passed-out Betty Jo and a mumbling Brown into Davor's tiny car, he had taken a taxi back to his hotel alone, wondering the obvious about the voluptuous Betty Jo Hunter.

The following day on Guam, Brubaker received a strange phone call from his boss Oliver Johnson in Washington, D.C. Johnson was nervous about Jimmy Carter's re-election chances and wanted to know if everything was okay with Brubaker and his troops.

After Brubaker said it was too soon to tell, Johnson abruptly told him to get rid of Puzo by dumping him on the T.T. government.

Brubaker asked what the problem was with Puzo, and Johnson said that Puzo wasn't a part of their Washington team anymore, and he didn't want Puzo to come back to D.C. Johnson was sympathetic to Brubaker's friendship with Puzo and said he would send a recommendation to the T.T. that they retain Puzo in Micronesia as a federal favor. Johnson figured Micronesia would be an ideal place for a stupid Reaganite.

Johnson then hung up, and Brubaker began to wonder if Puzo's previous support for Ronald Reagan had really caused this new development. Puzo was currently behaving himself for the most part, and he would have told him if he had really screwed up in Washington before they left for Micronesia.

However, whatever the case, Brubaker was told to transfer him somewhere in the T.T. operations by September thirtieth, and he decided to tell Puzo the bad news during his trip to Saipan in August.

Brubaker also realized that Puzo would probably do a double back flip right into a vat of tequila after he heard the news that he might be stuck in paradise for longer than he expected. But, who knows, Puzo might change and get to love the place after a few years or so.

Right.

15

ROSE DID IT AGAIN

FOR IMMEDIATE RELEASE
MONDAY, JULY 7, 1980
SAIPAN, NORTHERN MARIANA ISLANDS
TRUST TERRITORY HEADQUARTERS
UNCLASSIFIED
TO ALL TTPI GOVTS., GUAM, CNMI
PLEASE PASS TO ALL NEWS MEDIA

(HIGH COMMISSIONER WELCOMES TTPI LEADERS)

POLITICAL LEADERS AND REPRESENTATIVES FROM THE PALAU ISLANDS, FEDERATED STATES OF MICRONESIA (YAP, TRUK, PONAPE AND KOSRAE). MARSHALL ISLANDS AND THE COMMONWEALTH OF THE NORTHERN MARIANA ISLANDS (CNMI) HAVE ARRIVED TODAY ON SAIPAN FOR A TTPI LEADERSHIP CONFERENCE, WHICH IS BEING HOSTED BY HIGH COMMISSIONER RODNEY J. FINKEL. TOPICS TO BE DISCUSSED ARE: THE ADDITIONAL FUNDINGS FOR CAPITOL IMPROVEMENT PROJECTS (CIP);

INCREASES OF MONETARY ASSISTANCE FOR ISLAND GOVERNMENT OPERATIONS; PROPOSED REQUESTS FOR NON-U.S. INTERFERENCE WITH ISLANDS SEEKING FINANCIAL AID FROM OTHER FOREIGN COUNTRIES; RESTRICTIONS ON U.S. MILITARY PRESENCE IN THE ANCIENT, TRADITIONAL WATERS OF MICRONESIA; AND MULTIPLE MONETARY SUPPLEMENTS FOR THE GREATLY EXPANDING TECHNICAL ASSISTANCE PROGRAMS IN THE ISLANDS. GUEST SPEAKER PADDY POZI FROM THE U.S. DEPARTMENT OF INTERIOR WILL GIVE A PRESENTATION OF TECHNICAL ASSISTANCE PROGRAMS AND MULTIPLE FEDERAL MONETARY GRANTS. THE CONFERENCE WILL BE HELD FROM JULY 8 TO JULY 10 AT THE CONTINENTAL HOTEL.
(END OF RELEASE)
BT #00486

"Rose!" Puzo screamed in a hysterically loud voice. "Can you possibly tell me what the hell you're doing?!"

Puzo continued his rant: "And can't you get my name spelled right for once?!" Puzo was fit to be tied and was shouting on the phone the following Monday morning, after reading the latest press release from the T.T. public affairs officer.

"What? Who's this?" Rose impatiently asked.

Puzo screamed again, "It's Puzo, P.U.Z.O! Listen, I'm just here to do a few simple studies on technical assistance needs and you have me making public speeches and offering all kinds of federal money that I don't even know about."

"Wait a minute," Rose shot back, "are you trying to deny the fact that you're here because of a directive from the Assistant Secretary of O.T.I.A., in order to spread a little P.R. money around and get media support for the Democrats on the mainland?" Rose sounded miffed at Puzo's apparent naiveté of federal politics.

"Whatta you mean, Democrats! I'm not dumb enough to be a Democrat!" Puzo had little idea what Rose was talking about.

"Well, my friend, if you don't have any money to offer to these island leaders, you might as well pack your pencils and fly home. You get the drift?"

"Don't you guys think about anything else besides money, money, money out here?" Puzo blasted out. "How about building some self-respect and self-reliance in these islands?"

"I'm too busy to discuss your personal self-righteous policies in Micronesia, alright? I'm just telling you the facts, take them or leave them." Rose hung up.

Puzo was beside himself with anger and embarrassment. He wanted out, whatever it took. He would go back to Washington with his tail between his legs and take his chances on his future government career even after failing in paradise.

What's more, he was still holding onto his dream of possibly working for the National Aeronautics and Space Administration, where he wouldn't have to be involved with suck-ass social problems. He didn't realize at the time, however, that his superior at Interior had already terminated his future plans back in D.C.

The phone rang. It was Max Buford, the Hicom's special assistant. "Puzo? This is Buford. You're scheduled to give your full presentation at nine o'clock tomorrow morning. I've blocked two hours for you. Is that enough time?"

Puzo said without flinching, "Oh, sure, that's plenty of time. Is there anything special the High Commissioner would like me to discuss?" He was completely overwhelmed with a sense of losing all control and he forgot about D.C., NASA, and everything.

Buford nonchalantly answered him. "You don't need to say anything special. Just keep the island boys happy and you'll keep the Hicom happy. Bye."

After hanging up the phone, Puzo looked over and saw Jennings sleeping at his desk. He woke Jennings up, saying he needed some quick advice for a presentation he was giving the next day.

Jennings wisely told him that there was one basic rule to know for survival in Micronesia. "You gotta always remember that shit always flows downhill, so if you want to smell good in Micronesia, stay uphill of any soci-o, politic-o, economic-o piles of island bullshit." Jennings further exclaimed, "And don't get sucked into debates about how poor the islanders are, and how they deserve everything Uncle Sam gives them. Because they will always act like they desperately need, and will always demand their color TVs, air conditioners, new cars and swimming pools. Yes, even swimming pools on a small tropical island surrounded by water!" Jennings paused to loudly fart, then continued: "Of course, they will also bitch and complain that the U.S. is destroying their ancient ways and customs, in spite of all their new cars and air conditioners. But don't, I say, don't get sucked in, Paddy!" Jennings finished his dissertation with his hands raised to the ceiling and then his eyes became began rolling around and his head banged heavily back on the desk and he went directly to sleep or more probably slipped into a coma.

Puzo stared at Jennings, fast asleep or comatose already, and hoped the hundreds of cases of cheap booze he has drunk over the years hasn't harm him too much. He sincerely liked the old sewer expert, and decided to take his advice and dedicate the next day's presentation to him.

The following morning witnessed one of Puzo's finest performances. He had combined Brubaker's suggestions about writing everything down with the supporting theories of Jennings, and eventually he had the island leaders so confused that they imagined him to be unusually brilliant.

The main topic of the presentation was during the question and answer period. The questions were all centered around how much money the island governments would immediately get, and how much more money the island governments would later get.

Puzo completely agreed with all their demands for more and more money, which at times made the island boys a little suspicious because of Puzo's maniacal arm waving and goofy grins and jumping up and down, yelling, "Yes! Yes! More money for the islands!"

Puzo finally concluded the meeting by giving everyone Brubaker's home address and phone number on Guam, and encouraged them to call him whenever they felt like it.

Later that afternoon, just before leaving from work, Puzo decided to call Betty Jo and ask her for a dinner date. Betty Jo said sorry but she was busy, and maybe some other time. He accepted the rejection gracefully and left his office.

While driving in his recently acquired government staff car to his newly assigned staff housing, he was determined to forget about all social-racial conflicts, island politics, and everything else adversely connected with his present life. All he wanted to do was go somewhere that night to celebrate the minor victory he had scored during his morning presentation, because victories were hard to come by for island outsiders and a good drunk was in order.

The location he picked for his night time celebration was called Spam's Bar. It was owned by a retired Caucasian chief from the U.S. Navy by the name of Spam Jones, who had married a local girl after the American occupation of Saipan.

Puzo had discovered Spam's when he was shown his new T.T. living quarters on Navy Hill. His newest home would be an old, termite-infested Quonset hut that also served as a federal government-sponsored haven for cockroaches and various rodents.

But whatever his housing and work problems would be in the future, or even if Brubaker would never speak to him after a slew of island leaders eagerly called him about getting more federal money, he had soon blanked out everything in Spam's, except for the cold mug of beer and shooter of tequila that were sitting in front of him.

For the time being he was contently sitting at one end of a short bamboo bar that had been constructed by Spam in an old Japanese bunker from World War II. The noise was deafening in the bar, but it was somehow relaxing for anyone who was infected by small island fever. Besides, the best part about Spam's Bar was that it was an "American" bar, where statesiders could unwind and blow off steam about the craziness of Micronesia, without getting into heated debates with the local islanders about all their so-called privileges and rights to Fort Knox.

The drinking, pool shooting, juke box playing, dancing and occasional arguments over dice games in Spam's would usually end with the bar's nightly finale, i.e., "Spam's late night dissertation on life and how he single handedly captured the entire island of Saipan for the United States in 1944 during World War Number Two!"

But after Spam's historical tirade, he would always be reminded by the customers that the real part that he played during the invasion of Saipan was that of a U.S. Navy cook, whose unsavory meals probably drove the U.S. Marines onboard his ship into gladly accepting the risks of island invasions, rather than chancing the guaranteed food poisonings from Spam's infamous ship's galley.

Temporary insanity prevailed in Spam's every night, but it didn't seem to bother the patrons because it seemed a whole lot saner than taking the screwy island, and one's individual reason for being there, too seriously.

And by the time Puzo had left Spam's after midnight, he was drunk enough to even tolerate living in the lousy hut that was "temporarily" assigned to him, termites, cockroaches and rats included.

Well, at least he would try to tolerate it for his remaining stay on Saipan.

16

BRUBAKER

Brubaker finally made it to Saipan during the last week of August. He had been busy on Guam and postponed the trip until he was sure of getting a job for Puzo at T.T. Headquarters.

Puzo's performance at the July leadership conference had apparently gained him some brownie points with the T.T. and the island chiefs. So consequently, Buford had told Brubaker over the phone that Puzo could be picked up in early October for a stint in the T.T. Energy Office, which always had extra federal money for idiotic projects and for some extra idiotic project assistants.

Brubaker's arrival was on a payday Friday evening, and island paydays were always drunken celebrations, which he figured would help alleviate the sticky situation with Puzo and his sudden change of work status.

Brubaker had also decided on his plane ride to Saipan to lie to Puzo about his permanent switch of employment, and say that he would only be on temporary loan to the T.T. government until the end of the year. He would inform him about his termination at Interior at a later date, after Puzo had a chance to further acclimate himself to the island living.

Later that evening, Puzo picked up Brubaker at his hotel and they headed for Spam's. It turned out to be a bizarre and drunken payday night at Spam's and everyone was pretty blitzed by ten o'clock.

There was even a "drop your pants if you lose" pool tournament, and whoever lost had to drop their pants and underwear and moon the bar. Even Spam bared his ugly butt after losing one game, and his wife Rosey chased him around the bar with a machete for several minutes.

As the night further wore on, and after several beers and shooters of tequila were drunk, Brubaker decided to delve into personal matters and eventually told Puzo that Shirley had left him and went back to the states. Brubaker and Puzo talked about other island relationships and the repeated times that stateside couples had broken up over the wife's boredom and the husband's introduction and seduction of the beautiful women in the islands and other parts of Asia Pacific. Sometimes, they both laughed that it was the stateside wife who would dump the husband for a big brown islander stud. Brubaker eventually said he was okay and Shirley would be better off in a more civilized environment. He also wished out loud that his friendship with Puzo would last, no matter what happened in the future.

After nodding at each other in true friendship, Brubaker thought about switching the subject and telling Puzo about his upcoming change of work status. But Brubaker decided to wait and tell Puzo at the hotel just before leaving for his room. So after another beer and shooter, Brubaker asked to leave because he was tired.

Puzo agreed to leave but first wanted to ask Brubaker a very important personal question. Brubaker cringed at the thought that Puzo might know that he was going to be dumped on the T.T. government. Then suddenly Puzo grabbed a startled Brubaker and squinted at him in the eye and drunkenly asked, "Do you think Shirley will miss me?"

Brubaker burst out laughing, saying, "Jesus, Paddy, I really don't think so, and let's go, okay?"

They both paid their bills, and Puzo warned Brubaker to count his change, since Spam had a funny method of island accounting, especially if you were too shit-faced to even count to three.

They finally left Spam's and headed for Brubaker's hotel, arriving at the Continental about eleven o'clock. Brubaker invited Puzo for a short nightcap at the hotel bar, and they were soon settled into a dimly-lit lounge with a few Japanese tourists listening to a young Filipina singer.

They were seated at a corner table and ordered their drinks. Puzo noticed a thirty-something and fairly good-looking Micronesian girl from Truk Island stroll in and sit alone at the bar. He thought about making a pass, but decided to wait until Brubaker went to his room.

After a few minutes of light conversation, Brubaker decided to tell Puzo about his job switch, saying, "Paddy, there's been a slight change in your federal P-MAT status at the T.T. Beginning October first, you will be on loan to the T.T. O.P.S. section until the end of the year."

Puzo stared at Brubaker suspiciously and asked in a plaintiff voice, "What's up Ralph? Is this some kind of a joke? Yeah, you're just kidding because I gave those greedy islanders your phone number on Guam, right?"

"Wrong, Paddy, it's no joke. It's just a matter of inter-departmental relations between Interior and the Trust Territory. Johnson wants you to get some firsthand experience with the T.T. for later use."

"What later use? What happens in January, Ralph?"

"It's back to Washington," Brubaker said, hiding the real truth.

"Are you lying to me, Ralph? Please don't do that. You've never lied to me before, ol' buddy." Puzo began to sober up.

"Gimme a break, Paddy. Can't you see that it's really out of my hands what really happens to you. I've got you a good job at the T.T., and who knows, you could do wonders out here if you tried. Then you can write your own ticket with the feds. Listen, I'm trying my best to help you, and let's worry about January later. Okay?"

Puzo stared at Brubaker for a minute and finally asked with resignation in his voice: "All right, what will I be doing in O.P.S.?"

"You'll be assisting in the T.T. Energy Office."

"And how in the hell did I qualify for that?" Puzo inquired cynically.

"Apparently, your background in pumping gas in San Diego was a factor, and you know how the feds like to operate." Brubaker chuckled.

"I don't see the humor in this, Ralph. I'm beginning to get downright scared about how the U.S. government handles its personnel affairs."

"You'll do fine in the energy office, then you'll be back in Washington before you know it."

Brubaker ordered another drink, but Puzo declined, and said to Brubaker: "Hey listen, Ralph, I'm kind of beat. I'll see you later."

Puzo got up to leave, feeling strung out.

"Sure, Paddy. I'll talk to you later."

Brubaker watched Puzo leave the bar, and then he sauntered over to the barstool where the Trukese island girl was sitting.

17

THE REVEREND

The first of October signaled another brand new fiscal start for the Trust Territory government, and it was also a prime time of the year for island-style civic celebrations.

Exuberant Micronesian leaders could legally get their hands again on newly-appropriated federal funds, and it gave them yet another chance to wildly spend U.S. taxpayers' money and run up an entirely new deficit. This never appeared to be a problem for the island officials, since the new deficit was always tagged onto the previous year's deficit, and so on, and so on.

This phenomenon caused an unusual sense of accomplishment by the islanders, who felt compelled to emulate their wasteful congressional counterparts in Washington, D.C. They also felt they should receive some kind of presidential medal for maintaining the traditional ways of their American benefactors, whose bad examples conveniently took precedent in their own civic handbooks.

For Puzo, however, it meant the beginning of another new job at the T.T. and the lack of his true federal status. His first immediate task was adapting to his lost prestige around the place, like buying a used motorcycle that would replace his ex-staff car, which had been quickly assigned to someone else at T.T. Headquarters.

On Puzo's first day on the job as a planner for the T.T. Energy Office it had commenced with a short meeting with the director of OPS, Adrian Toddy, a tremendously fat and sloppy white statesider, who briefly met with him and the chief of the energy office, Doctor William P. Smith, another white statesider who was also known as the Reverend.

Following the brief orientation meeting, the Reverend took Puzo to another part of the OPS building where the energy office was located. The first thing Puzo noticed in his new workplace were the large windows for the Reverend's solar energy experiments, which involved little music boxes, fans and other mechanical thingamajigs run by tiny solar panels. If anything, the energy office, with its myriad of displays of solar experiments, sunshine posters, and indoor plants, was aesthetically more pleasing to the eye than Jennings' sewer charts and Wrench of the Month calendars from American tool suppliers.

After arriving in the energy office, the Reverend showed Puzo his desk, which was tucked away into a corner by a large window. There were several overgrown vines wildly growing from various wall planters and hanging pots that were hanging down on the desk's untidy surface, and Puzo randomly touched the vines and gave the Reverend an inquisitive look.

The Reverend responded to Puzo's silent request for an explanation to why his desk looked like an indoor jungle, by saying, "This desk hasn't been occupied since our last planner went outside the reef in his small boat equipped with an experimental, solar-powered outboard engine. Unfortunately, the young man took a case of beer with him and hasn't been seen for the last two months. He will either make it to the Philippines someday, or presumably drown in the name of environmental science. Meanwhile, his plants have been a growing shrine in his memory."

Puzo just kept nodding while the Reverend went on rambling about the rest of the office. As the Reverend rambled, Puzo casually began to gather up all the vines cluttering his desk, opened the nearby window, and stuffed the vines through the opening, leaving the window ajar.

After turning around, he noticed the Reverend give him a disapproving glance. The Reverend walked over towards him with an admonishing look and began lecturing.

"Oh, no, Mister Puzo. We can't have that. An open window allows the precious cool air to escape and wastes our very expensive energy resources."

Puzo nodded and located a pair of scissors and quickly proceeded to shear off the vines at the window, showering the area of Puzo's desk with dead leaves, and then closed the window.

The Reverend freaked out. "Are you insane?! Those precious plants are a living memorial!"

The Reverend just stared at Puzo until the Reverend fainted. Puzo then sat at his desk in disbelief.

But the Reverend suddenly jumped up and it scared the hell out of Puzo, after which the Reverend acted oblivious to everything and asked: "Is everything okay? How did your desk get so messy? Please try to tidy up."

The Reverend, a tall skinny man of fifty, with a ruddy face and long pointed nose, had previously received his bogus doctorate degree in Texas for the entire sum of fifty-two dollars. Furthermore, his doctorate wasn't even in science or any energy-related field, but in religious ministry--hence the nickname of the Reverend.

In the Reverend's past escapades, he had jumped on the energy conservation bandwagon after the Arab oil crisis of 1973, and started preaching the end of the modern world if everyone didn't start kissing the Arab's assets. He also crusaded frantically for mass bicycle transportation and the return of the wood-burning stove throughout the United States.

However, following a notorious and busted career on the U.S. mainland, he naturally ended up at T.T. Headquarters as another stateside misfit, and in charge of the half-witted energy office.

Once in Micronesia, it subsequently took the Reverend only a few short months before a majority of island leaders publicly swore that they were going to have him assassinated, for trying to disconnect the thousands of energy-wasting air conditioners that had been previously installed throughout all the islands.

The T.T. had continually constructed separate power plants to accommodate the energy sapping air con units on Saipan and throughout Micronesia, in order to appease themselves and the jealous islanders competing for air con supremacy.

After eventually apologizing to all the island chiefs for attempting to violate their sacred, traditional ways of keeping their sacred and traditional asses cool, the Reverend explained that he was only attempting to reverse the foolish trend set by previous T.T. officials, who had complained that the tropical breezes weren't comfortable enough for them in the modern age of split-unit air conditioners.

The threats on his life, however, had permanently changed the Reverend and made him a tad more flexible in his future dealings with the neurotic Micronesians, who felt that the air conditioners were godlike devices to keep their tropical butts cool forever.

Two days later, Puzo was shivering at his desk and inspecting the lower contents of his archaic desk. He lacked any real assignment and was idly passing through the time of day.

The Reverend suddenly appeared in front of him and began to preach about the present evils of excessive air conditioning at the T.T. Headquarters.

The Reverend hadn't totally given up on a personal mission to rid Micronesia of a least one excessive air conditioning unit, and he grandly announced to Puzo that he wanted the OPS building to become a special symbol of energy efficiency in recognition of "Energy Awareness Week." He was also attempting to win a free trip to Washington, where he would receive a pompous award from the U.S. Department of Energy. The award could then be parlayed into a contract to publish his first book, entitled, "Beware of Evil Energy."

So, the Reverend immediately instructed Puzo to do a Class "C" audit on the OPS building for overall energy efficiency. The two-week audit would be accomplished by figuring out the total square footage of the building and comparing it to the number of air conditioners operating throughout the entire facility.

"Energy conservation is serious business!" the Reverend would bellow, while ironically sitting in an energy office that had a temperature hovering around fifty-two degrees Fahrenheit, due to its being a part of the frigid OPS building.

Puzo seemed relieved to be tasked to do something to get away from the Reverend and a catatonic assistant planner, who hid in the office background behind a bunch of huge indoor plants surrounding his desk.

Puzo spent the rest of the day collecting his preliminary data, and he then compared his findings to an energy efficiency chart. After some quick math, he initially calculated that the OPS building was slightly warmer than the North Pole in the dead of winter. The building had so many air conditioners that Eskimos could have trained their dogsled teams in the corridors. He had also discovered later from a talkative stateside secretary, that whenever a new OPS director, chief, or supervisor got shifted around the building, another new air conditioner would be installed close to the person's new location. It was a matter of Air Con Supremacy! God forbid if a T.T. chief didn't have his or her own personal air conditioner, because on a small tropical island in the middle of nowhere, there weren't too many ways to show one's real importance in the scheme of things. And besides all the individual cooling devices, the OPS building had six central air conditioning units operating all the time, too!

Anyway, Puzo spent the whole two weeks, with the Reverend's advice, to milk a two-day assignment. And when Puzo finally submitted his overly critical report of the OPS building to the Reverend, it was quickly filed in the energy office's "overdone and overly critical" file that was discreetly kept away from OPS Director Toddy's prying eyeballs.

Following the past threats on his life, the Reverend had become a realist first, and a conservationist, second. Frankly, he didn't want to get his supervisors and the islanders too upset in Micronesia anymore, since he had a very lucrative T.T. contract to basically play with his solar toys and to keep the bothersome opinions of the energy office under wraps.

Moreover, Toddy, who kept his office so air conditioned that beef could hang in it for months without spoiling, had also advised the Reverend to be less severe with his energy conservation demands. It was widely known that Toddy had a complete distaste for sweating in the islands, which aggravated his constant crotch itch.

Overall, Puzo figured he was now doing God's work with the Reverend, and he would continue until he was someday blessed right off the frigging island for good.

A week later, after a gratuitous pat on the back by the Reverend for his wonderful energy audit, Puzo resumed his blurred assault on his remaining time on Saipan. This was partly accomplished by beginning his next project, which entailed the submission of a basic federal grant application for a load of money that was generated by the Emergency Energy Conservation Act of 1980 to write simple plans of action during petroleum shortages.

It happened that every time the U.S Congress passed a legislative act appropriating federal funds for state projects, the Trust Territory would usually qualify for a small chunk of federal change that was worth some big bucks.

In the case of the Energy Emergency Conservation Act, or EECA, there was over forty thousand dollars appropriated to the Trust Territory just to write a simple plan for any energy emergencies that might be caused by the possible oil cutoffs from the Middle East. But since the T.T. received their oil supplies from Malaysia, and its suppliers were not the targets of anti-U.S. sentiment from the Arabs, the EECA plan for the T.T. would eventually be another exercise in bureaucratic tomfoolery.

Puzo hadn't been thoroughly indoctrinated with the complete understanding of all these government shenanigans yet, so in his quest to make a reasonably coherent submission of the EECA application, he sought out the advice of the other energy office assistant, the catatonic white person hiding behind the plants with the name of Rob Bittle.

Bittle was a graduate in psychology from the University of California at Berkeley. He was twenty-six years old and an emaciated ex-drug addict. He was pretty much burned out on life at an early age, having lived a little too long in San Francisco.

He eventually ended up in Micronesia, like so many other lost souls from the U.S. mainland, and became a janitor for the local YMCA camp on Saipan. And after floating around Saipan for a few months, the Reverend got him a job at the T.T. Energy Office, because of Bittle's sensitivity towards conservation issues and for the fact that he wouldn't move for hours while listening to the Reverend's boring speeches on energy conservation.

The Reverend figured Bittle was truly spellbound with his public speaking, but in reality, Bittle didn't move because of the mostly catatonic state of his burned-out brain.

When Bittle did become semi-coherent, he was always in an anxious state of a near breakdown, especially when Puzo had decided to pull up a chair alongside Bittle's desk one day to questioned him about the EECA application.

After trying to ignore Puzo, Bittle began to fidget around and started smacking his lips.

Puzo pretended not to notice the early signs of a psychotic episode, and just wanted Bittle to help out with his next stepping stone to his eventual island departure.

Puzo grabbed Bittle's arm and asked: "How about helping me with my emergency energy application, then I'll leave you alone, okay?"

Bittle pulled back in paranoiac fear and blurted out, "I can't handle emergencies! Check the Northern Mariana Islands Energy

Office. I'm getting bad vibrations from you and I can't let myself suffer because of your existence. Why are you here, anyway?!"

"Uh, excuse me," Puzo replied, as he backed away from Bittle's desk. He then spoke to no one particular. "I'll just go back to my desk. And I really don't know why I'm here, but I'm sure trying my best to leave."

Bittle continued smacking his lips and staring into space.

Puzo then decided he had better just rummage through Bittle's files for information when he was out to lunch, which seemed to be most of the time anyway. And thinking about it, Bittle did ask him a reasonably good question: Why in the hell was he in Micronesia?

During the ensuing process of completing the EECA application, the Reverend was off-island and Puzo was winging it on his own. He mostly reviewed other grant applications for previous energy funds, and even took Bittle's advice and visited the Northern Mariana Islands (NMI) Energy Office for some extra needed assistance.

The Northern Mariana Islands had already completed their forty-page application to receive their funds, and had also completed their EECA state plan, which was ironically one fourth the size of the application, i.e., a simple, ten-page document that satisfied the feds and justified a tidy sum of grant money.

A senile energy planner for the Northern Mariana Islands gave Puzo a copy of the NMI EECA application, but the NMI planner had also inadvertently included their state plan by mistake.

Later on, Puzo realized he had a state plan already, so he used white-out to remove the Northern Mariana Islands' name, made Xerox copies of it, and then typed in the substituted Trust Territory of the Pacific Islands' name to complete its applicability to the whole T.T.P.I. region. He had figured that the Northern Mariana Islands' plan must be sufficient enough for the T.T.P.I.'s plan, since both dysfunctional government operations were located on the same damn small island of Saipan and they both administered other small isolated islands in the region.

Following this feat of clueless ingenuity, he naively included the modified T.T. plan at the back of the Trust Territory's EECA application, hoping to kill two bureaucratic birds with one coconut. He also hoped to make some points by submitting the T.T.P.I.'s EECA application with its state plan already included, thereby saving the feds some money.

Subconsciously, he was pushing the federal gods to smile on him and to hurry the process of his being officially commended and quickly transferred back to Washington.

However, his attempt to economize the system became a subsequent disaster for several T.T. officials, who would block any attempts by idiots who tried to change the bloated system.

The disaster started when Toddy quickly rubber stamped Puzo's finished EECA application without the advice and consent of the Reverend, who had been traveling throughout Micronesia and trying to soothe the tempers of some irate island leaders over air con issues. Unfortunately for the Reverend, the leaders had heard rumors that he was again planning to reduce the number of air conditioners in their island offices and homes, and the Reverend had quickly left on a tropical appeasement mission.

In Toddy's haste to make a deadline for more federal fun money, he had the mailroom expedite the EECA application by special messenger service to the Department of Energy's Region IX office in San Francisco. He also called his Region IX director friend in California, requesting that the funds for the T.T.P.I.'s EECA plan be sent to Saipan as soon as possible.

It was just another piece of federal pie for Toddy, especially after receiving a message from Region IX.

ZXCS MMU CRT-05 RE 0
KKW-990 OCT. 24, 1980
WWU CP MMOER 907 OO34-9984
SAN FRANCISCO, CALIFORNIA
2:00PM PST

TO: DIRECTOR ADRIAN TODDY, TTPI OPS
TRUST TERRITORY OF THE PACIFIC ISLANDS HQ,
SAIPAN, NORTHERN MARIANA ISLANDS 96950

DEAR ADRIAN:

RECEIVED AIR EXPRESS PACKET WITH YOUR TTPI
EECA APPLICATION THIS MORNING. WE HAVE
ALREADY WIRED YOUR FUNDING TO YOUR LOCAL
BANK. PLEASE SEND YOUR EECA PLAN BY END OF
NOVEMBER. KEEP UP THE GOOD WORK.

REGARDS,

F. RICHARD HIGGENBOTTOM, REGION IX DIRECTOR
U.S. DEPARTMENT OF ENERGY SAN FRANCISCO,
CALIFORNIA

CCT RCA

It was a week after this telex message was sent that a young federal employee advised Higgenbottom in San Francisco about an unusual problem with the Trust Territory's EECA submittal.

"Excuse me, Mister Higgenbottom, but that Trust Territory E.E.C.A. application you asked me to file, well, I read it and would you believe that the T.T. plan is already included. And it's the same as the Northern Mariana Islands' plan, with only the name changed."

"Why those idiotic bastards!" Higgenbottom shouted, continuing, "First, they steal the Northern Mariana Islands' plan, and then they have the gall to send it in with their stupid application! Don't they realize that our stupid taxpayers could find out about things like this, and then complain to our stupid congressmen about our wasting money on stupid energy plans. Send in my secretary! I want to send another telex to that idiot Toddy immediately!"

ZXVVW MMU CRT-11 PP 8
KKW*990 OCT. 31, 1980
WWO CO MMOER 907 0034-9984
SAN FRANCISCO, CALIFORNIA
10:00AM PST

TO: DIRECTOR ADRIAN TODDY, OPS
TRUST TERRITORY OF THE PACIFIC ISLANDS HQ,
SAIPAN, NORTHERN MARIANA ISLANDS 96950

ATTENTION MR. TODDY:

I WANT AN IMMEDIATE EXPLANATION TO YOUR ASKING FOR 40 THOUSAND DOLLARS TO WRITE A TTPI EECA PLAN THAT HAS ALREADY BEEN SUBMITTED TO MY OFFICE THAT YOU STOLE FROM THE NMI GOVERNMENT. I AM FREEZING THE FUNDING ALREADY SENT AND FURTHER ENERGY FUNDING WILL BE SUSPENDED UNTIL AN ADEQUATE REPLY FROM YOUR OFFICE IS IMMEDIATELY RECEIVED BY MY OFFICE. I ENCOURAGE YOU TO KEEP THIS EMBARRASSING MATTER CONFIDENTIAL.

F. RICHARD HIGGENBOTTOM, REGION IX DIRECTOR
U.S. DEPARTMENT OF ENERGY SAN FRANCISCO, CALIFORNIA

CCT RCA

"Miss Guzzard! Did you read this telex?!" Toddy screamed at his secretary, who had just handed him the urgent message sent by Higgenbottom.

"Of course not," smirked a less than trustworthy secretary, already relishing the future gossip to be spread.

"Well, if I find any Xeroxed copies of this telex on the bulletin board, you can plan on working with Jennings and his sewer charts for the rest of your stay on Saipan. Do you understand me, Miss Guzzard?!"

"I can't be blamed if that happens," Guzzard responded defensively. "What about the nosey people in the mailroom? I bet they have copies tacked up on their walls right now."

Toddy just sat in a seething trance, staring at a defiant Miss Guzzard. He then slowly instructed her to go immediately to the mailroom and confiscate any copies of the telex. She was also instructed to give her notorious angry looks to everyone, saying that heads would roll if this energy screw-up went public. Furthermore, Toddy wanted her to send an urgent telex to Yap Island, ordering the Reverend to get his butt back to Saipan pronto!

Toddy wanted this mess straightened out as soon as possible. His energy funding was in jeopardy, and it was his biggest source of bail-out money that could be easily reprogrammed into other projects that he usually fouled up, too.

Besides, his energy money could always be conveniently spent on "research trips" to the Orient and Europe, which he and his wife had always enjoyed so much.

After Miss Guzzard left Toddy alone in his office, he looked at the telex again and noticed how it was addressed to "Mr. Toddy," and that it was missing the friendly "Dear Adrian."

He lamented out loud, "It took me years to get close to Higgenbottom, and now it's back to 'Mister Toddy' again!"

He twisted the telex into a ball, put it on the floor, and proceeded to jump up and down on it, wailing, "Someone's going to pay for this! Someone's going to pay for this!"

18

THE WRATH OF TODDY

Immediately upon the Reverend's return to Saipan he was severely lambasted by Toddy, and the Reverend immediately went into acute schizophrenic shock. On his way out of Toddy's office, the Reverend collapsed into Miss Guzzard's arms, but she let him drop on the floor with a head-thumping bounce.

After regaining consciousness, the Reverend later took off all his clothes in the energy office and refused to put them back on until Toddy sent him a memo to get dressed and continue his sacred mission to eliminate evil air conditioners from Micronesia.

Toddy refused to write the stupid memo or even talk to the Reverend, so the Reverend was eventually restrained in a full-body straight jacket and placed in the local hospital on indefinite sick leave.

During all this commotion, Puzo had not been told the real reason for the Reverend's collapse, since Toddy thought that Puzo was too inexperienced to realize what he had done to screw up the EECA plan and jeopardize the future easy-peasy grant money.

Toddy had kept his wrath directed at the Reverend, who should have been checking the stupid EECA application before it even got sent to San Francisco, and not be visiting islands where he was hated.

With the Reverend hospitalized, the T.T. Energy Office was now under the dubious supervisory control of Bittle, who was in Toddy's office and instructed by Toddy to have the energy office do absolutely nothing until further notice. Bittle was a legitimate born again zombie in a wheelchair by this time, and after giving no response to Toddy's instructions, Toddy had to yell at Miss Guzzard to wheel the catatonic son of a bitch back to his desk.

Frankly, Toddy was actually relieved that at least Bittle was basically brain dead and incapable of doing anything to further screw up the current shit storm in the energy office.

Next on Toddy's agenda was that he quickly called Region IX about the unfortunate breakdown of the Director of the T.T. Energy Office, i.e., the Reverend, who had been under intense mental strain of being subject to multiple death threats by several of the island leaders. Toddy further explained that this was real reason that the pilfered EECA plan was prematurely sent in with the EECA application. He also promised Region IX that his energy office would never do that again, especially since the Reverend's contract would soon expire at the end of the year and he would definitely be replaced.

After the groveling and uncomfortable phone call to a Region IX junior administrator, since Region IX Director Higgenbottom refused to accept Toddy's call, Toddy started loudly banging his desk with the phone's receiver until he broke it into a dozen or so pieces.

He finally screamed: "Miss Guzzard!"

Meanwhile, Puzo, who seemed oblivious to everything except his seemingly near and dear departure from paradise, was passing his idle time away by experimenting with the Reverend's solar-power music boxes. He would sit at his desk shading the little solar panels with cardboard, listening to the theme song from "Doctor Zhivago" fluctuate from a normal sound to a slow musical death.

"Hey, Bittle," Puzo called over to where Bittle was sitting in his wheelchair at his desk, "do you think I could get a federal grant to study the Reverend's solar music boxes?"

There was no response from Bittle until Puzo pulled his chair over to Bittle's desk and began picking his nose and grunted at Bittle.

Bittle finally grunted back, and slowly took out some paper and began fumbling with an old IBM typewriter. To his credit Bittle miraculously got the paper inserted into the typewriter and finished typing a short bizarre memo and handed it to Puzo without saying a word.

TOOO: Energy Planer Puz
FRUM: Act. director BBittle
SUBJect: Temprary Asssssignment

I wil commanding u 2 do nothing nothing. until return of revrend diracter.

ccc: energi filer

Puzo read the memo and looked at Bittle, who began smacking his lips in triumph.

Puzo then made a paper airplane with the memo and tossed it out the window that he now kept open to let out the excessive cold air.

"Would it be okay then if I get patriotic," Puzo then asked Bittle, "and put a Reagan picture on the wall?'

Puzo had earlier read about Reagan's victory over Carter in the newspapers, and he was eager to rub it in around the Democratic-controlled T.T. Headquarters by hanging a framed picture of Reagan on the energy office wall near his desk.

Bittle just ignored Puzo and wheeled himself into the office closet and closed the door.

After hanging up Reagan's picture, Puzo returned to his desk and started playing with a solar-powered music box when all of a sudden a familiar voice startled him.

"Hey, wanna have a free lunch on me today?"

Puzo looked up quickly and broke into a smile, "Well, if it isn't Mister Brubaker himself. You come to Saipan to congratulate me in person for my fabulous work in the field of energy?"

Brubaker grabbed a chair and sat down, replying, "Yeah, you might say so," and he then began laughing, "I heard through the jungle grapevine about your submitting a premature energy plan, even before the T.T. government got its forty grand to write the idiotic thing. Congratulations, Paddy, only you would do something like that!"

"What in the hell are you talking about?"

"Didn't they tell you what you did?" Brubaker asked.

Puzo shook his head, "No, I'm not privy to most information around here."

"You don't write federal plans until the feds give you the money first." Brubaker lectured. "That's a big no-no around here since the T.T. directors know how to scam the federal grants for their big spending habits."

Brubaker finished talking and he noticed a newly-framed picture of President-elect Reagan hanging near Puzo's desk, and he quipped, "Reagan's crooked."

"You're changing the subject, Ralph," Puzo seemed perplexed, "and Reagan's not as crooked as other presidents we've had."

"No, I mean," Brubaker laughed, pointing at the Reagan picture, "the picture's hanging crooked."

Puzo went over to straighten the picture and asked Brubaker to continue explaining about his botching the EECA plan.

Brubaker nodded and explained: "Apparently your energy boss, the Reverend, took the fall for not preventing the sending of a plagiarized E.E.C.A. plan before Toddy even got the grant money." Brubaker elaborated some more, "They also figured you were too clueless to know better. Maybe that's why they grabbed at my offer to keep a closer eye on you."

"Wait a minute." Puzo jumped in. "It wasn't plagiarized, only borrowed, and what are you blabbering about an offer to keep a closer eye on me?"

Brubaker answered, "I've been hired here at the T.T. as the Deputy Director for O.P.S., and Toddy allowed me pick you up for a year as part of the deal. Even though Toddy was hired under the Democratic administration in Washington, it'll take a long time for the new Republican administration to remember about the remotely located T.T.P.I. and clean house out here," Brubaker began to chuckle, "and a paranoid Toddy doesn't want to mess with an apparent Reaganite like you, who might complain to Reagan himself and get Toddy prematurely fired."

Brubaker then watched Puzo's mouth drop open in disbelief.

Puzo finally blurted out, "What the fuck is happening to me?!" He hastily got up and stuck his head out the opened window and yelled: "What in the hell is happening around here?!!" He then turned to face Brubaker, wide-eyed, saying, "Seriously, you're joking again."

"It's no joke, again." Brubaker replied.

"What about your Interior job, Ralph? My future Interior job and my future G.S. Fourteen rating? Our going back to D.C. in January?!" Puzo slumped down and sat on the floor with his eyes closed.

Brubaker walked over to again straighten Reagan's picture that was hanging on a bent nail and said: "As you well know, with Reagan getting elected and my few donations to the Democratic Party being known at Interior, my future at Interior in Washington was a shaky proposition for the next four years. Frankly, I'm not really a Democratic or Republican supporter. Besides, I was getting tired of D.C. and I'm temporarily safe from stateside politics out here in this jungle isolation." Brubaker let out a sigh and continued. "You know, I think I discovered my true home out here in Micronesia. I hear Martinez even quit his T.T. job in American Samoa and now weighs nearly three hundred pounds. He also married a Samoan girl who is even heavier than him!" Brubaker returned to sit in an office chair.

Puzo opened his eyes. "And do you seriously think I'm staying on this volcanic funny farm with you? No way, Jose. I'm headed back to Washington to take my own chances with Interior."

Brubaker frowned. "I hate to tell you this, but I lied to you earlier. You must have done something to upset the Assistant Secretary back in D.C., and Interior had terminated you permanently over some Reagan story and your reputation for being a perpetual drunk." Brubaker then shrugged. "Anyway, face it, your only shot at a good job right now is here with me. So, why not work a year, save your money, and head back to the states with a decent bankroll?"

Puzo dropped his head, shook it a few times and looked up to the ceiling and said: "My nightmare has come true. I'm going to be stuck on this rock until I permanently crack. Even my NASA plans have now gone down the toilet. What am I going to do, Ralph? I'm broke and stranded in miserable paradise!"

Brubaker tried to cheer him up. "C'mon, Paddy, let's go have a beer and cheeseburger and talk some more."

Puzo replied, "Are you kidding? This place doesn't even have a good cheeseburger joint. The local islanders think spam is the best meat available on earth."

Brubaker feigned sympathy. "It must be rough living in the outer limits of civilization. How about an all beer lunch instead?"

Puzo nodded with mixed emotions. "I'll take you up on that offer." He then got up from the floor, asking, "Anyway, when do you, or we, get started on this new partnership at the T.T.? Christ, I guess I really am stuck here for another lousy year."

"January one," Brubaker answered. "You have some time left in the energy office, then it's E.D.A. time with me."

"E.D.A. time? I'll ask you later what E.D.A. stands for, probably 'Easy Dick Assignment'!"

They began to leave and Brubaker pointed back to Puzo's desk. "Reagan's crooked again."

"Who cares? He got me stuck here in paradise for another lousy year. Politicians! You can never trust any of them!"

They stopped for lunch at a small cafe on Beach Road, down from Capitol Hill and near the Northern Mariana Islands' Civic Center, which was the only place on the island to find a reasonable facsimile of a "cheeseburger." They ate their spam cheeseburgers and drank several beers in the hot, mid-day sun, and eventually wound up sitting on the beach sand, definitely feeling no pain.

"That girl…that girl in the attic," Puzo began mumbling. "Maybe she could have been my problem in D.C." He took off his shirt and lay back on the sand, using his shirt as a pillow.

"What girl?" Brubaker asked.

"I really don't know her name," said a squinting Puzo. "She was a girl I met in the attic of the Assistant Secretary's house on the night of our going away party. I was pretty drunk when I was with her and I blasted away at the big has-beens at Interior and leaked my support for Reagan."

"So that's what you did!" Brubaker began laughing. "THAT girl is the infamous and glamorous Rebecca, and she's the outgoing Assistant Secretary's spy-mongering secretary and highly paid mistress. She is rumored to have seduced some interesting information from unsuspecting foes of her boss, and I bet she's the one who got you defrocked at Interior." Brubaker then leaned back on the sand and continued laughing.

"It's not very funny." Puzo was miffed. "I suppose she was top secret, and you couldn't even warn your old buddy ahead of time."

"Believe me, Paddy, I didn't think you would cross her path in D.C., and you didn't mention anything." Brubaker started laughing again. "How did you find your way into the attic anyway?"

"Never mind!" He threw some sand at Brubaker. "As soon as Reagan takes office, I hope she goes right into the toilet with the Assistant Secretary and all those other Democratic jerk-offs at Interior."

Brubaker sat up and brushed off the sticky sand that Puzo had thrown at him, saying in a fake admonishing tone, "Very unprofessional of you to toss sand at your future E.D.A. boss, and as for Rebecca, she'll screw her way into a future Republican job for sure."

"Who cares about professionalism or Rebecca on a volcanic tit in the middle of nowhere?" Puzo took his shirt from under his head and began chasing several flies away that were getting attached to his beer-flavored sweat.

He stood up, put his shirt back on, and helped Brubaker get up from the sand with a pull, saying, "No wonder I didn't get a presidential medal for my work in the energy office."

They looked at each other for a moment and began laughing as they left the beach.

Both of them returned to T.T. Headquarters and then they went their respective ways.

Brubaker had met with Buford and later left for Guam. Puzo returned to his office and began playing with the solar music boxes again, which had been permanently left by the Reverend after his being transferred to Hawaii with a complete mental breakdown.

Puzo began looking for Bittle, and he finally found him jerking off in the closet. Puzo was glad that Bittle finally found something constructive to do with his life. But before he left Bittle playing with himself, Puzo loudly smack his lips at Bittle in symbolic retaliation against a sinister and crazy world and then closed the closet door and left for the day, not knowing when, or if, Bittle would ever leave the closet.

The last part of the year rolled by, and Puzo celebrated Christmas at Spam's, where a big turkey dinner was "generously" offered to the regular customers for a small cover charge of five paid drinks in advance. Of course, Puzo damned near drank himself into a coma.

It took a few days for him to finally sober up, and he decided then and there to seriously consider long-term sobriety, since he had caught a near fatal bout of severe bronchitis after sleeping drunk and nearly naked in a rainstorm all night behind Spam's bar.

While writhing in bed with a killer sickness on New Year's Eve, and deciding whether or not to drink a whole bottle of Nyquil to induce an over-the-counter anesthetic unconsciousness, he fitfully thought about his life, which had seemed to evolve into a dysfunctional living comic strip of sequential oddball affairs.

Well, 1981 and a new tropical job was still many hours away, since his first day at work was on January first and it, thank God, was a holiday, so he drank the bottle of Nyquil and passed out.

19

EASY DICK ASSIGNMENT

After his January arrival on Saipan, Brubaker was officially made the OPS Deputy Director and E.D.A. contracting officer for several very chaotic T.T. construction projects. The E.D.A. chaos was handed over to him to get him used to the Micronesian style of how things were unusually mishandled in the islands that were controlled by mostly unusual local island leaders.

Nevertheless, after spending a few days to get settled in, Brubaker looked real content sitting in the Deputy Director's Office for OPS, wearing a loose-fitting Hawaiian shirt, baggy Bermuda shorts, and rubber sandals on his bare feet.

With Brubaker continuously sitting at his desk with his hands clasped behind his head and a big grin on his face, he acted as though he had gone hatless in the tropical sun for too long. And while he enjoyed his present contentment, he also began to ponder about the morning meeting he had just finished with OPS Director Toddy. He had listened to Toddy explain about his duties and assignments, while all the time watching the director continually eat Danish rolls with the crumbs flying out of his mouth whenever he emphasized a point.

"Brubaker!" Toddy had said in a commanding voice during the meeting, "One of your first E.D.A. projects will be the redesigning of an international airport facility on a small atoll in the Marshall Islands. The local island leaders' plans call for an eight-thousand-foot runway with a terminal large enough to match the Honolulu airport terminal. However, we got problems. The whole atoll is barely five thousand feet long and has a total population of only ninety-three islanders!"

Toddy quickly ate another Danish and continued, "Apparently, this atoll has a very aggressive island chief who insists on having everything Honolulu has. The chief even planned to stage a nasty protest against the United States, if he didn't get his Hawaiian style runway. So, Interior finally gave in to a slightly modified version, with a new expensive house also being built for the island chief. Now we're stuck with the mess."

Toddy paused while looking for his next Danish victim and continued: "However, our boys in architecture and engineering have designed a coral strip of about four thousand feet and a scaled down terminal, which has an adjoining luxury apartment for the chief, too. Now it's up to you to sell it to this crazed and macho chief."

Brubaker was unconsciously nodding in agreement to the task, as Toddy added that his other major assignment was the completion of similar E.D.A. projects that were also in total chaos. Toddy further explained that the U.S. Economic Development Agency (EDA) had given the T.T. a large grant for several projects in the islands, and it was the U.S. EDA's philosophy to encourage local participation, which allowed the local contractors to get their hands on the fed money. However, this stroke of mad genius had turned the construction sites into vast monuments of mismanagement and misdirection. Toddy finally reminded Brubaker of the utmost importance to always put periods after each letter in E.D.A., for special purposes to differentiate the screwed up T.T.'s E.D.A. from the normal U.S. EDA. He then wished Brubaker good luck and finished eating his seventh Danish.

Brubaker was later sitting in his office and mulling over the last part of the meeting, in which he had faked enthusiasm by answering the foreboding challenge to try and make some progress with: "Sure, Mister Toddy, no problem." He had figured it better to keep it confidential that he couldn't even build a sand castle, let alone a frigging airport.

He further knew that in the islands a person's qualifications sometimes played second fiddle to just physically happening to being in the islands for whatever reason. The thought of Puzo and his previous energy escapades had attested to the fact that there was a severe lack of qualified people in far-far away Micronesia.

Following a quick study of the situation and realizing that it didn't take a genius to figure out what most of the problems with the E.D.A. projects were, Brubaker decided to visit Puzo and update him on their workload. He also decided to tackle the airport project in the Marshall Islands alone, thus preventing the unleashing of his anti-island-crazed friend on some unsuspecting macho chief on a small backwards atoll.

After lunch he went to Puzo's office, which was the same cubicle Puzo had previously shared with Jennings.

Unfortunately, Jennings was a missing item now. His liver had mostly quit functioning and they had shipped him to Hawaii for his remaining days. During which time he had peacefully entered that big beer bar in the sky.

Brubaker walked into Puzo's office, smiling, "We've got a few problems with the E.D.A. projects." He then grabbed a chair and sat down near Puzo. "But nothing we can't handle, right?"

Puzo looked up from an old Playboy magazine and whined, "You got problems?!" He was surveying the centerfold which was half missing. "I think my former cubicle-mate Jennings ripped Miss August in half and took the bottom with him to Hawaii."

Brubaker then noticed that the bottom half of Miss August was missing and said: "Jennings must have been a leg man. But seriously, let's talk about these projects for maybe a half-hour, okay?"

"Shoot. I'm all ears," Puzo replied, putting the magazine away.

"Well, first off," Brubaker explained, "we got two medium-sized projects in Palau, which are a fishery freezer unit and a fresh market facility that are being built by a crooked contractor who's very powerful in island affairs. From what I gather, he's had several legal problems with our T.T. attorney general over missing funds and he's decided to shut down the projects until he gets extra money for the slandering of his good name. He's also suing the T.T. Government, President Reagan, and the United States of America for damaging his impeccable reputation."

"Can he really stop the federal projects while being investigated himself?" Puzo asked.

"Sure, why not? He's a part of the T.T. free enterprise system, and he's free to do anything under the island sun. Did you know that the last T.T. attorney who came back from Palau had been beaten to a pulp by the contractor's office staff?"

"What did our gutless state department do about it?" Puzo inquired.

Brubaker responded, "The usual. They sent a letter of apologetic understanding to the contractor, his office staff of three women, and the people of Palau. They also promised to recommend to the battered attorney that he not be so insensitive the next time he tries to serve an arrest warrant on one of their community leaders."

"Sounds wonderful in Palau." Puzo picked up his Playboy again. "Keep going, I'm listening."

Brubaker had gone over to a chalkboard and had written on it "Palau" with a big question mark after it. He then wrote "Yap", shook his head, and continued, "Next, we have Yap Island, where there are problems with the Navy O.I.C.C. and the local Yapese contractor who gets paid by the T.T. but keeps going fishing all the time."

Puzo looked up from his magazine. "What's an O.I.C.C.?"

"Officer in Charge of Construction," Brubaker answered. "He's a Navy lieutenant who has had no real experience in construction. He reminds me of us in the inexperience category. Anyway, he's currently in charge of a different federal canned tuna project in Yap that's also a total nightmare because the cannery is located on a politician's land and he wants a few million dollars for the land. However, the O.I.C.C. has now tied up all the available equipment and local labor in protest until he gets a transfer to anywhere except in Micronesia. And besides that, the Navy's been pissed off because the T.T. got involved in the construction of its own E.D.A. projects and competing with the Navy projects in Micronesia. Our project in Yap is a small police and jail facility. But I guess there are bragging rights to who finishes its project first."

Brubaker then wrote a question mark and an exclamation point after the word "Yap" on the chalkboard.

Puzo slowly got up and went to the chalkboard and grabbed the chalk from Brubaker, He added the name "John Wayne" under the word "Yap", and handed the chalk back to him.

"That's the problem with the Navy," Puzo interjected, "just because John Wayne and the Seabees kicked some tail out here in the war movies, the Navy thinks they're still in charge of all the macho federal projects in the Pacific. Our strategy is to convince the O.I.C.C. and the local contractor into thinking we mean business, and that we plan to finish our project pronto. Then you can be a Micronesian hero, and I can get the hell back to Civilization."

Puzo returned to his chair and sat down.

Brubaker shook his head and challenged Puzo. "How in the hell are you going to mean business when you don't even know the difference between a six-penny and eight-penny nail?"

"Easy. The difference is two cents." Puzo confidently replied.

Puzo quickly ducked the chalk that Brubaker threw at him and Puzo pleaded, "Okay, okay! Don't get upset, Ralph. I don't know the exact difference, but I think it has something to do with the length of the nail."

Brubaker sighed, "Maybe there's hope for all of us after all," as he wrote "Ulithi" and "Truk" on the chalkboard and continued: "A little way from Yap is the island of Ulithi, and we have to finish a dental clinic there for an island that doesn't even have a dentist. Then last, but not least, there's Truk Island, and a warehouse that can't be finished because all the materials seem to be re-routed to various local government officials and their newly built homes."

Brubaker shook his head at the chalkboard and looked at Puzo, "What do you think, Paddy?"

"No problem, Puzo said intently, "let's just get a little dishonest and crazy like the rest of these islanders and fight fire with fire."

"Take it easy." Brubaker cautioned. "Remember, we're outnumbered out here, and the odds of our finishing these projects on time are rumored to be pretty slim. It seems the higher-ups don't really care that these projects are finished for some goofy reason,"

Brubaker then put the chalk on the chalkboard's bottom ledge and walked over to Puzo, saying, "Enough of the problems, I'll check you later, and plan on taking a little field trip to Palau and Yap soon. We'll need an eyewitness account of the problems there to gauge our possible chances for success."

"Sure, Ralph. I could use a trip…anywhere."

It was early February when Brubaker finally left for the Marshall Islands to negotiate the "long" runway project with an obstinate island chief, and he hoped he would return soon without any major problems.

Meanwhile, Puzo had gone on his field trip to Palau and Yap for onsite inspections. He would get to observe firsthand the political phenomenon of one of the most powerful nations in the world, namely the U.S. of A., being driven to international lunacy by a group of small Micronesian islands and their mostly friendly but definitely perplexing leaders.

Following Puzo's checking in at a quaint hotel in Koror, the capital of Palau, he was taken to a fish barbeque at the Palauan contractor's house, where he curiously observed that the house's back wall had been covered with fairly new aluminum siding.

The siding had the words "PROPERTY OF THE T.T.P.I." stenciled on the bottom of each panel, and he shook his head in amazement at the blatant display of thievery from the U.S. Trust Territory government.

During the barbeque, he listened to, and wisely agreed to, all points made by the contractor and his large, mean-looking assistants. He tried his best to sympathize with the poor, misguided Palauan contractor, who was supposedly being smeared by a white racist T.T. legal mentality. Puzo just kept agreeing and drinking with his adversaries until he was totally inebriated.

He wound up dancing all night with the contractor's nieces and nephews, depending on who was holding him upright at the time, and eventually passed out in a chicken coop in the contractor's backyard.

He woke up the following morning with a beauty of a hangover, and found himself staring at a discarded electrical panel in the corner of the coop that had some skinny chickens perched on its top. He sighed again in disbelief at the panel's stenciled letters of T.T.P.I. ownership, and then slowly raised himself to his feet.

As he walked out of the chicken coop he stepped over the prostrate Palauan contractor, who gave him a big, friendly smile.

Puzo nonchalantly said to the contractor, "Great party."

The contractor then replied with a slur, "You're okay, Mister T.T.," and then he passed out cold in a pile of chicken poop.

Puzo summarily spent the remainder of his short stay on Palau trying to convince the contractor that it would be better to finish the two E.D.A. projects first, and then sue the hell out of the racist T.T.

Puzo also hoped by the time the case came to court he would be long gone to the U.S. mainland, and the contractor and the T.T. government could spend the next forty years suing each other for all he cared.

Following Palau he visited Yap Island, where he found himself behaving in an overly pleasing manner to an aloof Navy Officer in Charge of Construction.

The Navy OICC was a real bona fide Lieutenant Fuzz-Brain, who kept calculating imaginary problems on his handheld calculator to keep busy and repeatedly admonishing Puzo with: "The Trust Territory government has no business doing construction projects in Micronesia. The United States Navy was here first."

"Alright, I agree with you," Puzo finally replied to the lieutenant in the OICC's office on the afternoon of his only day on Yap, "but if we don't work together, a greatly delayed U.S. project will be the object of continued foreign criticism."

Puzo had angled towards the patriotic side of the Navy lieutenant, and the lieutenant finally said he would try to help, only if Puzo bought him a new calculator and two cases of double-A batteries.

After leaving the OICC, his next assignment on Yap was to convince the Yapese T.T. paid contractor to postpone his fishing trips for a while. The Yapese contractor initially balked at the thought of not fishing every day, but after Puzo bought him a new rod and reel out of his E.D.A. emergency money, the contractor finally gave his promise to reduce his fishing trips to every other day.

All in all, his minor dishonesty in dealing with his E.D.A. objectives was justifiable in his own opinion, and the eventual trip back to Saipan was a pleasant flight filled with champagne and peanuts. It was also filled with thoughts of a big trip that he would eventually take back to Civilization.

Puzo arrived on Saipan with the feeling that his first trip to the district islands was very enlightening, although he felt like he had just returned from outer space.

On the plane ride back he had come up with the nutty theory that future astronauts could maybe train on some of the outer, less inhabited islands of Yap or Palau, by exposing themselves to environmental isolation and alien get-togethers, hosted by the extraterrestrial islanders who lived there.

Hmmm…maybe NASA would be interested.

After his return to T.T. Headquarters, he spent a couple of days writing a glowing report on his field trip to Palau and Yap. It was nearing the first of March and he began to wonder why Brubaker hadn't come back from his field trip to the Marshall Islands.

Another week later, Brubaker finally returned from his extended trip, where he had successfully negotiated a compromise with the Marshallese chief of the airport atoll. The atoll's international airport would be justifiably shorter than originally planned, but not until Brubaker had promised to get the chief a brand new fire engine with white-walled tires and a French horn. Apparently, Brubaker had to use the same bargaining devices as Puzo did on Yap, which they had both discovered were quasi-federally-approved ways of doing business in Micronesia.

The reason for Brubaker's delay, however, was a side trip he had reluctantly agreed to take to an isolated, backwards island called Kosrae.

He had got stranded on Kosrae for two weeks because of transportation difficulties, and being stuck on Kosrae had a very unusual effect on Brubaker. He was never quite the same person after his confinement on Kosrae, since "overly primitive" Kosrae mostly operated around the customs and culture of the fourteenth century.

During the whole month of March, Puzo decided to devote most of his time to the procurement of everything necessary for the completion of the E.D.A. projects. He estimated that the shipments of construction materials would all arrive by the latter part of April, and he bribed all the appropriate personnel with free cases of beer on each island to make sure that they would secure the arriving shipments until they were ready to use. He didn't want to be a spoilsport, but he roughly calculated that the T.T. government had already supplied the various island officials enough building supplies to construct hundreds of houses, including the entire Taj Mahal.

The shipments of E.D.A. materials were eventually being processed and promptly delivered as the month of April began, and Puzo kept sitting relaxed at his desk, circling the months on his calendar and dreaming of his future departure from Saipan. He didn't want anything to upset his remaining days in paradise, and prayed that the whimsical nature of the islands and islanders would not disturb his speedy and uneventful exit back to the U.S. mainland.

Brubaker had let him run his own show on the various project scenarios, and Puzo seemed more and more secure about his future fate, especially after nearing the project completion of some long-running headaches for the Trust Territory government.

Later in May, Puzo had officially and surprisingly finished all the projects, by accomplishing these feats using the islanders' skills and abilities, as long as an outsider knows how to tap into their inner souls.

However, he had unintentionally challenged and upstaged the T.T. power boys, who previously couldn't get the projects completed. They had diabolically decided to give the E.D.A. mess to Brubaker earlier for a punishment in bringing a stateside lunatic named Puzo out to Micronesia to mess up their self-serving and status quo T.T. affairs. The Hicom and Toddy wanted to scrub the E.D.A. fiascos and tactfully blamed the islanders for being incompetent and uncooperative nincompoops, to cover their own T.T. incompetence.

Puzo's methods for completing the E.D.A. projects involved bonding with the islanders in special friendly ways, but a few bonding actions had bordered on being legally questionable, and his suspect activities would soon cause him difficulties with the T.T. higher-ups.

For example, he facetiously promised to be a character witness for the Palauan contractor in his future lawsuit against the T.T., in exchange for finishing the projects in Palau.

He then forced the Navy OICC in Yap to cooperate with him by convincing the Yapese governor to tell the OICC that the sooner the T.T. finished its project there, the sooner one less U.S. government agency would be bothering the people of Yap. It had to be noted that the OICC feared the Yap governor and his large and forceful assistants.

On Ulithi, he had turned the dental clinic into a small sports recreational hall and eliminated several time-consuming and costly requirements. He also traded unused dental equipment for sports equipment. The Ulithians were happy as hell to get an indoor basketball court and they gratefully signed off the completion notice to satisfy the E.D.A. acceptance documents.

On the island of Truk, Puzo persuaded the local officials to give their utmost efforts to finishing the warehouse project. He accomplished this feat by smuggling in beer and whiskey in the T.T. packing crates. Truk was supposedly a "dry" island, but as long as the proper officials received their drinkable duty, then projects like the E.D.A. warehouse stood a chance to get completed.

Consequently, the surprising news of the E.D.A. completions was ironically accepted with shaking of heads and the wringing of hands around T.T. Headquarters.

By completing the projects, which had been a T.T. embarrassment for years, it had now been reported to Washington that after the T.T. Headquarters had been informing the feds in D.C. about the 'slim to none' chance of ever completing the chaotic E.D.A. projects in Micronesia…how in the hell did they now complete them all in five months?! The completions were now an even more embarrassing subject for the pompous higher-ups at headquarters, who had already written off the projects as true examples of the island leaders' ongoing fuckup-abilities. This manifestation of islander incompetence in turn kept T.T. higher-ups secure in their high-paying jobs and overseas benefits by justifying their positions by blaming the islanders for the whole mess in Micronesia.

High Commissioner Finkel, who had vociferously given up on the completion of the E.D.A. projects, had now been upstaged by an upstart, and a Republican upstart for that matter.

To exacerbate the situation, Puzo's pictures of President Reagan in his office had always irritated the Democratic-appointed Finkel, who was still in charge of the T.T. Empire because Reagan's people hadn't nominated their own Republican candidate for the High Commissioner position yet. Furthermore, Finkel hated anything to do with Republicans, and he was very leery of Puzo and the new wave of Reaganism that was infecting the minds of loyal Democratic Americans, and he felt it was his Democratic duty to combat such dangerous patriotic ideology.

The Hicom consequently called Brubaker into his office during the first week of June and told him about his decision to terminate Puzo, due to his questionable E.D.A. conduct, like the illegal supplying of liquor to the Trukese officials and other Reagan-inspired screw ups. Moreover, no complaints would be filed against Puzo if he left the T.T. in a peaceful manner and didn't go public with his own version of the whole chaotic E.D.A. affair. The Hicom then instructed Brubaker to immediately tell Puzo about his firing, and to tell him to take his goddamn picture of Reagan with him. Apparently, the HiCom didn't give a rat's ass about Puzo's overrated connection to the new president.

But Brubaker had mixed emotions about Puzo's predicament, asking, "Do you think it's fair to fire him? He did finish the projects and saved us from future criticism by the leaders and people of Micronesian."

"You really don't understand the balance of power in Micronesia, Mister Brubaker," the Hicom replied. "If we finished all the projects, then we wouldn't be needed out here. And if we're not needed out here, well, we would lose the ordained power of having to be here to protect these simple-minded islanders, who are the reason things don't get finished in the first place."

Brubaker frowned at the Hicom's line of reasoning, and the Hicom continued, "We can always blame the Micronesians for not completing projects, since they love to show their own imaginary power over us by using their delaying and incompetent tactics. But it's we who are in real power, as long as we are just physically here. And people like Puzo can't be allowed to be here and interfere with our systemic T.T. superiority."

The HiCom paused, and repeated, "Tell him he's terminated immediately so he doesn't sabotage anything, and I called the C.I.A. to keep an eye on him. He can stay at his government quarters until tomorrow to clean out his belongings. Now, do you have any problems with Puzo's termination, Mister Brubaker?"

"No, I guess not. I told him already that he's on his own from now on."

"Good. By the way, Brubaker, you'll soon be receiving a C.I.A. personal commendation in honor of the Democratic Party for the completion of the E.D.A. projects. That will be all for now."

The Hicom's final remark left Brubaker stunned.

He then walked out of the Hicom's office and stopped at Betty Jo's desk, saying, "I don't believe it. Puzo's going to get fired for finishing the projects on time and I'm getting a C.I.A. commendation. By the way, do you know if the C.I.A. is a part of the Democratic Party?"

Betty Jo replied, "C.I.A. and the Democratic Party? What the hell are you talking about? And don't worry about Puzo, Ralph, that's life out here in the crazy T.T. jungle. Besides, Paddy's a big boy and it probably won't be the last time he gets fired."

"I just don't know sometimes about the craziness of U.S. politics," Brubaker muttered, "and forget about the C.I.A. question," Brubaker whispered out loud. He oddly shook his head at a confused Betty Jo, and then left to notify his friend about his immediate termination.

Betty Jo sighed, "Puzo, the C.I.A. and the Democratic Party, and Brubaker acting strange. I think I need a drink."

20

WHAT, I'M FIRED?!

Before a thoroughly dumbfounded and fired Puzo departed the T.T. Headquarters, he made five hundred copies of his termination letter and ripped them into confetti. He dumped all the bits of paper and a bunch of greasy ball bearings from Jenning's desk into a large cardboard box and then proceeded over to the Hicom's office.

Upon his arrival at the Hicom's office, he walked briskly past Betty Jo Hunter and barged unannounced into Finkel's office. He stopped in front of the glaring Hicom, and then went directly over to the Hicom's precious plants.

He smiled at Finkel and violently dumped the contents of the cardboard box all over his plants. Then he roughly placed the box over the Hicom's prized begonias and gave the box several heavy punches with his fists.

"Just a little T.T. fertilizer for your stupid-ass plants!" Puzo said with a salute. He quickly pulled down his pants and mooned the HiCom, and then walked out of the office and passed by Betty Jo again, stopping to give her a wink and a wry smile.

After the savage attack on his begonias, the Hicom scurried over to his plants, screaming, "Get me security!"

Fertilizing the Hicom's plants got Puzo thrown out of his government quarters the very same day, and he luckily found a place to stay that evening at Spam's.

Spam had laughed so hard about the vicious attack on the Hicom's plants that he gave Puzo a free place to stay. It was one of Spam's spare tool shacks which had been converted into living quarters for one of his former Filipino workers. The happy Filipino was now working as a security guard and staying in a barracks full of Filipina "exotic" dancers. Spam told Puzo that he could stay there until he got squared away and decided what to do.

A couple of days later, Puzo sat profusely sweating in his tropically-heated tin shack that had no air conditioning, cringing about his present situation, and then realized that his future situation didn't look too appetizing either.

He figured it best to head back to the mainland as soon as he could, although first he needed to get a decent job to pay the expensive plane fare back with some extra money to start his life over again.

He thought about asking Brubaker for a loan, but Brubaker's financial situation was shaky too, caused by the divorce from Shirley and his new Micronesian girlfriend with her borrow-borrow relatives.

Spam eventually let him clean around the bar for a few extra bucks, but he kept drinking his earnings every night and it turned into a drunken cycle of getting nowhere.

Puzo desperately needed a plan, and it was his consequential living away from the T.T. environment that eventually seeded the plans to help his current, barren situation.

Being forced to survive on his own had made him more aware of the local community and its overwhelming socio-political structure of government jobs, and this awareness might hopefully lead him towards home in the states.

It happened that the island of Saipan, home of the T.T. Headquarters, was also the major island in the newly-formed U.S. Commonwealth of the Northern Mariana Islands, which was haphazardly nurturing new island bureaucrats in a wonderland of federal aid. The Commonwealth had more U.S. aid sent to them than they knew what to do with, and had quickly created a similar system of overlapping government agencies and too many repetitious jobs just like the feds did. The Commonwealth even had jobs for some lucky statesiders, who knew how to read and write English well enough to write lucrative U.S. federal grants and glowing press releases for federally-crowned island leaders.

Surely there was a spot for Puzo to fill, and all he needed was a simple political connection. Furthermore, with its second general election coming up for the Commonwealth's gubernatorial and legislative branches, certain opportunities were ever so ripening.

The only problem was to pick the right political party, because if you picked wrong, then you could kiss your employment opportunities right out to sea.

As Puzo observed the local leaders in both parties, he saw that their election strategies were finally shaping up by the end of July. It appeared a sure bet that the local Republicans would win most of the elected positions that year, since the Democrats had made a real mess of the young government. And with the Republican Ronald Reagan winning the previous presidential election in the U. S. mainland, it was highly probable that the local islanders would elect Republicans in the Commonwealth. This, of course, would guarantee favorable financial conditions with President Reagan appointing Republican territorial staff in Washington to handle the islanders' big bucks.

Armed with his booze-laced observations and the knowledge gained in Spam's bar about the Republicans being favored that year in the Commonwealth, Puzo decided to invest most of his meager savings into some well placed ads in the local papers. The ads were fairly cheap and they made it known that he was supporting the local Republicans that year.

He advertised about his receiving an official membership in the Republican Presidential Task Force in Washington, D.C., which came about after his name was placed on a Republican mailing list when he had sent in a dollar contribution to Reagan's 1980 Election Committee.

What the hell, he thought, it looked impressive when he mentioned his fancy "Task Force" membership in his ads, and the local politicians wouldn't know any better. He was now a big-shot Republican supporter with mainland clout.

The word soon began to spread on the small island that Puzo had some connections in D.C., and the local politicians, who were prone to excessive rumor mongering, soon had him regarded as a secret advisor to President Reagan himself.

Although he seemed destined for a definite piece of the local action, Puzo didn't really consider himself that important in the island scheme of things, and he knew his outsider's white boy status was still a big liability.

However, he was proud of the subtle effect he was having on the local political scene, and graciously thanked his old friend Jennings, God love him, for teaching him the secrets of beautifully engineered bullshit.

The following months became "Campaign Showdown" in the Commonwealth, and the place was a political nuthouse. Automobiles with gigantic speakers on their roofs were blaring all night long for their respective candidates, and village meetings invariably turned into contests of who had the loudest sound systems.

The incumbent Democratic governor, an arrogant and aloof Felix T. Yamoreyes, was frantic about his poor chances in the upcoming election. He furiously erected gigantic signs all over the island, falsely claiming that every building, streetlight, water fountain, and public toilet ever built, or installed on Saipan, was due to his great administration.

But the campaign kept going bad for Yamoreyes, and his Republican opponent, Regino J. Gustomacho, was looking good in the early returns.

Meanwhile, Puzo had gone to work for the Marianas Daily News as a news stringer, replacing the reporter Jim Morrison who had gotten a job as a singing bartender at a local strip club. Puzo's editor at the Marianas Daily News, Freddie Huston, told him that his Republican connections wouldn't hurt in getting some inside information about the favored Republicans. The newspaper job was also important to Puzo's plan to gain better access into the inner circles of Republican local leaders, and he used the opportunity to the fullest.

As it turned out, Yamoreyes failed miserably with his last minute attempts to gain royal recognition, and Gustomacho and his fellow Republicans easily won all the November elected positions.

It was now a new ballgame in the Commonwealth and Puzo's position in life was hopefully going to change come January.

However, knowing that statesiders were always jerked around in the islands, he still kept his low-paying job at the newspaper, for he knew his new lease on life was still languishing in loco island limbo.

21

PLEASE, GOVERNOR GUSTOMACHO

January of 1982 was civic carnival time on Saipan with Governor Gustomacho's inauguration highlighting the island's festivities. The inauguration occurred on Commonwealth Day, a very popular holiday for the Northern Mariana Islands. For on this day in 1978, the United States and the new U.S. Commonwealth of the Northern Mariana Islands had officially created another federally-sponsored welfare wonderland, and the islanders enjoyed temporary U.S. status that would soon become permanent full-fledged U.S. citizenship with all the benefits included.

One of the main attractions of the inauguration was the parading of outlandish outfits by Micronesian politicians, who were bent on serious, mind-boggling one-upmanship. The star of the parade was a politician from an outer island somewhere in southern Micronesia, who kept sashaying around in an outfit that was designed by a cross-dressing, color-blind tailor from Fiji. The politician's sartorial get-up consisted of a yellow straw hat laced with red and purple flowers, an orange and green plaid sport coat, a purple shirt with a white and pink tie, blue and white checkerboard-striped polyester pants, red rubber sandals on his bare feet, several gold and silver chains draped around his neck, a silver nose ring, a large green earring in one ear, and monstrous, mirror-finished, white-framed sunglasses. The whole attire seriously challenged the naked eye to look at it for more than a split second at any one stare.

Besides showing off their wild garb, the region's political leaders who were attending the inauguration enjoyed another favorite pastime, which was coming to Saipan to show Pacific island unity, and to embellish "Brown Brotherhood" with the unilateral declaration of: "Let's make sure all those damned white outsiders don't take over!"

Throughout the inauguration, Puzo's assignment was to cover the highlights for his newspaper. Near the end of the day he finally gathered his wits and approached Governor Gustomacho after the festivities. He nervously said: "Great inauguration speech, governor. You had them hanging on every word."

The governor then came closer to Puzo and said with a smirking smile, "I might have a job for you in my administration if a great story of my inauguration appears in your newspaper."

Puzo took the hint and responded: "I'll do my best, governor."

Actually, the long-winded speech sucked, and it did have one clear message for the people, i.e., it was highly recommended that a certain long-winded speech writer should be thrown to the sharks, because the too damn long speech delayed the islanders from gorging on the gigantic tables of great island food and other goodies.

As a rule, most speech writers for the island leaders were burned-out stateside attorneys, who normally had an adequate command of the English language and, simultaneously, a very inviting fifth of bourbon on their desks. They could make a Micronesian politician sound either like a brilliant island statesman, or a boring buffoon, depending on the amount of alcohol saturating their brains during last minute writing sessions.

For what it was worth to Puzo's future, his next day's story of Gustomacho's inauguration teetered on the edge of stupendous reporting, realizing, of course, that a desperate man was writing it.

Three days later, Puzo anxiously sat at his desk in the newspaper office and the phone rang. "Hello, Puzo here," he quickly answered.

"Mister Puzo. The governor liked your story and sends his regards. Goodbye." The phone call ended just like that, and Puzo felt crestfallen.

Where was the offer for a good job? What about his future plans to escape back to America?!

Oh, well, with the money he earned working at the newspaper he could eventually leave Saipan around the year 2042. Aaaaahhh!!!

But at least the islanders seem to get his name right.

In the last part of January, Gustomacho selected his Cabinet and other staff members. It was the changing of the guard around the Commonwealth, and political payoffs and close family relationships played a major role in the governor's selection process.

The staffs of all Micronesian leaders, however, normally included a few white, U.S. statesiders, who were thrown in for certain communication skills, legal expertise and, apparently, for quasi-mental balance. The statesiders were also hired because island leaders felt it was a good public relations idea, since all their federal spending money came from the U.S. of A., where they thought only white people paid their taxes.

Overall, Gustomacho made some classic choices for his administration's Cabinet. The choices were definitely dictated by island custom and not by common sense. He filled almost the entire Cabinet with his immediate family and in-laws, no matter if they had been in jail and were immediately released upon selection, or had previously escaped from jail, or had the I.Q. of a ripe papaya.

Some of his relatives' qualifications for civic duty were also based proportionally to the length of their prison records. And certain crimes, like embezzling federal funds or beating up on visiting statesiders, were ranked pretty high on the local list of community achievements.

Compared to other local island leaders, it was widely known that Gustomacho had some very high-ranking relatives, and that the Commonwealth was destined to be temporarily ruled by a group of U.S.-approved, local law-breaking lunatics.

It soon became mid-February, and still no lucrative government job for Puzo. He was still working for the local newspaper, but the low pay had forced him to seek another source for his future traveling funds.

While scanning the advertisements in the newsroom one afternoon, he noticed a local radio station was advertising for an all-night deejay on the weekends. He figured he could combine the night job with his day job and increase his meager income.

He immediately went over to the radio station, and after a quick, one-minute interview, got the job and would begin that same night. He wasn't really qualified for the deejay job, but no one else wanted to fill the graveyard shift.

The radio job paid a whopping $1.35 an hour, which was the minimum wage in the Commonwealth, and he could now leave paradise for Civilization around 2041, instead of the year 2042.

Aaaahhhhhhhhhhhhhhhhhh!!!!!!

Puzo was now getting more and more anxious about his dire predicament on Saipan, but he was also getting somewhat pissed at his repeating misfortunes and, consequently, he was ready to attack his fate and diligently work his way out of his current dilemma. He was hanging onto this shaky confidence until he got back to his newspaper office after his deejay interview and talked to his more informed editor about his new job as a weekend all-night deejay.

"Did you notice the isolated location of the radio station at the top of Navy Hill?" asked Houston, who was a likable guy who originally hailed from Tennessee.

"Yeah," Puzo replied.

"Did you also ever wonder why the station was off the air most Monday mornings?" Houston then asked with a grin.

"Not really, I can't even afford a radio right now to check."

"Well," drawled Houston, "the place has a nasty reputation for being a weekend drinking place for the local teenage hoodlums, who get this crazy notion they're deejays about three in the morning. Their favorite night seems to be always on Sunday when they do a real foot-stomping finale on the station and, sometimes, on the hapless deejay. So, every now and then, radio K-P-A-N closes down for a few minor repairs, and I get an ad for another deejay."

"Are you serious, Freddie?"

"About as serious as a bobcat with hemorrhoids," Houston deadpanned.

"Hey, Freddie?" Puzo implored, "Can you loan me about two thousand dollars until payday?"

"Sorry, I know what you make, and it'll take you too long to pay me back. Besides, I have a feeling you'd be sending me a postcard from somewhere in France, telling me my money was well spent."

"I wouldn't do that. French people are pains in the ass. And what did you mean about the bobcat?" Puzo asked.

Houston just smiled and left the office.

The first couple of weekends as a deejay were certifiably bizarre sessions for Puzo. He had taken several NoDoz tablets to stay awake and turned into a rambling idiot who kept playing records with the audio switches in the wrong positions. And about the only person listening to his show was a retired U.S. Coast Guard chief with insomnia, who would invariably call him early in the morning and chew his butt out for being an idiot.

The one good and healthy thing about the job was that he would bring two six packs of beer on Sunday nights and spike the beer with tequila. He would then hand out the tequila and beer to the teenagers and, fortunately for him, he would watch the island teens, who were not use to the Mexican loco brew, do cartwheels down the hill all night and end up not beating him up. The bad thing was the beer and tequila put a big dent in his miniscule earnings. But for Puzo and his travel fund, his future was about to rapidly change.

Houston was the first to know at the newspaper that it had been quietly reported that Governor Gustomacho had an opening for a Public Information Officer, since his first appointee for the PIO job accidentally shot himself in the balls while practicing quick draws with his loaded pistol. The poor bastard with the perforated nutsack happened to be the governor's nephew, and they had to evacuate him to Hawaii for emergency reconstructive surgery.

The recovery period was unknown and the governor needed a PIO in a hurry. So, the governor decided to take a chance with Puzo, who did have some media experience for a whopping couple of months.

The governor didn't really trust white guys with too much experience and smarts, because they would give him a pain in the ass like his long-winded stateside speech writer. Puzo, who had been frequently hanging around the governor's office with an eager grin on his face every chance he could, seemed to fit the governor's statesider qualifications of being just smart enough to do the PIO job without causing too many problems for the island leaders.

When finally contacted at the newspaper office, Puzo had to swear complete support for Gustomacho and his entire administration. But Puzo didn't care. He would have sworn his parents were childless.

The only problem was his appointment was that it wasn't received very well by some islanders on the governor's staff, who preached "jobs for locals only."

But the governor soothed his relatives by saying that the appointment was only temporary until his nephew recovered and could walk correctly and speak with a deeper voice.

It didn't take long for Puzo to quit both of his jobs and move out of Spam's shack into a tin house by the beach. He would begin work at the governor's office on April first, which was appropriately April Fools' Day.

22

P.I.O.

On the first day of the PIO job Puzo called Rose, the Public Affairs Officer at the T.T., and requested some confidential information for Gustomacho. Eager to get revenge, Puzo prodded a reluctant Rose into giving him some sensitive data, which he would save for a rainy blackmailing day.

But after giving Puzo the data, Rose had insisted on knowing why he needed the information.

Puzo finally replied to Rose's demand with a whispered: "April Fools!" which made Rose go into a frenzy.

Puzo then listened to Rose's numerous threats, until he made him back off with his own threats of later blaming Rose for the possible leaking of sensitive T.T. information to the press.

Rose was finally coerced into writing a glowing T.T. press release about Puzo's new job as the governor's PIO and to get the name spelled right. At that point, Rose finally screamed a stream of obscenities and hung up.

Puzo was all smiles. He had waited a long time to get revenge on Rose. But now he had to finish his first release about Gustomacho in the next half-hour.

So he got busy looking at the file of old Commonwealth releases and quickly roughed out a draft for the governor's eventual approval.

CNMI PRESS RELEASE
(GOVERNOR REGINO J. GUSTOMACHO DECLARES NO MORE FISCAL WASTE IN STATEMENT TO VISITING FEDERAL OFFICIALS)
SAIPAN, COMMONWEALTH OF THE NORTHERN MARIANA ISLANDS, APRIL 1, CNMI/P10---

GOVERNOR REGINO J. GUSTOMACHO HAS DECLARED THERE SHALL BE NO MORE FISCAL WASTE IN HIS ADMINISTRATION, EXCEPT FOR OCCASIONAL TRAVEL EMERGENCIES. DURING AN OFFICIAL VISIT THIS WEEK FROM THE INSPECTOR GENERAL'S OFFICE OF THE U.S. DEPARTMENT OF INTERIOR, GOVERNOR GUSTOMACHO WAS SHOWN THE INTERIOR'S FINANCIAL AUDIT OF THE COMMONWEALTH, WHICH POINTED OUT VARIOUS PROBLEM AREAS OF LOCAL FISCAL IRRESPONSIBILITY. THE GOVERNOR MADE A SOLEMN PROMISE TO LOOK INTO THESE SERIOUS MATTERS AT ONCE AND FURTHERMORE, HE WISHES TO POINT OUT THAT THE PREVIOUS DEMOCRATIC ADMINISTRATION IS TO BE BLAMED FOR ANY FISCAL PROBLEMS IN THE COMMONWEALTH. THE ASSISTANT INSPECTOR GENERAL FOR INTERIOR, HORACE T. BUSHBOTT, AND HIS STAFF ARE PLEASED WITH THE GOVERNOR'S CONCERN OVER THIS MATTER, AND THEY SPOKE HIGHLY OF GOVERNOR GUSTOMACHO'S ADMINISTRATION AT THE BIG BARBEQUE GIVEN IN THEIR HONOR AT THE GOVERNOR'S MANSION. (END OF RELEASE)

Gustomacho seemed apparently pleased with Puzo's first release, although it was basically the standard release that was always given by the local leaders to appease visiting federal authorities.

Later in the day, however, Puzo received a very obscene phone call after the press release had been distributed. The call was from an irate Democrat, who was currently out of work as an ex-legislator, and who was extremely incensed over Puzo's press release.

The ex-legislator vehemently denied that his Democratic Party was to blame for any mother fucking deficits! He also advised Puzo to get his facts straight before he released anything else about the Democrats, or there would be swift and serious revenge, like burning down his tin house at the beach with maybe his white ass inside!

Welcome to local island politics, Puzo thought. Then he shuddered at the idea of it being only his first day on a job that was again promising to put him, a fairly nice white person on the road to racial recovery, right in the middle of a dangerous, tropical island-style, anti-whitey, socio-politico shit storm!

A week later, Puzo received a packet of incoming information from various sources, and he was amused to see that Rose had taken him seriously about his press release. Among the inter-department memos and government documents was a short and semi-glowing T.T. press release about his recent appointment as the new PIO for the Commonwealth of the Northern Mariana Islands. He reveled in his sweet revenge over Rose and ceremoniously tacked the T.T. release to his bare bulletin board. Armed with a desire to share his current fortune, he decided to phone Brubaker, in an eager attempt to regain some of the friendly spark of their previous relationship.

Puzo phoned the T.T. Headquarters and reached Brubaker. "Ralph? Paddy here. I just wanted to tell you that I'm sorry we lost touch."

"No problem, Paddy. These things happen."

"Talk about things happening," laughed Puzo. "Did you read the release from Rose's office about my PIO appointment?"

"Yeah. It was a dumb thing for Rose to do, considering the Hicom's feelings about you. But Rose didn't think he had to clear it with the Hicom's office because the Hicom was off-island. But the first thing the Hicom did when he found out about it was to transfer Rose to an isolated island somewhere near the Marshalls."

"You mean the Hicom sent him to Kosrae?"

"Please don't mention the name of that island, okay, Paddy."

"Sorry, Ralph, I forgot about your bad experience there. Hey, and forget about Rose, too. Tell me about yourself."

"Well, I had my contract extended two more years, partly because I, I mean you, finished the E.D.A. projects that were made into a success story by the T.T. higher-ups to cover their pompous butts, and by the way, my Trukese girlfriend Terra and her whole family moved in with me. She's already got seven previous children and she's expecting our baby soon."

"Sons-a-bitch,' Puzo exhorted, "you're going to be a poppa! Congratulations. How many did you say are living in your government house now?"

"Around ten to fifteen, depending on who's visiting from Terra's island of Truk--" Brubaker was abruptly cut off by Puzo.

"Wait a minute, you mean to tell me that you got the glory for the E.D.A. projects, and I got the shaft!"

"It was only fate, and maybe your support for Reagan." Then Brubaker assured him. "Anyway, it gave the Republican gods a chance to find you a better position with the governor."

"Yeah, I guess the political gods work in strange ways. But I still got shafted by a crap-for-brains Hicom. Tell me one thing, Ralph. Did you agree with him?"

"What do you think?" Brubaker asked.

Puzo replied, "I don't think it really matters to tell you the truth. I probably deserved what he dished out to me."

An islander secretary then interrupted Puzo with a message, and he said, "Sorry, Ralph, the governor wants to see me right away. Talk to you later."

Puzo hung up, grabbed his note pad, and swiftly headed for Gustomacho's office.

In the ensuing meeting, the governor informed Puzo about the upcoming U.S. congressional budget hearings to be held in Washington, D.C. These hearings were the financial lifeline for the local islands, and Gustomacho wanted the proper press coverage to successfully establish his strategic fiduciary assault straight into Uncle Sam's pockets.

Puzo was instructed to arrange a big press conference for all the media the following Friday at noon. The governor then questioned Puzo's abilities to arrange such an important and historical event, and Puzo shuddered, and then said in a cracked voice, "I, uh, I can do it, governor."

In reality, Puzo knew only what he had previously seen on stateside television about news conferences, since he never got the chance to cover any of the local press conferences when he worked for the Marianas Daily News. That was his boss Huston's job.

But he, like millions of other TV-trained scholars, was a bona fide expert in quite a few fields of professional endeavors. For instance, after previously watching "Marcus Welby, M.D." for a season or two, he could have probably applied for medical residency at the Mayo Clinic.

He eventually left the governor's office with a feeling of cautious confidence. He knew it would be a major feat to seduce every reporter to a boring governor's press conference on a Friday at lunchtime. It would also be a miracle for them to be on time during their all day break, even with free donuts included. The problem was the local media didn't publish the news over the weekend. So all the reporters were basically on a break from Friday until Sunday night when they just published old news and miscellaneous stuff for Monday's editions.

Besides the Marianas Daily News, there were a few reporters from smaller local papers, and a radio reporter. At the time Saipan had no television and only a small radio station.

Most of Saipan's reporters were young statesiders, who were mostly lackadaisical potheads, since marijuana was legal on Saipan at the time. His former boss, Freddie Houston, had recently hired an ex-Peace Corps bum from the outer islands, and he was reported to be quite cynical about island leaders, which could cause Puzo some problems. Houston said he wanted to help Puzo with his first press conference and be there to lend support, but Huston said he had moving plans that day.

Puzo knew that the more serious news-gathering on Saipan was normally scheduled during the reporters' Monday through Thursday news timeframe and not during long noontime beer drinking sessions on Friday paydays. Further Friday activities for reporters were smoking cannabis zig-zagers and taking long tropical naps. And naturally, against Puzo's later advice, the governor insisted on scheduling his press conference at noon on a payday Friday. It was widely known that if Japan or Russia attacked Saipan on a Friday, it wouldn't be reported until the following Monday or Tuesday.

No matter what the day or hour, the governor demanded that all the media be present, and it was Puzo's job to get their journalistic butts in the governor's office, and on time!

Following a week of cajoling and begging and promising plenty donuts for a marijuana-induced media group, Puzo received sworn assurances that all the news people would show up early for his first attempt to make Gustomacho a media celebrity, excepting his loyal friend, Houston, who was moving to Bali.

But it was now already ten minutes past noon on Friday press day, and he nervously stood at the governor's door. He inwardly squirmed at the stinging stares he was receiving from Gustomacho and some of his hoodlum Cabinet members, who were also close relatives of the governor.

The Cabinet members in attendance that day were the governor's chief administrative officer (CAO), Roque Gustomacho, a hulking, local thug with visions of becoming the Crown Prince of the Commonwealth; the planning and budgeting officer (PBO), Kobiashi Gustomacho, a half-caste Japanese Chamorro who knew his figures and how to juggle them for the governor's benefit; the legislative affairs officer (LAO), Joaquin Gustomacho, an ex-con who could blackmail any legislator into doing a favor for the governor's office; and the governor's legal counsel, Barry Fishblatt, a sleazy stateside attorney from Washington, D.C., who excelled in every scheme available to make both the governor and him wealthy island politicians.

Also in attendance at the already delayed press conference was the lieutenant governor, Gabriel Flores, who was a member of an influential local family and the governor's brother-in-law because Gustomacho had married his very rich and very fat sister. Flores was a guaranteed fruit loop, but his family's wealth convinced Gustomacho to pick him as a very generous monetary running mate.

Twenty minutes after twelve, the news media finally arrived with the strong smell of beer and marijuana smoke emanating from their midst. The governor, who had been sitting in a catatonic fit of rage, angrily reviewed the motley group as they immediately sauntered over to the free donuts. They were an oddball assortment of characters, and they possessed shaky media credentials of being both semi-literate and now semi-coherent.

After being coerced to take their seats by an anxious and prodding Puzo, the mostly drunk and stoned news corps finally began to question Gustomacho on his upcoming trip and budget requests to the U.S. Congress, which was twice as much as the previous year's request.

"How can you justify such an increase in the Commonwealth's budget?" the radio reporter seriously asked. "Especially after last year's congressional report criticizing the excessive spending here."

"That's easy," replied a smiling governor. "My planning and budgeting officer, Mister Kobiashi Gustomacho, has spent plenty time to make our budgets okay. He will explain to you."

A sleeping Kobiashi was bumped by the CAO, who loudly whispered in his ear, "Hey you, wake up. Tell them the budget's okay."

"Our budget is okay," blurted out a bad-tempered and freshly-awakened Kobiashi, "but you can blame the increase on the stupid Democrats." He closed his eyes again and went back to sleep.

Following a few more questions about what kind of fancy official car Gustomacho was planning to order, and how many young Filipina maids were employed at the governor's mansion, there was one last question by the Peace Corps freak from the Marianas Daily News. He asked the governor if he planned to criticize the United States before the U.N. Trusteeship Council, which was having a meeting right after the U.S. congressional hearings in Washington.

The governor shrewdly replied in his best, federal aid-seeking tones, "Of course not. The United States is our close friend. We are a U.S. Commonwealth now. We are family, and here in the islands it is not respectful to attack one's family."

The Peace Corps reporter pressed on. "What about the broken water system that Saipan inherited from the U.S. Department of Interior, which I might add, governor, has never been repaired by the U.S. government or the local Commonwealth government even with generous amounts of U.S. monetary aid?"

"That's another matter!" Gustomacho shouted. "We want the lousy U.S. government to fix our water system immediately, and stop ridiculing us about minor fiscal mismanagement!"

Puzo could see the sparks fly in the later news coverage on the following Monday, about Gustomacho blasting the U.S. for their insensitivity and total disregard of the infrastructure needs for the islanders when, in fact, the federal government was continually dumping millions of dollars into the Commonwealth's water and power systems.

The real problem was not only the bad press with the governor blatantly criticizing the U.S. government, but it was also the reported misspending of the federal money that would always be reprogrammed for more essential local island needs, like new cars, fishing boats, and shopping trips around the world.

The press conference finally ended with a photo session of Gustomacho and his Cabinet members mugging for the media cameras, and as Puzo started to take some shots with his PIO camera, he suddenly realized his camera didn't have any film.

In his nervous haste to attend the press conference he had forgotten to load his camera with film.

Now he would be forced to buy some extra photos for his office from a grinning reporter, who naturally would want a special favor later. He cringed at the thought of media blackmail, and after faking the photo session with several empty clicks of his camera, he awkwardly left the governor's office and his very first press conference, fervently hoping that the governor didn't have another one for at least a year or two. On the bright side, at least the governor would be leaving the next day for Washington and wouldn't be reading his bad press the following Monday and screaming obscenities at a rattled PIO.

23

OH, NO, FLORES IS IN CHARGE

Gustomacho and his large entourage left for Washington, D.C. and the budget hearings right after the disastrous press conference in mid-April, and the travel-happy group wasn't scheduled to be back until the first of June. Gustomacho's absence consequently made Lt. Governor Flores in charge as "Acting Governor," and everyone around the governor's office groaned in antsy anticipation to what Flores might do while he was temporarily in charge.

Flores was an educated imbecile, who always bragged with a noticeable lisp about his master's degree in music from UCLA, located in Los Angeles, California, where he specialized in organ playing. Most people, however, recognized his true talent of being real handy around organs of another male variety. For those who had to work around him, he was a mean, vindictive bastard, or bitch, whenever confronted and not allowed his way.

In the following weeks, Flores scheduled daily, pain-in-the-ass Cabinet meetings, which prompted a few of the more homicidal members of the Cabinet to contemplate an early assassination for Flores.

During the daily meetings of the Cabinet, Flores would constantly walk around the meeting table, dressed in outlandish bisexual outfits, and constantly lecture the various department heads about their ineptitude. He would also hand out inane assignments to everyone, which included the orders to decorate everyone's offices with flowers and semi-nude paintings of men, which were from Flores' personal collection during his time at UCLA. He also wanted multicolored lighting in all the offices.

To add to Puzo's attempts to diffuse the assassination rumors about Flores to the media, he was further being driven nuts by all the photo sessions Flores demanded. Puzo spent hours taking pictures of Flores doing everything from getting out of his chauffeured car to washing his hands in his official lace-trimmed restroom. Apparently, Flores wanted a complete historical photo album of his entire, hysterical time in office, and Puzo kept patiently clicking away his camera, while mentally calculating how many more paychecks it would take to leave Saipan.

Time dragged on for everyone in the governor's office and it was now creeping past mid-June, but Gustomacho still hadn't returned from his trip.

The governor had decided to extend his trip to cover a Rum Producers' Convention in the Caribbean, and he wouldn't be back until sometime in mid to late July. This news sent Flores into a rampage, because the governor had promised to return earlier so that Flores could take a trip to Paris for a meeting of the International Order of Males with Males.

As a result of his bitch fit, Flores doubled everyone's assignments, especially for the upcoming Liberation Day festival, and ordered that no one could take any off-island trips until the governor returned from his lengthy junket. Flores knew that by denying trips to everyone it would surely cause a panic that would force the governor to promptly return.

Well, the travel restrictions did cause a panic, most notably in the jittery attorney general's office, which had to urgently handle a substantial increase in the number of assassination threats against Flores.

The attorney general frantically called Gustomacho in Trinidad and pleaded with him to return as soon as possible. Gustomacho reluctantly agreed with the seriousness of the Flores situation, and said he would return to Saipan by early July.

As promised, the governor finally did arrive on July third in the early evening, and Puzo and the LAO, who were both driven to the airport by the governor's personal driver in the governor's limo, were there to greet Gustomacho at the airport

"Welcome back, governor." Puzo said, as he noticed the wary look in Gustomacho's eyes.

"Where's Flores?" Gustomacho demanded.

"He left for San Francisco at noon today," replied Joaquin Gustomacho, the LAO, adding, "and Senate President Mongo has been screaming all afternoon that he's the official acting governor until you returned."

"What?" Gustomacho yelled. "That crazy Mongo can't be trusted. Has he done anything stupid?"

The LAO frowned. "Yes, he did, governor. Mongo got the joint legislature to pass a quick bill to increase the legislative budget by another hundred and fifty percent. He then signed the bill as acting governor about two hours ago."

"I'll kill Flores when he gets back!!" the governor screamed. "What can we do, Joaquin?!" The governor was steamed, and Puzo kept clear of the heated conversation and retrieved Gustomacho's suitcases.

"Don't worry, I've got some pictures of Mongo when he was in the Philippines attending some stupid fashion seminar," the LAO answered. "Mongo was drunk in one of those high school apartments for young prostitutes, and his wife would kill him if she saw the pictures."

The governor then slyly remarked to the LAO, "Lanya, you tell that sneaky Mongo you're going to show his wife the pictures if he don't tear up that bill he just signed."

The word "lanya" was a local islander phrase loosely meaning in English: son-of-a-bitch.

Gustomacho and the LAO were now approaching the governor's limo in front of the airport, as the LAO suddenly laughed out loud, "Don't worry, Reggie, I already showed Mongo the pictures, and he tore up the bill in a big hurry. I just wanted to see you go crazy like you did when we were in high school."

The governor flopped down in the back seat of his chauffeured Cadillac limo and scowled at his cousin the LAO, who was still standing outside the car. "I don't like your joke and don't call me Reggie anymore. You ride back to the office with Puzo."

The governor hastily ordered his driver to pull away, leaving Puzo chasing behind it, throwing the last suitcase of the governor's into the opened trunk. The car continued moving out of the airport with the trunk lid flapping at every bump in the old road.

Puzo then turned and looked at the LAO. "Joaquin, I forgot to tell him about his speech tomorrow for Liberation Day."

"Screw Reggie," replied an angry Joaquin. "You take me back to the office! And don't call me Joaquin!"

"Okay Mister LAO, but I can't take you back. Remember, I rode here with you in the governor's car."

They both stared at each other and simultaneously blurted out: "Lanya!" and they futilely began looking for a ride in the hot tropical sun.

An hour later, they hitched a ride with a tour bus, and they then had to walk a mile to the governor's office, with the LAO angrily repeating to himself, "Lanya, screw Reggie, lanya, screw Reggie…"

The Commonwealth of the Northern Mariana Islands always celebrated Liberation Day on July fourth, because that was the day the local islanders, who were initially Japanese collaborators during World War II, were finally released from U.S. internment camps on Saipan right after the conclusion of World War II. The U.S. internment camps actually gave safe haven to the local islanders, who were caught in the middle of the conflict and were being shot by Japanese troops when they started switching allegiance to the Americans, who were beginning to win the battle for the island of Saipan.

Ironically, Liberation Day also shared the same day as U.S. Independence Day on July fourth, and this invariably set the Saipan stage for coinciding American and anti-American activities.

The local islanders regarded July fourth as their special liberation day to remember their release from the alleged American "concentration" camps after the war. They would emphasize the point that day with emotional speeches about the dastardly Americans, who still owed them continuous international apologies and millions of dollars of reparations each year, since the Americans had imprisoned them when they were the poor victims of war.

But in fact, they were America's enemy until they realized the U.S. was winning the war, and then they switched waving their Japanese flags to American flags in a hurry.

The current Liberation Day on Saipan was very unruly that year, and Puzo was on hand to officially record it with his notebook and camera, praying it would be the last Liberation Day he had to endure.

The U.S. Navy band had flown in from Guam to entertain the island residents during the all-day "Independence Day" festivities, and they were again tasked to spread some U.S. military public relations among the islanders with their American flag-waving rock and roll music.

But it was only a small military band that came this time, because the Navy commander in charge of the area, Rear Admiral Clayton Blowntoggle, was still angry about the last Liberation

Day celebration when the local politicians gave emotional speeches that repeatedly blasted the diabolical U.S. government about the "concentration" camps after the war. He was also mad because the Navy softball team was attacked by swarms of local hoodlums after the Navy team had beaten the island favorites.

So after the previous year's debacle, Blowntoggle had a very short fuse with the Marianas' islanders, and this was compounded by the fact that during the war, when he was a young Navy ensign on Saipan shore duty, he was shot in the ass by a crossed-eyed Saipanese islander, who at the time was a Japanese scout.

Following the usual activities of the current festivities, and the repeated caustic speeches by local leaders, the 1981 disjointed Liberation and Independence Day eventually ended with the Navy band being pelted with breadfruit and mangos by a crowd of angry islanders, who objected to their playing of "America the Beautiful," instead of the local favorite "Marianas Forever," which caused Blowntoggle to become ballistic again.

Blowntoggle also refused to play the local Commonwealth anthem, "Mauleg Toto Marianas," which roughly translates into "We are all friendly islanders." He abruptly ordered his Navy band to pack up and they promptly left the island again, to keep the annual mini-war between the Saipan islanders and the U.S. military alive and well for another year.

24

WAKE UP, SAIPAN!

"Wake up, everybody! It's a beautiful August day in paradise! And this is Charlie Volcano, your morning man here at K-PAN radio, where the latest hits keep coming. Yeah, as long as the record shipments arrive on time! Ha, ha, ha. Yazoo, you great-looking islanders, gimme a call here at good old K.P.A.N., and I'll play your request! Call me now, as you all listen to the great Jerry Lee Lewis and "Great Balls of Fire"! Yeah! Yazoo! Yeah! Call me now!"

"Hello? Charlie Volcano? Do me a favor, okay?" A sleepy voice was on the line.

"Sure. You got a special request?" Volcano shouted.

"Yeah! Why don't you jump into a goddamn active volcano!" Puzo slammed the phone down.

Puzo had called Charlie Volcano because the raucous deejay had startled the hell out of him that morning, because Puzo had accidentally left his clock radio in the radio wake-up mode the night before with the volume full blast.

After a few minutes Puzo whispered into the darkness, "It's August twentieth already and I'm thirty-four years old today, and I'm still stuck on this miserable tropical rock."

He slowly turned his bedroom light on and then he struggled into the bathroom to relieve himself, while the radio kept playing a much lower sounding "Great Balls" in the background.

Following a cold shower in low pressure and reddish water, since his water heater was an early victim to the rust problems in Micronesia, he sat at his rickety card table in the kitchen, staring at a bowl of half-eaten corn flakes. He had run out of milk and was slowly eating his cereal dry, washing it down with lemonade.

He finally looked at his watch, spit out the last mouthful of corn flakes, and quickly left for another day at the governor's civic madhouse.

While driving to work, he figured that maybe by his next birthday he should have enough money to leave Saipan forever. It was a "maybe" situation because his paycheck kept getting hefty deductions from the local Republican Party. As a result, it would be a whole year before he could possibly leave the islands.

He realized that he needed a diversion to get his mind off the compounding pressures of his present predicament.

Moreover, if he didn't relieve the mental pressure soon, he might find himself in jail for publicly urinating on the governor's new statue, which had been recently placed on top of the administration building. The large ornate statue, which the governor would become incensed when the birds shit all over it, had been built after Gustomacho jealously read about President Marcos and all of his statues all over the Philippines.

In late September, Puzo finally found his diversion at the local airport, and he shrewdly arranged a way for his PIO transportation allowance to pay for it.

Having justified that his official duties occasionally included the traveling by air to the sparsely-populated outer islands of the Commonwealth, in order to take pictures of the resident mayors and all their special assistant flunkies, he transferred the cost of more expensive commercial traveling to the outer islands of Tinian and

Rota for the cheaper cost of his taking flying lessons and visiting the islands during training sessions.

It was a definite mind-blowing diversion, and Puzo never thought that he would be bouncing around in the wild blue yonder, seemingly in control of a small airplane. What better way to temporarily escape the demanding doldrums of earthbound island living, and this was flying with a flight instructor who was ranked very high in the area of non-boring.

During one rough flight in high winds, his colorful flight instructor, Clancy Moore, had yelled out to Puzo over the sound of the rushing wind through the wired-up open cracks in the plexi-glass side windows of his Cessna 172: "Yeah, Paddy, my fine featherless friend, if God meant us to fly, He would have given us frigging wings!"

Moore, an ex-Vietnam chopper and fixed wing pilot, who wound up on Saipan after a bad marriage or was it a bad drunk, was Puzo's flight instructor and airborne philosopher.

Moore continued, "And don't ever drink and make low passes over the nude sunbathers on nearby Managaha Island, because you don't want to lose focus and ruin God's earthly handiwork when you crash and burn in a bunch of coconut trees."

Moore could scare the morning Wheaties out of someone with his combat style of flying, as Puzo soon found out while taking his flying lessons.

Even so, the extracurricular flying activity did accomplish its mission. It definitely gave Puzo a diversion from his tropical maladies, especially when Moore flew upside down and low over the Japanese tourists sunbathing on the beach, singing, "Bridge Over Troubled Waters."

One flying day in particular, while practicing landings in a nasty seat-sucking crosswind, Moore quickly took over the controls from Puzo, who had the look of shear panic in his glazed eyes. Puzo wanted a diversion from his job, but this was ridiculous. He could kill himself!

As they were bouncing around in a sudden tropical windstorm, Puzo knew that they were in deep kimchee, and maybe his departure from the island would now be in a pine box. But Moore began casually whistling the theme song from 'The High and Mighty," and reached for a bottle of Jack Daniels whiskey under his seat. He drank a mouthful of whiskey, then yelled, "Geronimo!"

Moore suddenly crabbed the epileptic plane towards the runway like a possessed banzai pilot, and at the last moment, just before seriously ramming into Mother Earth sideways, he adroitly righted the cockeyed plane into a beautiful piece of bouncing landing work.

As they taxied in, Puzo looked at Moore with a sigh of relief, sweat seeping out of every pore of his body.

Moore nodded at him when they finally parked the plane and said nonchalantly, "Piece of cake, Paddy. But don't ever drink when trying to land in a bitch of a crosswind. You could hurt yourself monumentally."

Puzo shook his head, and then weakly smiled. "I'll try to remember that, Clancy."

Puzo left the airport and went straight to the nearest bar.

The workload in the governor's office slowed down during the latter part of the year, and the administrative staff spent most of their time planning for the upcoming holidays in December.

Following several weeks of avoiding the airport, Puzo finally began flying again, and received his pilot's license a week before Christmas.

He felt unusually proud about being a pilot, and even offered to fly Gustomacho around to visit the outer islands anytime he wanted.

The governor quickly declined Puzo's offer, saying that anyone who learned to fly from that crazy statesider Clancy Moore must want to die before his time.

The governor liked to gamble, but he wanted to definitely finish his term alive and become a gubernatorial legend in the Micronesian islands and his own mind, simultaneously. And speaking of gambling, Puzo was quickly ordered to write an emergency press release just before Christmas.

CNMI PRESS RELEASE
(GOVERNOR REGINO J. GUSTOMACHO SIGNS ANTI-GAMBLING BILL) SAIPAN, COMMONWEALTH OF THE NORTHERN MARIANA ISLANDS, DECEMBER 23, CNMI/P10---
GOVERNOR REGINO J. GUSTOMACHO SIGNED SENATE BILL NO. 3-016 INTO LAW THIS MORNING, MAKING MOST FORMS OF GAMBLING ILLEGAL IN THE COMMONWEALTH. THE CONTROVERSIAL BILL WENT THROUGH WEEKS OF DEBATE IN BOTH THE SENATE AND THE HOUSE OF REPRESENTATIVES, BEFORE IT FINALLY REACHED THE GOVERNOR'S OFFICE EARLY THIS WEEK. LAST MINUTE ATTEMPTS BY A GROUP OF CHINESE BUSINESSMEN, WHO WANTED TO OPEN A GAMBLING CASINO ON SAIPAN, FAILED TO SWAY THE GOVERNOR FROM KEEPING HIS PROMISE TO MAINTAIN A MORAL SOCIETY ON SAIPAN. THOSE PRESENT AT THE SIGNING WERE LT. GOVERNOR GABRIEL FLORES, SENATE PRESIDENT JESUS T. MONGO, HOUSE SPEAKER DAVID P. SOBLAN, AND MONSIGNOR FRED MONGO OF SAINT JUAN'S CATHOLIC CHURCH. MONSIGNOR MONGO HAD EARLIER MADE AN EMOTIONAL PLEA FOR THE GOVERNOR TO SIGN THE BILL, WHICH DOES ALLOW FOR THE CHURCH TO HAVE WEEKLY POKER NIGHTS, COCKFIGHTING, BINGO AND A SPECIAL CHURCH LOTTERY RUN BY THE MONSIGNOR.

THE GOVERNOR AND MONSIGNOR MONGO ALSO
WISH EVERYONE A MERRY CHRISTMAS AND ASK THE
ISLAND RESIDENTS TO TRY AND REDUCE THEIR NON-
STOP DRINKING THIS YEAR DURING THE HOLIDAY
SEASON. THE MONSIGNOR ADDS THAT HIS DAILY
HOLIDAY BINGO AND POKER TOURNAMENT HAS
ALREADY STARTED AND INVITES EVERYONE TO ST.
JUAN'S CATHEDRAL TO PLAY.
THE GOVERNOR ALSO ANNOUNCED HE WAS TAKING
ANOTHER TRIP IN JANUARY. (END OF RELEASE)

While Puzo wrote the anti-gambling release, he fretted over
another Gustomacho trip and he also had to wonder about the
behind-the-scenes events surrounding the good Monsignor Mongo
and his sneaky half-brother, Senate President Mongo.

Monsignor Mongo had forced his half-brother to write the
Senate bill by threatening to tell his parishioners, who made up about
ninety-nine percent of the voting population on Saipan, that Senate
President Mongo actually supported the evil ways of the gambling
outsiders, especially the atheistic Chinese from Hong Kong.

In writing the bill, the Senate President was fit to be tied. The
Hong Kong boys had previously made him a shareholder and board
member of their casino project, and they also promised him a twenty-
thousand- dollar personal campaign contribution if he could keep
casino gambling legal in the Commonwealth.

But Mongo knew what his half-ass-brother the Monsignor would
do, if casino groups moved into the Catholic Church's gambling turf.

So, he angrily wrote the bill and silently cursed his brother
for days, until he was publicly blessed by the Monsignor during a
pre-Christmas High Mass. The Senate President was later privately
"blessed" by getting a sanctified promise of a nice share of the
church's bingo profits.

Church and state cannot be separated always, the good
Monsignor preached, and Senate President Mongo couldn't have

agreed more, especially when he planned to travel to the Philippines for a lengthy young girl screw-a-thon as soon as he got his first share of the bingo profits.

It was another hot and muggy Christmas night in the islands and there was some serious drinking in Spam's that whole evening.

Puzo had been huddled over a cold beer and a tequila shooter during the middle of a rambunctious pool game, when he suddenly heard a very loud announcement breaking the normal din of bar noise. The very loud announcement directly involved him.

"I bet anyone in Spam's a hundred bucks a pool game!" Takahashi Vierra yelled.

Vierra was a Japanese-Portuguese construction contractor originally from San Pedro, California. He continued his announcement: "And I'll even play partners with the lousiest shooter in the whole damn place!"

"Who's that?" asked another pool player loudly.

"From what I know, it must be Puzo!" Vierra yelled back.

Everyone laughed as Puzo spit out his beer and turned around, facing the pool table area.

"Whadda you mean, a hundred dollars a game!" Puzo bellowed. "I can't afford it because I got travel plans."

"Don't worry, Paddy, I'll put up the whole hundred," Vierra boasted, and then he screamed at the ceiling, "because I'm mad as hell right now at our stupid, stinking, local fucking government!"

He quickly looked at Puzo. "And when I get real mad I just don't lose at the pool table. So get your butt over here, Paddy!"

"What the hell. It's not my hundred bucks." Puzo shrugged and he joined the game.

And like Vierra said, he could shoot great pool when he was mad, and he was extremely mad at the local government for previously rejecting his low bid on a federally-funded housing project, which was being administered by a corrupt Commonwealth housing authority.

The bid award had gone to a Saipanese relative of the governor who was also a local administrator in the housing authority, and the relative's bid was naturally much higher than Vierra's. Furthermore, the governor's relative didn't even have a construction company, but the relative won the bid anyway. And naturally, the whole project ended up in the toilet.

Fortunately for the local contractor, he did manage to illegally pocket a huge chunk of the federal funds and buy a nice home in Southern California, and also make a nice donation to the governor.

Unfortunately for Vierra, the system does work for those who are fortunately connected to the governor via local bloodlines.

Furthermore, what later angered Vierra even more was the indifferent attitude displayed by the jackasses at the U.S. Department of Housing and Urban Development (HUD) in Region IX headquarters in San Francisco. The HUD feds continually ignored his complaints about the improper bidding procedures and the illegal expenditure of federal funds on Saipan.

HUD would inevitably dismiss Vierra's complaints by saying, "We must encourage local and minority participation at whatever cost, and people like you must realize it's for the good of our American socio-economic system to forcibly integrate the less fortunate into the higher establishment of capitalism without straining their abilities."

"Bullshit!" Vierra shouted at a liberal fuck nut and a stateside Trust Territory employee, who was drinking at the bar and who was defending HUD and the local government for its legitimate right to help the poor islanders and also screw the American taxpayer.

Following the short HUD debate, Vierra got so mad that he broke his custom cue stick over the T. T. employee's head, and continued shooting pool with the "modified" stick like a madman.

Puzo occasionally made a few easy corner shots, and they eventually prevailed over their opposition and won three hundred dollars.

The only problem for both of them was they had to pay for their total bar bill, which had to cover for the bar damages because of Vierra's extracurricular exuberance. The bill would be almost four hundred dollars, as Spam figured it, because it included a new felt top for the pool table which had been triumphantly ripped off by Vierra after the last game.

After the crowd had urged Puzo into paying for his share of the inflated damages to Spam, who had further hiked up the cost because of the mental strain on his wife Rosey, Puzo finally left the bar for his tin shack by the sea without a dollar in his pocket.

On the way home, he didn't really regret the drinking and the costly bar damage, although he imagined what it would be like if people like Tak Vierra and Clancy Moore ever teamed up and challenged the locals to a winner-take-all contest for the island. He gave a slight edge to Vierra and Moore, and wished it would actually happen someday within his remaining days on Saipan.

25

THE CABINET MEETING

ACTING GOVERNOR'S CABINET MEETING

MINUTES OF JANUARY 23, 1983.

MEMBERS PRESENT WITH ACTING GOVERNOR GABRIEL FLORES: SPECIAL ASSISTANT FLORENCIO GUSTOMACHO; PERSONNEL OFFICER GUILLERMO GUSTOMACHO; CHIEF ADMINISTRATIVE OFFICER ROQUE GUSTOMACHO; PLANNING & BUDGET OFFICER KOBIASHI GUSTOMACHO; LEGISLATIVE AFFAIRS OFFICER JOAQUIN GUSTOMACHO; CAROLINIAN AFFAIRS OFFICER JUAN MANAYO GUSTOMACHO; DIRECTOR OF PUBLIC WORKS IGNACIO GUSTOMACHO; DIRECTOR OF NATURAL RESOURCES JOSE GUSTOMACHO; DIRECTOR OF COMMERCE & LABOR RAMON GUSTOMACHO; DIRECTOR OF FINANCE GREGORIO GUSTOMACHO; DIRECTOR OF PUBLIC SAFETY ANTONIO GUSTOMACHO; DIRECTOR OF TRADITIONAL AFFAIRS LORENZO GUSTOMACHO; DIRECTOR OF PUBLIC HEALTH FELIPE GUSTOMACHO;

DIRECTOR OF CIVIL DEFENSE RAFAEL GUSTOMACHO; DIRECTOR OF PUBLIC SCHOOLS LOURDES GUSTOMACHO; GOVERNOR'S SECRETARY GUADALUPE GUSTOMACHO.

OTHERS PRESENT
GOVERNOR'S LEGAL COUNSEL BARRY FISHBLATT; ATTORNEY GENERAL WADSWORTH BEXFORD III; PUBLIC INFORMATION OFFICER PADDY PUZO; AND SHINARO NAKAMURA, A VISITING SHINTO PRIEST FROM JAPAN. NOTE: PUBLIC DEFENDER BILL O'BRIEN WAS ABSENT.

**THE MEETING CAME TO ORDER AT 9AM AND ACTING GOVERNOR FLORES INFORMED THE CABINET THAT GOVERNOR GUSTOMACHO WOULD NOT BE ARRIVING FROM HIS JANUARY TRIP UNTIL APRIL. THE ACTING GOVERNOR ALSO MENTIONED HIS DISPLEASURE OVER THE LONG ABSENCE OF THE GOVERNOR AND NOTED THAT THE STATESIDER OWNED NEWSPAPERS HAD PUT PICTURES OF THE GOVERNOR ON THE FRONT PAGE WITH CAPTIONS THAT READ: "GUESS WHO THIS PERSON IS AND WIN A FREE NEWSPAPER SUBSCRIPTION." THE ACTING GOVERNOR SEEMED AMUSED BY THE MEDIA ATTACK ON THE GOVERNOR, BUT ASKED THE DIRECTOR OF PUBLIC SAFETY TO INVESTIGATE THE WHITE-OWNED NEWSPAPERS IMMEDIATELY FOR BIGOTED AND SUBVERSIVE ACTS AGAINST THE ISLAND GOVERNMENT.
**THE ACTING GOVERNOR THEN INTRODUCED MR. SHINARO NAKAMURA, A SHINTO HIGH PRIEST FROM JAPAN, WHO IS COORDINATING A SPECIAL CEREMONY TO BE HELD ON SAIPAN IN EARLY JUNE THAT WILL COMMEMORATE THE SPIRITS OF DEAD JAPANESE

SOLDIERS AND THEIR SAIPANESE COMRADES, AND THE JAPANESE CIVILIANS WHO COMMITTED HONORABLE SUICIDE BY JUMPING OFF SAIPAN'S SUICIDE CLIFF DURING WORLD WAR II. NAKAMURA UNVEILED A SPECIAL MINIATURE DISPLAY OF A COMMEMORATIVE PAVILION TO BE BUILT AT THE BOTTOM OF SUICIDE CLIFF AT THE NORTH END OF THE ISLAND. THERE WILL BE PLAQUES HONORING THE JAPANESE SOLDIERS, THEIR SAIPANESE COMRADES AND THE JAPANESE SUICIDE LEAPERS, ALONG WITH TWO PAVILION STATUES OF THE CURRENT GOVERNOR AND THE LIEUTENANT (ACTING) GOVERNOR. THE ACTING GOVERNOR THEN ASKED HOW BIG HIS STATUE WILL BE, AND HE WAS TOLD THAT IT WILL BE LIFE-SIZE, APPROXIMATELY FIVE FEET TALL. THE ACTING GOVERNOR THEN OFFICIALLY REQUESTED THAT THE STATUES BE AT LEAST TWENTY FEET TALL, AND NAKAMURA FINALLY AGREED AFTER THE ACTING GOVERNOR THREATENED TO RESTRICT ALL FUTURE TRAVEL VISAS FOR JAPANESE TRAVELERS TO SAIPAN. THE ACTING GOVERNOR GRACIOUSLY THANKED MR. NAKAMURA FOR HIS WILLING COOPERATION AND THEN ASKED HIM TO LEAVE THE MEETING IMMEDIATELY.

**NEXT THE ACTING GOVERNOR ANNOUNCED THAT HE HAD INSTRUCTED THE DEPARTMENT OF PUBLIC WORKS TO INSTALL TIME CLOCKS IN EVERYONE'S OFFICE. THE PLAN WAS CONCEIVED BY THE PERSONNEL OFFICER AND APPROVED BY THE ACTING GOVERNOR, WHO AGREED WITH THE PERSONNEL OFFICER THAT BEING ON TIME WOULD BE A SIGN OF RESPECT TO THE ACTING GOVERNOR. THE ACTING GOVERNOR ALSO ASKED THE PUBLIC WORKS DIRECTOR TO MAKE SURE ALL THE DISGUSTING EMPTY BEER CANS AND DIRTY BABY PAMPERS WERE PICKED UP ALONG THE

HIGHWAYS. HE SAID IT MADE HIM NAUSEOUS TO SEE THE MESS WHEN HE DROVE TO WORK IN THE MORNING. THE DIRECTOR OF PUBLIC WORKS SAID HE REGRETTED THAT THE ACTING GOVERNOR GOT SICK ABOUT THE DIRTY DIAPERS, BUT REPORTED THAT THE HEAVY FLOODING ALL OVER THE ISLAND WOULD SOON CARRY ALL THE TRASH OUT TO SEA. THE PUBLIC WORKS DIRECTOR ALSO SAID THE TREMENDOUS RAINSTORMS WERE PREDICTED TO LAST ANOTHER WEEK, BUT PUBLIC WORKS WAS STILL HAVING A PROBLEM OF GETTING THE RAINWATER INTO THE PUBLIC WATER SYSTEM. THE ACTING GOVERNOR THEN ORDERED PUBLIC WORKS TO CONSTRUCT TWO WATER TANKS AT HIS OFFICIAL GOVERNMENT RESIDENCE AND PLACE A WATER TANKER AT HIS OFFICE BECAUSE HE INSISTED ON SHOWERING THREE TIMES A DAY.

**FOLLOWING THE PUBLIC WORKS COMMENTS, THE DIRECTOR OF PUBLIC SAFETY REPORTED THAT HIS GOVERNMENT POLICE CAR WAS STILL MISSING AND PRESUMABLY STOLEN. HE ALSO REPORTED THAT THE FIRE SUBSTATION IN THE SOUTHERN PART OF THE ISLAND BURNED DOWN LAST WEEK DURING A DRUNKEN EMPLOYEE BARBEQUE AT THE REAR OF THE BUILDING.

**THE DIRECTOR OF FINANCE THEN REPORTED THAT THE COURT CASE FOR THE EMBEZZLING CHARGES AGAINST HIM WOULD BE HELD NEXT WEEK. HE STILL INSISTED THAT HE IS INNOCENT, BUT ANNOUNCED THAT HE WOULD BE MOVING TO THE PHILIPPINES SHORTLY, AND INFORMED THE ACTING GOVERNOR OF HIS IMMINENT RESIGNATION.

**THE DIRECTOR OF NATURAL RESOURCES STATED THAT HIS FEDERALLY-FUNDED AGRICULTURE FARM WAS RAIDED BY THE FBI FROM GUAM, AND THAT

SEVERAL MARIJUANA PLANTS WERE DISCOVERED GROWING BEHIND THE MANGO TREES. BECAUSE THE U.S. FEDS FORCED THE COMMONWEALTH TO PASS A LOCAL LAW, WHICH MADE MARIJUANA ILLEGAL NOW, THE DIRECTOR SAID THAT ALL OF HIS EMPLOYEES, WHO WERE CURRENTLY IN JAIL, WERE NOW MAKING CLAIMS FOR EXCUSED LEAVES OF INCARCERATED ABSENCES AND DEMANDING THEIR PAYCHECKS.

**NEXT THE DIRECTOR OF CIVIL DEFENSE SINCERELY WANTED TO APOLOGIZE TO EVERYONE FOR NOT WARNING THEM AND THE WHOLE ISLAND ABOUT THE SNEAKY TYPHOON THAT STRUCK NEAR SAIPAN THE PREVIOUS SATURDAY. HE BLAMED IT ON HIS 24-HOUR, SEVEN DAYS A WEEK STAFF OF THE EMERGENCY TYPHOON WARNING COMMAND POST. HE STATED THAT THE WHOLE STAFF DECIDED TO HAVE A WEEKEND BARBEQUE ON THE NEARBY ATOLL OF MANAGAHA, WHICH WAS DURING HIS EXTENDED SHOPPING TRIP WITH HIS WIFE LAST WEEK TO HAWAII AND, UNFORTUNATELY, DURING THE FINAL CHANGE OF DIRECTION OF THE TYPHOON TOWARDS SAIPAN, THE TYPHOON WARNING COMMAND POST WAS TEMPORARILY CLOSED FOR THE STAFF'S BARBEQUE. HE SAID HE WOULD FIRE THEM ALL, IF THEY, AND MANAGAHA, WHICH WAS DIRECTLY IN THE TYPHOON'S PATH, WERE EVER LOCATED AGAIN.

**THE PLANNING AND BUDGETING OFFICER STATED THAT THE PROJECTED CALCULATIONS ON THE GOVERNMENT'S SPENDING WOULD BE SIXTY MILLION DOLLARS BY THE END OF THE FISCAL YEAR 1983. HE ALSO REPORTED THAT THE PROJECTED LOCAL REVENUES AND FEDERAL ASSISTANCE WOULD ONLY TOTAL THIRTY MILLION DOLLARS. HE THEN SAID THAT THE GOVERNMENT WOULD HAVE A PROBLEM

WITH A SLIGHT SHORTFALL OF THIRTY MILLION DOLLARS, DEPENDING ON LOCAL ALCOHOL SALES.

**THE ATTORNEY GENERAL REPORTED THAT THE LAWSUIT FILED BY THE CAROLINIAN AFFAIRS OFFICER AGAINST THE GOVERNMENT FOR NOT HIRING MORE CAROLINIANS IS PROGRESSING. THE A.G. ALSO PUBLICLY APOLOGIZED FOR CALLING THE CAROLINIAN AFFAIRS OFFICER A JERK FOR FILING A LAWSUIT AGAINST HIS OWN COUSIN, THE GOVERNOR. THE ATTORNEY GENERAL ALSO SAID HE WOULD DROP THE ASSAULT CHARGES AGAINST MR. GUSTOMACHO FOR PUTTING HIM IN THE HOSPITAL WITH A BROKEN NOSE AND VARIOUS OTHER INJURIES.

**THE CHIEF ADMINISTRATIVE OFFICER AGAIN REMINDED EVERYONE ABOUT THE EXTRA FIVE HUNDRED DOLLARS THAT EACH CABINET MEMBER WILL CONTRIBUTE TO THE GOVERNOR'S OFFICE FOR HIS ENTERTAINMENT EXPENSES. THE CAO SAID THAT THE MONEY WOULD BE PERSONALLY TAKEN CARE OF BY HIM.

**THE ACTING GOVERNOR FINALLY ASKED WHY THE PUBLIC DEFENDER WAS MISSING FROM THE CABINET MEETING. THE ATTORNEY GENERAL THEN REMINDED THE ACTING GOVERNOR THAT MR. O'BRIEN WAS IN COURT DEFENDING THE GOVERNOR'S BROTHER FOR THE ALLEGED DOUBLE RAPE OF A JAPANESE HONEYMOON COUPLE.

THE CABINET MEETING ADJOURNED AT 10:25 A.M.

Governor Gustomacho arrived back from his January trip on the twentieth of April, thereby establishing a new travel record for a Micronesian governor.

Soon after the governor's arrival, Puzo had to officially explain to the news media about the importance of Gustomacho's lengthy trip and his "crucial" meetings with other world leaders in such important places as Hawaii, Las Vegas, Tahiti, Hong Kong, Bangkok, Manila, Singapore, and oh yes, even Bali on this particular trip.

The news media loved watching Puzo squirm through the governor's trip report. They also knew that an inexperienced PIO like Puzo would invariably butcher the spin control. Thus the governor would invariably look foolish in the news reports mainly due to the naiveté of a rookie public relations man, and not because the governor spent almost four months junketing around the world.

As expected, the next day's news stories of Gustomacho's trip were not very flattering, and the CAO dragged Puzo into the governor's office and Gustomacho blasted him for his ineptitude.

The governor was very miffed at the negative image his trip had received, and he was very disturbed that the reporters somehow misconstrued the importance of his travels, too.

"I want you to do a better job with my trips in the future," Gustomacho demanded, "because I'm planning to leave again for Washington in a few days, and I don't want any more bad stories about my traveling too much."

Puzo sighed at the mention of the governor leaving again so soon and said, "I'll do my best, governor."

"You'd better" the governor barked. "I hear my nephew is recovering from the bullet fragments lodged in his balls and he should be coming back from the hospital in a couple of months."

Puzo knew what the subtle mention of the return of the governor's nephew meant, and he hoped the little bastard got severe scrotal complications. Puzo didn't want to lose his job until he had at least enough money to securely leave Saipan. Furthermore, the political deductions from his paycheck were already prolonging his escape plans for a lot longer than he wished. He just had to hang on for another six months or so.

Before leaving the governor's office, Puzo and the CAO were given a demonstration by the governor of his new hydraulic, elevator shoes, which he had specially made in the Philippines.

Gustomacho, who was just over five feet tall, bragged. "Those Filipinos can make anything. Just watch this!"

At the flip of a hidden switch on the governor's belt, the soles of his shoes began to automatically elongate, eventually adding six inches to the governor's height. His pants also became longer, which discreetly hid the weird-looking, monstrous, white shoes.

Puzo bit his tongue trying not to laugh, and the CAO quickly advised the governor to practice in them in private before wearing the shoes in public.

"Don't worry about me," the governor confidently replied, eyeballing Puzo, "I just want to show the American statesiders that they're not the only tall people around here."

On their way out of Gustomacho's office the CAO glared at Puzo's grinning face and reminded him that his five-hundred-dollar contribution hadn't been delivered to his office yet.

"Next payday I'll give a partial payment." Puzo replied cautiously, and he added, "I hope you guys don't charge interest."

The CAO just glared again--glaring was the CAO's favorite pastime--, and Puzo gamely smiled back and returned to his office.

After he closed his office door and thought about the governor's shoes, Puzo laughed so hard he began to cry. He then cried even harder when he thought about the current situation he was in.

About a week later in the first part of May, Gustomacho departed for Washington for the U.S. congressional budget hearings concerning the Commonwealth of the Northern Mariana Islands. Before leaving, he said he would try his best to be back in time for the Liberation Day celebration in July and naturally, the lieutenant governor freaked out when he heard that Gustomacho was going to be away so long. Flores swore that he would somehow teach Gustomacho a lesson.

On the day Gustomacho left Saipan, Puzo carefully provided a brief news release to an office full of media types, which had the following information about the governor's latest ongoing trip:

(SAIPAN) May 7...Governor Regino J. Gustomacho left for Washington on May third with a group of twenty aides, several traveling companions, and his two personal secretaries. The governor will speak next week before Congress about the desperate needs of Commonwealth's poor islands. The following day he will also address the United Nations to complain about the cutbacks of U.S. aid. The governor will then travel to Europe for several weeks to meet with the leaders of Liechtenstein to discuss the advantages of tourism and tropical ski resorts on Saipan. (End of Release)

After reading again what he had just announced to the media, he knew he was in a no-win situation.

How could anyone logically explain why a governor would take nearly fifty people on an expensive trip to Washington to ironically plead the island's poor financial situation? And then on top of that, go to Europe on a money-burning junket to meet with leaders in the Swiss Alps to discuss recreational ski resorts in the goddamn tropics!

Two days later, he had to further explain to the media why Acting Governor Flores ordered the governor's new black Lincoln limousine to be painted fluorescent lime green with silver flakes.

At the end of the month, Puzo was adroitly avoiding the acting governor. To stay at of harm's way, he volunteered to help with the final preparations for the Shinto memorial service, which would also commemorate the new statues of Gustomacho and Flores. Puzo was relieved with the chance to be out of the office, and he enjoyed the time he spent outdoors at the isolated northern end of the island.

The upcoming ceremony would draw several dignitaries and businessmen from Japan, who would join with the local Saipanese in remembering their past togetherness and comradeship during World

War II, and to also capitalize on Japan's future business plans for Saipan.

It didn't take much to figure out the ulterior motives of the Japanese, who felt like they were still the rightful owners of the Northern Mariana Islands. They were still pissed about turning over the islands to the Americans after the war, and they wanted to cajole the local leaders into a multitude of partnerships and mutually beneficial agreements.

After several more days of preparation, the day of the Shinto Memorial Service finally arrived in early June, and a large crowd was anxious to see the new memorial pavilion with its newly-erected statues of the island's two top guys.

The tall, slanted-roof pavilion jutted out from the base of Suicide Cliff, and underneath the large roof were the two tall statues, which had been covered for a later unveiling.

Situated directly above the pavilion at the very top of the high cliff was the famous Suicide Cliff Memorial Park. The park had been previously built by the Japanese for the remembrance of those Japanese who had jumped to their deaths from the cliff after the Americans had occupied the island back in 1944. The Suicide Cliff Memorial Park was located right at the edge of the cliff, and it had a large observation platform sticking out approximately ten feet from the edge.

Unknown to everyone down below, a lone observer was looking straight down one thousand feet from the hilltop platform, scanning the top of the new pavilion at the base of the cliff. He looked down for a moment or two, and then disappeared.

The ceremony soon began with speeches from both the Japanese and Saipanese dignitaries. Then a Shinto priest began a long, emotional ceremony to mourn for the dead, especially all those poor bastards who had leaped to their deaths in 1944. It was ironic that the same Shinto fanaticism displayed that day during the ceremony probably drove most of the Japanese leapers in 1944 to their deaths in the first place.

With the Shinto ceremony finally concluded, the Japanese mayor from Tokyo invited Acting Governor Flores to come to the pavilion area and pull the rope that would unveil the covered statues of Governor Gustomacho and himself.

Flores bowed to the audience and quickly pranced up to the statue area dressed in an all-white suit with a pink hat and lavender shoes. He thanked the mayor repeatedly, and then gave the startled mayor a big kiss on the lips. Following a short speech of self-indulgence, Flores hastily pulled the rope and let out a squeal of delight. The statues looked magnificent, and he ran over and immediately began to hug the base of his statue.

Simultaneously, a loud explosion was heard from above, and everyone looked instantly towards the billowing smoke and dust emanating from the observation platform at the top of Suicide Cliff.

It seemed like a dream sequence, but from out of the smoke and dust that enveloped the platform, a very large cement truck had crashed through the platform's protective railing and was now descending in graceful slow motion towards the pavilion below.

Everyone began screaming and running from the pavilion area, and the Japanese mayor began shouting, "Banzai! Banzai!" He then screamed at the acting governor to get out of the covered pavilion.

Unfortunately, Flores didn't understand a word of Japanese. So, he just stood in a frozen trance next to his statue.

Meanwhile, Florencio Gustomacho, the acting governor's special assistant and Flores' lover, was also yelling at him from a distance.

But it was too late. The cement truck crashed into the top of the pavilion with a thunderous explosion of broken concrete and debris, and after the dust settled, the acting governor's special assistant ran towards the demolished pavilion, screaming, "Gabby, darling! Gabby!"

Ironically, Flores had been miraculously spared from death by his own fallen statue, which had made a partially protective barrier over him with the help of Governor Gustomacho's crumbled statue.

As he was loaded up in the ambulance, Flores' first words after recovering from the initial shock were that he wanted the cocksucking culprit behind the cement truck attack to be shot on sight.

Flores ended up in the hospital with several major contusions and a multitude of broken bones throughout his entire body, and he kept screaming between morphine shots that he wanted his attacker found, tortured, and thrown into the shark-infested channel at the southern end of the island.

It took about two weeks, due to the lack of investigative prowess of the local police force, but the culprit was eventually apprehended. It wasn't too difficult to solve the case because the perpetrator's name was on the side of the cement truck and he had announced his revenge on the governor's office all week in Spam's Bar and other public places.

The would-be assassin was of course Tak Vierra, the hot-tempered contractor, who was arrested and charged with attempted murder with a cement truck. Vierra was immediately thrown in jail, then convicted and sentenced by the Honorable Judge Jose P. Gustomacho for nearly two hundred years, with no parole and no time off for any kind of good behavior.

Even though Flores almost got killed, Governor Gustomacho continued his trip throughout Europe after being informed about the accident. Acting Governor Flores now had to painfully run the government from a hospital bed while suspended in mid-air by various cables and wires.

For the next several days Flores sent numerous telexes to Gustomacho, pleading that he come back and help him with the administrative duties. Flores also needed help with the local Republican Party and the upcoming Liberation Day celebration. He repeatedly reminded the governor that it was a mid-term election year for their fellow Republicans in the local legislature, and that Liberation Day was a big political event on Saipan.

Gustomacho finally telexed Flores from Paris, saying he would try his best to return by July fourth. He furthermore asked Flores to make sure a Liberation Day speech was prepared for him, just in case he did make it back in time for the festivities.

Flores angrily tore up the telex with the only two parts of his body that were not in a cast, which were his mouth and right hand, and he then screamed for another shot of morphine.

26

REAR ADMIRAL BLOWNTOGGLE

During the rest of the month of June, the island of Saipan prepared for another dysfunctional Liberation and Independence Day celebration.

Puzo was busy, too, coordinating the arrival again of the U.S. Navy Band and Rear Admiral Blowntoggle, who had officially advised the local government that he wasn't going to tolerate any more anti-American nonsense. Blowntoggle further reminded the local leaders that the Northern Mariana Islands were not their own personal commonwealth, but a frigging commonwealth of the United States of America.

Accompanying Blowntoggle would be two "fact-finding" U.S. congressmen, who wanted a free taxpayers-sponsored trip to the Caribbean but somehow ended up with a less desirable trip to the Western Pacific islands. But a free trip is a free trip, so the congressmen decided to head for Saipan.

The stage was now set for another showdown between some politically-dazed leaders of Uncle Sam and some politically-crazed local leaders on Saipan.

In the early morning of July fourth, a military C-130 loaded with Blowntoggle, the two U.S. congressmen and their aides, and an even smaller U.S. Navy Band landed on schedule at the Saipan airport.

Puzo had arranged for two buses to transport the band members and their equipment to Civic Center Park, where the Liberation Day activities were to take place. He also had three air-conditioned government limousines ready on the airport tarmac to take Blowntoggle, the two congressmen, and their aides to the park.

While waiting for the plane to finally park at the gate, Puzo sat in one of the limousines reading a press release about the visiting congressmen.

One of the congressmen was a Democratic Representative from Michigan by the name of Howard Herdson, and the other congressman was Representative Robert Bryant from Florida.

Bryant, who was a Republican, was also the Chairman of the Science and Space Subcommittee in the U. S. House of Representatives. He was apparently very influential with NASA and other spacey matters and, needless to say, Bryant was of special interest to Puzo, who swore that this would be his last Liberation Day on Saipan.

Puzo wanted to quickly befriend the congressman and create some good connections at NASA, for he had a scheme cooking for his future. Moreover, he knew he had better take advantage of his PIO position before he got axed and lost any chance to meet influential federal VIPs.

After observing the congressional group headed his way, he got out of the limo and quickly arranged with the police escort that Puzo himself would personally drive Bryant and his aide to the Civic Center Park in the governor's newly painted lime green Lincoln.

He went back and patiently waited in the driver's seat of the governor's limo, while a police officer escorted Bryant and his aide to the garishly decorated puke-green car.

The police officer opened the back door of the Lincoln, and as Puzo turned around to greet the congressman and his pretty assistant, his mouth suddenly dropped. The congressman's aide was none other than that traitor whore of a spy: Rebecca of D.C.!

Puzo wondered how in the hell did she switched from a Democratic honcho to a Republican congressman, although he guessed like Brubaker had said earlier that her sucking abilities and anatomical assets outweighed her Democratic deficits.

Anyway, Rebecca was busy wiping the tropical perspiration from all over her face and didn't see the surprised expression on Puzo's face. Puzo quickly looked straight ahead and maintained his composure while his passengers got comfortable in the back seat of the Lincoln.

Puzo nervously started up the car and mumbled, "Welcome to Saipan."

"Oh, thank you." The congressman seemed disinterested in small talk and tired from his long flight.

"Pleasure to have you here on Saipan," Puzo mumbled again. He then adjusted the rear view mirror and quickly eyeballed Rebecca for a split second, as he proceeded to drive hastily out of the airport and lead the other vehicles to their civic center destination.

Rebecca, who was still fairly young and attractive, stared at the back and side of Puzo's head for a moment and suspiciously asked, "Do I know you from somewhere?"

"I don't think so," Puzo replied. He remembered that she was pretty zonked out on marijuana when they met, and his stateside looks had changed measurably during his ordeals in paradise.

Rebecca then looked at Congressman Bryant and shrugged, "I guess I made a mistake."

Puzo felt relieved that he wasn't recognized so that Rebecca might later bad mouth him to Bryant.

As the motorcade moved down the bumpy road, Puzo began fishing for favors with, "By the way, congressman, did you know that I work for the Republicans here, and I regularly read your chairman reports on your space subcommittee work. I want to commend you for your support of my favorite federal agency, NASA."

"Uh, thank you," answered a slightly impressed Bryant, "and you can send me some of your comments about our NASA space program if you like." Then Bryant asked, "By the way, who picked the god-awful color for this car?"

Puzo replied: "It's a long story and you've had a long trip, so I won't bore you with the details, but I think there are plans to get it painted back to black real soon. And thanks for saying I could send you my comments about the NASA space program." The part about the NASA space program and sending comments was giving Puzo a mini erection.

The remainder of the trip was spent in silence as he occasionally spied the congressman and Rebecca in the rear view mirror. They both looked very tired and seemed uninterested in the mostly undeveloped sites of Saipan in general. But Puzo was getting antsy and wondered if it was now a good time to bring up his unique NASA plan with the congressman and his desire to work for NASA in the U.S. mainland. Although it would probably be better to discuss it later when Bryant wasn't so tired and feeling less miserable over the fact that he could have been on a trip to a much closer and the more exciting Caribbean.

Everyone got safely delivered to the Civic Center Park, and the Liberation Day celebration soon commenced with the singing of the national anthems of both the Commonwealth of the Northern Mariana Islands and the United States.

During the U.S. national anthem, however, a local policeman from Saipan intentionally hooked the American flag upside down and then raised it half-mast with a smiling face to the visible chagrin of Rear Admiral Blowntoggle. The stage was now definitely set for a return military engagement between a re-incensed rear admiral and the entire island of Saipan.

Following the flag incident, the governor, who had arrived just in time for the festivities, threw away his prepared speech and gave an impromptu speech about the dastardly United States government.

Because he had to cut his trip short, the governor was in a foul mood, and he was also super pissed off because his beautiful black limo got an outrageous new paint job. To further his rotten mood, he had returned from his long trip with his constantly nagging wife, who had joined him in Europe to shop, and to later come back with him to Saipan. She usually stayed most of the year in their beautiful U. S. subsidized home in California, but she had decided to tour Europe and then visit her jailed brother on Saipan, who kept bugging the governor to pardon him since he had only fourteen rape convictions out of twenty-two arrests. So due to his ongoing family stress and other matters, the governor was angry with everyone, especially the U.S. government.

While in Washington, he found out that there would be no more excessive federal handouts coming to Saipan, and he thereby decided to take some Liberation Day swipes at Uncle Sam on his local island turf and in front of his own people, and especially in front of Blowntoggle and the two visiting U.S. congressmen.

After Gustomacho's speech, he was followed to the podium by a very drunk local politician, who expertly picked up where Gustomacho had left off.

The sloshed local politician began haranguing all the Americans about the U. S. being too stingy to care of all their island needs, namely, large salaries, new cars, plenty of booze, and free trips to Manila and Hong Kong. It took only about forty-five seconds of the drunken politician's speech to make Blowntoggle order his men back to the airport for an immediate departure.

To calm the strained U.S. and Commonwealth relations, both Congressman Herdson and Bryant decided to stay and try and patch up the cracked relationship between the local leaders and the U.S. military.

But before he left, Blowntoggle told the congressmen, "Fine, suit yourselves, but find your own way back to Guam, because the next time I fly to Saipan, it'll be in an armed and loaded B-52!"

Blowntoggle then abruptly left with his band and successfully continued the ongoing traditional Fourth of July war between the U.S. military and the island leaders.

During all the commotion, Puzo quickly offered to help by reserving seats for the next available commercial flight to Guam the following morning and hotel rooms for both the stressed-out congressmen and their aides. The congressmen gladly accepted his offer, and Puzo felt he was back on track in his quest to befriend Congressman Bryant.

Puzo hurriedly left the festivities to call the airlines and the best hotel on the island for his overnight VIP guests.

"NASA, here I come!" he kept saying to himself, adding "Lord, don't screw me now!"

Around thirty minutes later during the continuing festivities, Blowntoggle's anger was still very evident. He had ordered his military C-130 to buzz the Civic Center Park during the coronation of Miss Liberation Day, and the very low-flying buzz job blew everyone and everything, including the two U.S. congressmen, in about sixteen different directions.

In the middle of the C-130 mess, Gustomacho was running and shouting obscenities at the plane.

Suddenly, one of his elevator shoes activated, and a news photographer got some great shots of the governor, stumbling around on his unevenly-matched set of limbs and throwing rocks at the C-130 while madly cursing Blowntoggle.

Gustomacho swore he would get even with the U.S. someday, while he continuously pounded on the waist button of his Philippine-made and slightly defective hydraulic elevator shoes.

"This lanya la puta insult will not go unanswered!" the governor kept shouting.

Unless, of course, the U.S. government gave him several millions to soothe his civic embarrassment and buy him a new pair of elevator shoes.

Later that same day at the hotel, after all the commotion had died down, Puzo attempted to impress a slightly disheveled and severely intoxicated Congressman Bryant, who was downing several scotches in the late afternoon to forget the island political chaos and the strafing he had just endured. Puzo had decided to invite Bryant and a reluctant Rebecca to go on a flying tour of the island. They weren't leaving until the next day, and an inebriated Bryant felt somewhat obligated to appease Puzo after he had arranged for their transportation and for securing the nicest rooms on the island.

So, a half-hour later during intermittent heavy winds, they were all strapped into Clancy Moore's semi-dilapidated Cessna-172, with Puzo at the controls.

For all the right reasons, Rebecca had become frozen with fear in the cramped back seat. Besides having bouts of claustrophobic fits, she was now having delusions of somehow knowing a nervously grinning Puzo, who was currently holding her life in his not-so-well-trained aviator's hands.

While Rebecca chewed her lips and Bryant sat anxiously in the front seat of the wind shaken airplane, Puzo got his clearance to take off and taxied to the runway.

In a few minutes they began rolling down the airstrip in continuous gusting winds.

Just as the plane broke away from the ground, a violent downdraft slammed the Cessna back on the runway. The plane then bounced a few more times and finally became airborne with everyone on board tightly clenching their teeth.

While climbing out through the increasing turbulence, a shaken and getting sober Bryant finally asked: "How long did you say you've been flying?"

"About three months, give or take a few weeks" Puzo replied with a weak smile, "but my instructor says I have the potential to be another Chuck Yeager."

With the forced pressure of trying to gain favor with Congressman Bryant in a limited time frame, Puzo realized his big screw-up and said under his breath, "I should have never gone up in this killer wind."

As the plane continued its feeble attempts to gain altitude and as they erratically flew out towards the open ocean, Puzo suddenly said loudly, "It's a bit rough up here, congressman. Do you mind if we just get back into the landing pattern and set her down?"

"Go right ahead!" Bryant's voice cracked with semi panic.

Rebecca just clasped her hands over her face and was whimpering out loud.

Puzo nervously battled the winds, which had blown the plane further out to sea, and the added downdrafts made the plane come dangerously close to the water's white caps. He somehow brought the plane back towards the airport and he entered the downwind leg of the landing pattern.

He then watched the windsock dance around like a whirling dervish and mumbled, "Oh, God!"

Following a few diabolical downdrafts, he finally made his base turn for his final approach, but a fierce crosswind quickly blew him off course. He made a small, rapid turn into the crosswind, added power, and began crabbing in like a herniated lobster. The plane was now pointed across the runway diagonally as it lurched around the last few descending feet in want of a merciful crash.

With another downdraft the plane hit hard on the runway, and then it was back up again, and then it quickly hit crossways and mercilessly bounced in the air again, and then back down again with a loud thud.

Rebecca screamed.

Bryant screamed.

Puzo closed his eyes and then he screamed.

The plane finally skidded to a noisy halt, and Puzo fumbled around to shut off the engine. He squinted through the front plexiglass, which was covered with debris, and he noticed that the plane had ended up off the runway and had somehow terminated its flight against the windsock stand. The windsock itself had been thoroughly shredded by the plane's propeller.

He checked his passengers, who were both passed out, and then he stumbled out of the plane. He walked around with wobbly legs to the front of the plane and slowly removed the shredded windsock remnants from the propeller. He pushed the plane back from the windsock stand and moved to the tail section and turned the plane to face the runway. Finally, he walked back to the passenger side and opened the door to allow fresh air to circulate around the cabin, in order to revive his passed-out passengers.

Meanwhile, an airport fire truck was now rushing to the scene and Puzo quickly got in and tried to start the plane's engine. He wanted to taxi to the hanger area unassisted, so he would avoid being overcharged by the airport authorities for any emergency assistance. But the damn engine wouldn't start.

Furthermore, the airport fire department had a reputation for over demonstrating their latest equipment and, subsequently, they eagerly sprayed foam on the entire plane and its occupants. The blast of foam aroused Bryant and Rebecca and they began screaming again. Puzo just silently sat in the plane covered in foam as it was towed to the hangar.

The plane was finally parked, and Puzo helped his two zombie-like passengers into his car. He had left a note on Clancy's plane that he would check him later to pay for the damages, and he also signed an airport official's report, promising them a new windsock, three barrels of foam, and four cases of beer.

While driving his shocked and foam drenched passengers back to the hotel, Puzo decided he had nothing to lose by asking a stunned Bryant to help him with a NASA proposal that he planned to send in later.

Bryant grotesquely grinned at Puzo, shouting, "Sure, by all means! Excuse me, where are we, in the Carribean?!"

Early the following morning at 2 a.m. Puzo yelled in his sleep and woke up in a sweat. In his sleep he had taken the pillow case off his pillow and had ripped the inside stuffing into shreds. He had dreamt that he was a plane that had just reproduced his infamous landing the afternoon before, windsock and all.

It took him another three hours to fall asleep again, because he kept fretting about what Bryant might do if he ever came out of shock.

Later the same morning, Bryant and Rebecca checked out early to leave Saipan. At Rebecca's request, they didn't wait for Puzo and took a cab and they both left parting messages for Puzo.

Puzo later stopped by the hotel to take Bryant and Rebecca to the airport, but was just given the two departing messages and he read them warily.

Congressman Bryant's message read: "I believe I promised to help you with some kind of NASA proposal. Contact me later when I'm feeling better."

Rebecca's message read: "Both the congressman and I will never be the same again, thanks to you. The congressman is now acting very strangely, and he even thinks you're a NASA expert and some kind of hero for apparently saving our lives at the airport. I can't remember too much about the flying fiasco, although you somehow remind me of an idiot that I once met in an attic in Washington!"

Puzo felt that a strange island climax was brewing for him. He would either be gone from Saipan in the near future in a straightjacket, or he would be stranded on this island asylum like a forgotten castaway, who should be properly punished for messing with with a U.S-sanctioned territorial nuthouse that was once a simple and fairly pleasant tropical island.

He the read the messages again and went for a long walk along a deserted beach that was littered with some Liberation Day posters that were blown there from two miles away.

27

BETTY JO HUNTER

"Do you think the world's gone completely crazy?" Betty Jo Hunter asked her favorite bartender, while nursing a gin tonic in Spam's a few nights after Liberation Day.

"Yes and no," Spam grunted. He then popped open a can of Budweiser and served it to his only other customer at the opposite end of the bar. His other customer, named Ernie, was a white ex-Marine who had served on Saipan during the war and who was now an outspoken critic of the local government for its anti-American attitudes.

He returned to Betty Jo and continued his answer. "Yep, the whole world's acting real crazy. But I'm not. I'm just stuck on this godforsaken rock with a group of mixed-up islanders and stateside drunks...excluding you, Betty Jo." It was early and he checked his watch anticipating his later crowd.

"I appreciate your excluding me." She teased.

"Well, you know you're my secret sweetheart, Betty Jo," Spam replied with a big grin, "and if it weren't for my Rosey, I'd be sending you flowers every day and even give up drinking."

He then poured himself a big dose of Canadian Club over some ice and innocently looked at Betty Jo with his big glass of whiskey in his hand, saying, "It's early, but I need a little pick-me-up." He then took a big slurp of his drink, smiled, and asked, "Why are you here by yourself?"

She began to toy with the ice in her drink. "I agreed to meet Paddy here. He said he would be a little late because the governor wanted him to pack up a pair of special shoes for some urgent repairs in the Philippines."

"You know that boy's slightly shy of a full head of smarts," Spam cautioned.

"I know. But he's harmless." She continued to toy with her ice.

Spam then served another beer to the grumpy ex-marine, saying back to Betty Jo, "Ernie here thinks the world's crazy because we're in the 'Darkie Ages."

"What ages did he say?" Betty Jo asked.

"The Darkie Ages!" Ernie shouted. "Because of all the darkies, like blacks, browns and white wannabees, who are running our stupid fucked-up government right now!"

Spam looked at Ernie and inquired with his famous grin, "Hell, what's going to happen then to us real white folks, Ernie?"

"Read your history books about what happened to the stupid Roman Empire after they turned it over to all the slaves and social workers," he bitterly replied and gulped his beer, "and I don't care what happens to you or anyone else. I'm taking care of only me, and I need another beer!" He turned to the wall and became sullen and quiet.

Spam walked over to Betty Jo and whispered to her to not worry about Ernie. Spam then opened a warm case of beer and began loading it into an extra beer cooler for the late night crowd.

The phone rang, and Spam answered it. "Hello, Spam's Bar, yeah...okay, hang on."

He turned to Betty Jo, "It's for you."

She walked behind the bar and took the phone from Spam and listened to the voice on the other end.

"Betty Jo? This is Paddy." His voice sounded tired on the other end of the line. "I'm going to be another hour late. The governor wants me take his special shoes later to the airport for the last flight to Manila. And I need to work on my NASA proposal. Could you meet me at my place in about an hour?"

"What do you have in mind?" she coyly inquired.

"I just want to be alone with you tonight for a while."

"Can I trust you to be a gentleman?" she asked.

"You know you can, Betty Jo." He started to react warmly to her friendly grilling.

"Well, okay. I'll meet you there in an hour. How do I get to your place?"

"Just drive north on Beach Road until you pass the House of Bamboo Bar, then turn left on the first coral road towards the beach. It's the small tin house near the lagoon with a large coconut tree growing through the roof. You can't miss it, and if you get there before me, there's a key to the front padlock under the stone by the front steps. Go on in and make yourself at home until I get there, okay?"

"Okay, Paddy. See you in an hour or so." She hung the phone up and returned to her bar stool.

She smiled at Spam, who always listened in on phone conversations in his bar, and coyly asked him, "Do you think I'll be safe going to Paddy's house alone?"

"Like you said before, the boy's harmless." He then acted jealous. "But you're going to break my little ol' heart, Betty Jo."

"Aw, c'mon over here," Betty Jo chuckled, "and let me give you a big kiss." She leaned over the bar and gave him a kiss on the cheek.

Suddenly, out of the kitchen flew Spam's wife with a large frying pan, and she swatted him hard on the butt.

"You watch it, lover boy!" Rosey shouted. "Next time I hit you with my machete!" She abruptly returned to the kitchen to resume cooking Spam's late night dinner, while Spam gently rubbed his painful rear end.

"Sorry." Betty Jo whispered with a surprised look on her face. "I didn't mean to get you in trouble?

"Never mind Rosey," Spam softly replied as he checked through the kitchen door window to see if Rosey was spying on him again. He added, "It does her good to get the blood boiling every now and then. The extra heat might melt off some of her extra weight, if you know what I mean."

"Shame on you, Spam." Betty Jo scolded him with a grin, then asked: "By the way, I always wanted to know how did you ever get the name Spam in the first place?"

He laughed. "About ten years ago some local punk challenged me to an eating contest for fifty bucks. I agreed, and was dumb enough to let him choose the food. The little bastard picked spam because he knew I hated it from my military days, but I beat him anyway by eating seven cans of the lousy stuff. I was sick for three days and the rest is history."

Betty Jo giggled and Spam asked her if she wanted another drink. She replied: "How about a banana daiquiri for a change."

Spam said he didn't fix any tooty-fruity drinks in his bar because it was against his principles, and a man has to be a man with some principles, he would always say.

She nodded and waited for him to mix her another gin and tonic and casually inquired: "Do you know anything about a NASA proposal that Paddy's working on?"

"NASA proposal? Oh, yeah, Paddy tried to explain it to me a couple of nights ago, after telling me about a nasty landing he had at the airport some time back. He seemed a little shook up." He served Betty Jo her drink, asking, "Are you sure you want to hear about his hair-brained scheme? It's supposed to be confidential, but I'll tell you if you want."

"Please do. I think I might have to deal with it later tonight." She drank some of her gin and tonic and rested her chin on her right hand that was propped up on the counter.

"Okay, I'll try and make it short." Spam threw down a double shot of Canadian Club and twitched a few times. "The boy's scared of no future job in the states when he leaves here, and he says his being white don't help him in a time of politically-correct minority hiring. So he's concocted an elaborate plan to impress NASA into hiring him as some kind of information specialist. He figures the NASA space program offers more opportunities for white folks, because its scientific projects don't include basketball and hip-hop dancing yet."

"Doesn't he realize that NASA has minority-hiring policies, too?" she interjected.

"I don't think he wants to believe it," Spam answered. "He feels NASA can't afford to have any unqualified people in such a challenging field as space exploration, even if certain unqualified people try to get the great-paying jobs only because they're qualified for being mostly Mexican or all Negro." He paused, and then decided to fix himself another double C.C. on the rocks.

"So," Betty Jo implored, "what's his plan?"

Spam stumbled over the next few words with his eyes going a little glassy, and slowly saying, "Assim, assimi, assimilated and simulated spaceman environments or something or other for astronauts, who will stay right here in some isolated islands in Micronesia." He belched and said excuse me.

Betty Jo quizzed Spam some more: "Would you mind explaining that a little more?"

"Sure, why not." Spam pulled up a stool behind the bar, swayed a little, and sat down. "He believes the remote islands have similar living conditions as space, like, uh, isolated living conditions and constant temperatures...and the presence of alien things, like betel nut, Peace Corps pukes, and the offspring of some unusual Micronesian islanders. So why not stick an astronaut-trainee on a lonely atoll out here and bingo! The feds could get some cheap studies done on outer space living right here on earth. The only loser would be some poor space trainee who got stuck on a stinking atoll in the middle of Micronesia, with nothing to do but play with himself, sweat, swat flies, and get severely sunburnt for several months." Spam gulped down his double C.C., quipping, "Strange plan, huh?"

"Well, I've heard stranger plans on the T.T. hill. So how's he fit in with the proposal and how did he come up with such big words?" Betty Jo asked.

Spam replied, "He figures NASA has to hire him to explain his brilliant idea to the people back in the states, and he'll be based there to write fancy big-worded reports with the dictionary I gave him."

Spam just shook his head and was about to chug another drink when suddenly Rosey flew out of the kitchen again in the direction of his whiskey glass. She knocked the glass of C.C. out of his hand, shouting, "You drink too much, then try to make baby all night with no good whiskey dick!" She took her machete and broke Spam's bottle of Canadian Club.

"Ah, Rosey, not my C.C.," Spam pleaded, "hit me instead."

Rosey concurred and took a swing at him as he quickly jumped back. "Good to see you move fast," she mockingly said. "Maybe you lose weight, too!" She faked another swing at him and then returned to the kitchen.

Spam twitched while sobering up a bit. "That woman scares me sometimes with her spooky hearing and spying." He started to clean up the broken glass and spilled whiskey when four new customers walked in.

They were Ralph Brubaker and three of his girlfriend's cousins from Truk Island. They all sat down next to Betty Jo and said hello to everyone, even Ernie, who was cracking his knuckles and mumbling to himself.

'Howdy, Ralph," greeted Spam as he hastily dumped the broken glass into the trash can and reached across the bar and shook Brubaker's hand. "Long time, no see. Who are your friends?"

This is Johnwayne, Nabisco, and Texaco," replied a scruffy-looking Brubaker. "They're cousins of my girlfriend and they just moved in with us."

"How'd you guys get the unusual names?" Spam asked while trying to sneak some Jack Daniels into a hidden glass.

Johnwayne looked at his two cousins, who nodded their approval, and then he explained. "Our parents think good American names help us with future American financial aid programs."

After hearing that remark Ernie angrily butted in. "It's going to take more than funny names to help you fucking island freeloaders!"

Then Spam quickly jumped in. "Okay, gentlemen, we've got a lady present. Let's keep it friendly."

"Kiss off, Spam!" shouted Ernie. "You Navy sissies always hide when there's a real fight!"

Brubaker asked his friends to pay no attention to the drunk ex-Marine, but Texaco said to Ernie, "Somebody tell me that white ex-Marines out here always eat dog shit because they want to be brown like us!"

Well, about thirty minutes later, the local police carted off three Trukese islanders and one ex-Marine, after they had all displayed a fairly decent re-enactment of the WWII battle for Saipan.

During the entire melee, Spam just protected his bottles of booze and yelled at the combatants not to break any of his glasses.

Meanwhile, Betty Jo hastily excused herself to leave for Puzo's place earlier than she had planned. She decided it would be much safer there than in the middle of an island bar brawl.

When things finally quieted down, Spam uncharacteristically gave Brubaker a free beer, and began giving his late night dissertation again on how he had single-handedly captured Saipan and was consequently awarded two Navy Crosses and three Purple Hearts...

After arriving at Puzo's tin shack of a house, Betty Jo unlocked the front door and went in. She had some time to kill, so she ended up washing the dirty dishes that had been in the sink for a week and tried to straighten out the place a bit. It was a hopeless task, but at least it improved the atmosphere slightly.

Following her volunteer house work, she slowly took a shower in a heavy trickle of water that sporadically spurted out of an old rusty spigot. She then laid down wrapped in a towel on a creaky couch in the living room.

She peered at the coconut tree that had grown through the roof and wondered if the make-shift rain gutter around the tree kept most of the water out, although she didn't want to find out while she was there. She then spied a book on the plywood coffee table and began idly reading "The Martian Chronicles."

Soon she was yielding to drooping eyelids and was soundly asleep within minutes. She had a busy day at work and an interesting night in Spam's Bar and the sleep was very welcomed.

An hour later, Puzo silently crept around the insides of his house when he discovered Betty Jo was sound asleep on his couch. She looked contented and he carefully placed a bed sheet over her. He didn't want to disturb her--not yet anyway.

Feeling dirty and sticky, he tried to take an adequate shower to rid himself of the oily sensation that the island humidity gave him, but ended up giving himself a sponge bath out of the toilet tank.

He then spread some light blankets on the floor next to the couch and turned off the light. He set his alarm for seven o'clock in the moonlight filtering in through the roof and quietly crawled under one of the blankets, while the old floor where he lay creaked and quivered with possible collapse. His eyes meandered over towards Betty Jo's serene face and voluptuous upper body, which was partially exposed by a shifting towel and bed sheet, and the sensuality of her presence put him into a deep, R-rated sleep.

Fortunately, he would have no nightmares about volcanoes, plane crashes or any other calamities that night.

28

THE NASA PLAN

At seven o'clock the next morning the alarm clock rudely aroused Puzo from the depths of a very relaxing sleep. He unconsciously threw the loudly ringing clock against the nearest wall and it shattered with a crash. He finally realized that he had company and rapidly rolled over to look at a smiling Betty Jo.

"Good morning, Mister Puzo. Did you sleep well down there?" she asked with a twinkle in her eye.

"Pretty good, considering." he said with a grin. Suddenly two termite-infested floorboards gave way and his butt sank through a gaping hole in the floor. He awkwardly pulled himself out of the broken pieces of flooring and asked, "You know any good carpenters?"

She shook her head, smiling. "Is it safer in your bedroom?"

He then took a deep breath and carefully crawled over some weakened floorboards towards the couch, wearing only his white boxer shorts covered with little red hearts and flowers. He climbed halfway up on the couch and lightly kissed her.

She gently pushed him back, saying, "Nice shorts." She then pulled him forward and gave him a big passionate kiss.

Puzo quickly reacted by picking her up in his arms and looking intently into her eyes--just like the movies he hoped--and then he started to carry her into his bedroom. But he accidentally stepped into the newly-created hole in his floor, which was hidden from view by a rumpled blanket, and they both fell down in a crashing and laughing heap.

After wisely deciding to walk separately into the bedroom, they finally snuggled up on Puzo's waterbed, skipping any small talk, especially about Puzo's NASA plans.

They spent some time adjusting their body positions to the wave action of the under-filled mattress bag, which added some unnecessary adventure to a nervous host, but true paradise for Puzo was eventually attained, compliments of Betty Jo Hunter.

Because of the morning festivities, Puzo was happily an hour late to work, and he even kissed his surly secretary on the cheek when he finally did arrive at his office.

Instantly, his temperamental secretary threw her wastepaper basket at him for kissing her. But he successfully ducked it, commenting sarcastically, "You need a little more practice."

As a consequence, she angrily called her two hoodlum brothers who loved to display their homicidal tendencies, and Puzo spent the rest of the week worrying about what her demented brothers swore they would do to him once they sobered up enough to find him.

The remainder of August rolled by with not much happening on Saipan, which can happen quite often on a small Micronesian island.

Puzo fought off the symptoms of island doldrums by spending most of his idle time reworking his NASA proposal. His proposal, however, was giving him minor attacks of anxiety, by forcing him to delve into the higher levels of proposal justifications and making him to try and understand the mysteries of federal thinking and using big words. Furthermore, his future plans were precariously riding on not only his questionable proposal, but a mentally-deranged congressman.

Like it was previously said, August rolled by on Saipan in a listless fashion. And nothing really exciting happened that month, except an obvious case of arson that totally destroyed a certain staff car assigned to Puzo. The car was set afire in the governor's parking lot in broad daylight, right next to the local police station.

When the fiery commotion had finally died down, Puzo found a cryptic note on his desk which read: "Next time, white boy, we put you in burning car if you ever kiss our sister again!"

He read the note twice and felt his neck getting tighter and tighter, so he quickly looked for the address for Congressman Bryant. His time spent on Saipan needed to be rapidly shortened.

While Paddy busily pursued his NASA objectives in early September, the details of the annual meeting of the Association of Pacific Island Leaders (APIL) were being finalized, and the local political machine on Saipan was actively setting the stage for Governor Gustomacho's chance to publicly blast the United States for not responding to his exorbitant demands for more monetary assistance.

Financially speaking, the governor wanted about a zillion dollars a year until around the year 2092, or longer, depending if the Northern Mariana Islands had somehow attained self-sufficiency by that time.

Moreover, if the United States didn't entertain his outlandish monetary requests, a mentally-delirious Gustomacho threatened to look elsewhere for new political and economic relationships.

Besides his upcoming money mongering during the APIL meeting, he also wanted to vehemently protest the life-threatening strafing he had received by Admiral Blowntoggle during the previous Liberation Day.

Adding to the fun, another event would also be coinciding with the APIL meeting that month, namely, the meeting of the Pacific Region Financial Council (PFRC).

The PRFC was primarily a lobbying organization for most of Micronesian islands and it was based in Hawaii. It also had certain U.S. congressional pull in Washington, but not that much pull.

Over the years, however, the Pacific island leaders were getting tired of paying the PFRC's costly dues--money which they could more easily spend on themselves.

So for this reason, the PFRC meeting was hastily scheduled by its executive director to begin a day before the APIL meeting, in order to quell any unrest about the membership dues being too expensive. The meeting would also try to repair the simmering racial problem of a PFRC identity crisis with the island natives, because its executive director was a very white boy from North Carolina by the name of Jimmy Lee Thompson.

Thompson was a smooth-talking, former lobbyist for the U.S. tobacco industry, who had jumped on the idea of lobbying for the Micronesian islands when he observed their leaders struggling around Washington in want of prudent directions, especially the prudent directions towards the United States federal vault.

"More money spent creates more needed money to spend!" Jimmy Lee would always exhort his island council members when explaining the high PFRC membership dues. But he would dare not tell them that his big salary was necessary for his swinging lifestyle and three broken marriages that were costing him a fortune.

Jimmy Lee was on borrowed time and he didn't fully realize it yet.

Two weeks later, Saipan welcomed the arrival of the APIL members, some PFRC representatives, and a slightly shook Jimmy Lee Thompson, who worried about the next day's PRFC meeting.

Upon his arrival, Jimmy Lee immediately sought out a fellow white boy who was currently working as the governor's PIO.

Jimmy Lee anxiously checked Puzo on the weather conditions of the local political climate. Thompson had always been pretty confident going into previous PFRC meetings, but Puzo noticed that he had a strange look on his face for this one, and it wasn't a bit cocky either.

Jimmy Lee was absolutely petrified that his money making council was about to quickly sink into the Marianas Trench, and with the tobacco industry being accused of giving cancer to everyone and everything that ever lived, he just didn't want to think about another lobbying stint with a paranoid group of wild-eyed tobacco growers.

"Are you sure that Gustomacho won't sabotage me?" Thompson nervously asked as he sat in Puzo's office, while twisting his straw-hat into a distorted lump, adding, "Because I've heard rumors he's planning weird things nowadays."

"I can't guarantee anything," Puzo replied. "Nobody can figure out what he plans to do in the next few days, or years, although I have a suspicion that he wants to embarrass the U.S. into immediately giving him more federal money and several apologies for the dastardly Blowntoggle military stunt and a cheap U.S. congress."

"Well, Jimmy Lee exclaimed, "I still think I can shake loose Uncle Sam for some extra change for these islands."

"You don't understand completely, Jimmy Lee. The governor's on an anti-American and anti-white people tirade. And you're American, and appear mighty white to me."

"Then how come you still got your job?" Jimmy Lee asked.

Puzo sighed. "Believe me, it's not for long."

"If you asked me," Jimmy Lee scoffed, "I think your crazy governor is bluffing. He still needs me to officially beg for some federal assistance."

Jimmy Lee got up and confidently headed for the door, saying, "I'm going back to my hotel and relax. I've got a date later tonight with a sweet young thing that I met on the plane. See you later, Paddy."

Puzo said goodbye, and then received a call to prepare an immediate press release for the governor.

FOR IMMEDIATE RELEASE
(NORTHERN MARIANA ISLANDS PULL OUT OF PRFC)
SAIPAN, COMMONWEALTH OF THE NORTHERN
MARIANA ISLANDS, SEPTEMBER 26, PI0--

GOVERNOR REGINO J. GUSTOMACHO ANNOUNCED
EARLY TODAY HIS DECISION TO IMMEDIATELY PULL
OUT OF THE PACIFIC REGION FINANCIAL COUNCIL
(PRFC). HIS REASONS ARE: 1) THE PRFC DIDN'T FULLY
REPRESENT THE PACIFIC ISLANDS' NEEDS AND
CULTURE; 2) HE COULDN'T JUSTIFY THE COSTLY
ANNUAL DUES BECAUSE OF HIS OWN FISCAL WANTS
AND NEEDS; AND 3) THE PRFC WAS TOO AMERICAN FOR
ITS OWN DAMN GOOD. THEREFORE, THE GOVERNOR
HAS IMMEDIATELY STOPPED PAYMENT ON THE
RECENT CHECK SENT TO THE PRFC, AND REQUESTS
THAT ALL HIS FELLOW MICRONESIAN LEADERS JOIN
HIM IN HIS BID TO RID THE ISLANDS OF GREEDY,
STATESIDER ORGANIZATIONS. THE GOVERNOR ALSO
WANTS TO OFFICIALLY WELCOME ALL THE PACIFIC
ISLAND LEADERS TO THE ANNUAL "APIL" MEETING
BEGINNING TOMORROW AT THE NEW COCONUT
TREE HOTEL. (END OF RELEASE)

The big tidal wave of local revenge which had given Jimmy
Lee Thompson recurring nightmares finally hit with a fury, as all
the other PRFC members followed the lead of Gustomacho. They
all announced their immediate terminations with the PRFC and
promptly demanded back all their membership dues for the entire
year.

Later, Puzo got an urgent phone call from Jimmy Lee.

"Those bastards, those sons of gonorrhea-infected, banana-
sucking bastards! They've really done it to me!" shrieked Jimmy Lee
on the phone while he yelled a bunch of obscenities and continued,

"Just wait until they come crawling back to me after Reagan starts cutting back all the federal freebies to these blood-sucking, betel nut republics."

"Jimmy Lee? Are you okay?" Puzo inquired.

"Am I okay?" Jimmy Lee sobbed and asked, "Can you give me the directions to Suicide Cliff? I feel like jumping off a few times."

"Take it easy," Puzo said, sympathetically. "Maybe the governor will reconsider after he gets a few U.S. monetary apologies and things return to semi-normal."

"Damned betel nut republics!" Jimmy Lee screamed and suddenly slammed down his phone.

Puzo shook his head, looked at the wall calendar, and continued rewriting a section of his future-saving NASA proposal.

It was halfway through the first session of the APIL meeting the following day when Jimmy Lee made his loud, drunken entrance. He burst through the flimsy, sliding partition of the meeting room at the Coconut Tree Hotel, and fell forward onto the podium, where Governor Gustomacho was ranting away with his "Give us the money now, Uncle Sam, or we'll leave you later" speech.

Both Jimmy Lee and the governor tumbled forward as the podium collapsed into a crashing heap.

Then, in the spirit of APIL togetherness, several humongous Pacific island leaders leaped on Jimmy Lee and nearly beat the entire white out of him.

During the entire process of Jimmy Lee's complete loss of consciousness and the removal of pieces of his body, the governor kept screaming as more large and very rotund Pacific island leaders kept jumping into fracas.

As a consequence, the APIL meeting was suspended indefinitely, while an ambulance carted off both the governor and Jimmy Lee to the local hospital.

After being admitted to the hospital, Gustomacho angrily lamented that he never even got a chance to wear his new Cuban formal wear to the cancelled APIL dinner dance that evening, and now he was in a very painful and boiling rage over the latest American attempt on his life.

Before visiting hours were over, Puzo visited Jimmy Lee in the hospital and told him it was highly advisable to leave Saipan as soon as possible, since the governor had issued an executive order for his public hanging.

Jimmy Lee, who was in a full body cast, nodded his head in complete agreement with Puzo.

The next morning, Jimmy Lee was fork-lifted into the front cargo bay of a Boeing 727 and began his painful journey back to Northern Carolina.

His second wife had agreed to temporarily take care of him for a nominal charge, which was paid for by a wealthy tobacco grower who was glad to see Jimmy Lee back from the heathen jungles of the Pacific.

As for Governor Gustomacho, he had broken his left leg and both arms in the APIL fiasco, and he was painfully agonizing over his plight in his hospital bed. His bed was strategically placed next to Lieutenant Governor Flores, who was still recuperating from the cement truck attack.

Subsequently, they both ended up just staring at each other with glazed eyes, screaming for more morphine shots.

For the next few days it was a tongue-biting experience not to laugh when Puzo brought the morning mail to a glaring Gustomacho, while Flores whined to the governor about his itchy butt.

The only thing that kept Gustomacho from declaring that all statesiders on Saipan should be shot for his horrendous condition was the fact that he had been continually fed heaps of Valium, Darvon and morphine by a nervous stateside doctor.

Before Puzo left the hospital one particular morning, the governor whispered to him: "I'm not going to fire you yet, because I'm going to make you suffer a long time like I am."

"How's that, governor?" Puzo anxiously inquired.

"Somehow I'm going to make all statesiders suffer when I get out of this hospital."

"Do you plan to declare war on the United States, or something?" Puzo asked.

"Maybe. I don't know yet. But something will come to me." Gustomacho's face began to twitch.

Puzo left, figuring his job was safe for now as long as the doctor kept giving the governor enough pain-killers and tranquilizers to keep him in a deep twilight zone. But he also decided that he'd better spend much more time to finish his NASA proposal and his emergency plan for a safe departure from paradise.

While Governor Gustomacho convalesced in the hospital, the local legislative campaigns went into high gear for the upcoming November mid-term elections, and everything on Saipan seemed secondary in importance, excepting the governor's growing appetite for more drugs.

The November election was originally scheduled for the first day of the month. But in mid-October the Republican legislators hastily drafted their only piece of legislation in the previous six months to have the election conveniently moved from the first of November to the fourth of November, a government payday.

This change of the election day would hopefully guarantee a much happier group of voters, who would happily receive their paychecks and then happily vote for the hardworking and civic-minded Republican incumbents.

At the same time, the Democratic candidates were delirious about the possibility of getting back their lucrative jobs. With one week left before the election, there was campaign chicanery everywhere.

The Democrats were wisely traveling to village meetings with truckloads of free beer, and the drinking masses began shouting that the Democrats deserved another chance. Furthermore, it really didn't seem to matter to the Republican President Reagan about who was actually in charge of the newly formed and "financially struggling" Commonwealth, since the U.S. federal funds were continually being sent to the dysfunctional Commonwealth, albeit not quite enough money to satisfy Governor Gustomacho's monumental lust for more. Besides, what really politically mattered to the islanders on Saipan was that the local Democratic Party offered more free beer than Gustomacho's stupid self-serving Republican Party.

It appeared to be political flip-flop time again on Saipan, and the Democrats smelled victory like hungry sharks circling a group of fat-ass swimmers.

A week later, while Puzo was applying the finishing touches to his NASA proposal, he got the news of the election results. It was wipe-out time for the Republicans in the Commonwealth.

They lost every one of the legislative seats in both the Senate and the House of Representatives and, consequently, many out-of-work Republicans would be soon after his PIO position. And on top of that, the governor's nephew had reasonably recovered from his ball-shooting accident, and he was headed back to Saipan.

The same day he received the election results and the news of the governor's nephew, he sent his NASA proposal to Congressman Bryant---by Special Delivery!

29

GUSTOMACHO'S REVENGE

Although having mostly recovered from his injuries, the governor's pain made him later stay in his governor's mansion while still fuzz-brained on Valium overdoses. But he was forced to return to his office on November seventh, three days after the election massacre of his Republican party.

Previously, with both Gustomacho and Flores in the hospital at the same time, the governor's office had been placed on hold until one of them could be released.

But with the Democrats now in control of the legislature, the Republican Party coerced Gustomacho back into office to do battle with the opposition, although all he had on his raging mind was to retaliate against the U.S. government and statesiders like Jimmy Lee Thompson!

Upon his return, Gustomacho's first official act was to declare that all statesiders on Saipan had to wear traditional, Saipanese loin wraps, which were made out of breadfruit leaves and woven coconut fronds, and which barely covered one's crotch and bare ass. He also decreed in a later proclamation that all statesiders on the island must give him fifty percent of their earnings, which would compensate him for his recent pain and suffering.

In response to his wild demands, most statesiders on Saipan knew about his excessive drug abuse, so they didn't take Gustomacho too seriously.

But Puzo took Gustomacho seriously and feared that the governor's lunacy might enter into the next totally bizarre stage real soon, so he kept avoiding the governor and anxiously awaited word from NASA.

Two weeks later in a raucous Cabinet meeting, Gustomacho was currently incensed by the Caribbean Basin Initiative that had been recently signed into U.S. law by President Reagan.

It was a lucrative, twelve-year economic program designed to revitalize the sagging economies of the Caribbean and Central American nations, but it also initiated a wave of jealousy in Micronesia, especially in the Northern Mariana Islands.

Gustomacho, who was running extremely low on painkillers, was in a foul and frenzied mood. He yelled at his Cabinet members: "To hell with those crooks in the Caribbean! They've been stealing a long time already from the United States. Why don't America take care of its Marianas' children instead?" He began stamping his feet on the floor and beating his fists on the table until tears came to his eyes.

Puzo was taking mental notes of the governor's latest verbal tirade against the United States, and it was apparent that the shortages of painkilling drugs at the hospital had taken its toll on the overly irritable governor.

Gustomacho was so tense that the tendons in his neck visibly bulged out. He suddenly glared at the local hospital director, yelling, "And speaking of taking better care of our Marianas' children, I wanna know why the hospital ran out of my drugs again!"

The local hospital director looked at the governor and began fiddling with an old stethoscope that was always dangling around his neck. He figured it added to his professional qualifications of being a hospital director, ever since he had been thrown out of a nursing school in Tahiti for lack of basic brains.

"I'm sorry, governor," the local hospital director finally said, "but the funding for medical supplies had to be diverted to cover the travel expenses for my last medical convention in Rio de Janeiro."

The governor's neck stretched out even further, to give him the appearance of an enraged cobra. He put his hands up in the air and demanded, "I don't care about your stupid Rio trip, what about my drugs?!"

"Why don't you check with the supervisor at the prison?!" The hospital director shot back in frustration, adding, "He seems to always have a better supply of drugs than our own pharmacy."

"Alright, I'll do that! Right after this meeting!"

The governor's vocal chords were now stretched to the max as he howled: "I want all statesiders on island to be notified that they are my official hostages until I get my millions from the U.S. congress!"

With that remark, Fishblatt, the governor's creepy stateside legal counsel, who had been a nervous wreck for weeks, screamed and ran out of the room.

Before the meeting adjourned, the governor, who was running out of barely coherent relatives, appointed his goofy cousin as his new director of finance and instructed him to immediately fly to Hong Kong and place ads in their daily papers, notifying the entire world that Governor Regino J. Gustomacho and the soon to be "FORMER United States" Commonwealth of the Northern Mariana Islands were looking for a new political partner!

The Hong Kong ads drew immense laughter from the Hong Kong residents who never heard of Governor Gustomacho, and even the U.S. State Department was in hysterics knowing about Gustomacho's drug-induced craziness.

By the latter part of November, the governor had already traded his Lincoln for a month's supply of Valium from the prison supervisor. But at the rate he was gobbling up the stuff, he would be out of stock by Christmas, and every director was now worried about losing their staff cars to the prison parking lot.

At least Puzo didn't have to worry because his staff car was already incinerated history, and his current PIO vehicle was an unwanted, rusted-out pickup from the public works garage. He did worry about one thing, however, did his NASA proposal ever reach Congressman Bryant, and would it save his butt from this ongoing island insanity?

Nine thousand miles away in Washington, D.C., a previous visitor of the islands was also going through a very questionable crisis in his life.

Following his traumatic visit to Saipan, a seriously disturbed Congressman Bryant had decided to wear a NASA spacesuit at all times in his office at the Capitol Building. He feared that he would be infected by all the millions of earthly germs that were trying to infiltrate into his loftier views of future cosmic coexistence.

It was early morning in his office, and Bryant was reviewing Puzo's NASA proposal after he had lifted the mirror-finished sunshield on his space helmet. He kept gazing at the assimilated-simulated spaceman plan for Micronesia and eventually leaned back in his chair and tried to put his arms around his head. But the bulky suit was making it difficult.

One of his assistants tried to help force his arms behind his head, but Bryant finally waved the assistant away and motioned for him to get a NASA walkie-talkie. Bryant wanted to communicate with the assistant via his space helmet communicator.

"This is Congressman Bryant, calling Legislative Assistant Price. Over." He impatiently motioned for his assistant to respond.

"Yes, congressman, this is Price. Over."

"Price, I want you to inform NASA that a special Micronesian space program is to be implemented as soon as possible. Over."

"But, sir, Rebecca and I thought this Micronesian proposal was a big joke. Over."

"A joke! A big joke!" Bryant exploded over his communicator. "I suppose Berner Von Braun was a big joke, too! That's why the Russians beat our butts into space! We must never let any of our geniuses down again! Over and out!"

"Roger, sir! I'll contact NASA immediately! And Von Braun's first name is Werner, sir. Over and out, sir!" Price immediately rushed out to start the federal gears turning.

Meanwhile, Bryant asked himself, "Who's Werner?"

VIA WUI

6611 '12/2 #

CMCAA SAIPAN 113

DECEMBER 2, 1983

TO: THE HONORABLE REGION J. GUSTOMACHO
           GOVERNOR, NORTHERN MARIANA ISLANDS

FROM: NATIONAL AERONAUTICS & SPACE
           ADMINISTRATION
           Washington, D.C.

RE: MICRONESIAN ASSIMILATED-SIMULATED
           SPACEMAN STUDY (MASSS)

THIS IS TO INFORM YOU THAT THE NASA HAS BEEN PERSUADED TO IMPLEMENT A MICRONESIAN ASSIMILATED-SIMULATED SPACEMAN STUDY (MASSS) IN YOUR ISLANDS FOR RESEARCH INTO THE ISOLATED AND ALIEN CONDITIONS OF SPACE. FURTHERMORE, SINCE YOUR OFFICE IS DIRECTLY RESPONSIBLE FOR THE ORIGINAL MASSS PROPOSAL, WE FELT IT APPROPRIATE THAT YOUR OFFICE BE ESTABLISHED AS THE MAIN LIAISON CONTACT FOR THIS RATHER UNIQUE PROJECT.

AT THIS TIME, HOWEVER, WE ARE SHORT OF AN ASTRONAUT-TRAINEE TO BE SENT TO YOUR REMOTE ISLANDS. THEREFORE, FEEL FREE TO SELECT A MASSS CANDIDATE IN YOUR AREA TO SATISFY THE HUMAN

ASPECTS OF THIS TWO-YEAR STUDY. AFTER WE HAVE
BEEN NOTIFIED OF YOUR CANDIDATE'S SELECTION
AND THE ISOLATED ATOLL THAT YOU HAVE PICKED
FOR THIS MASSS PROGRAM, ADDITIONAL INFORMA-
TION AND THE APPROPRIATE MAJOR FUNDING WILL
BE IMMEDIATELY SENT TO YOU WITHIN FIFTEEN (15)
DAYS.

REGARDS,
WILLIAM I SNAFUNE
DIRECTOR OF NASA PLANNING & STUDIES
DCCAA WASHINGTON, D.C. VIA...WUI

Governor Gustomacho read the telex alone in his office,
gobbled up a handful of Valium, and read the telex again. He then
grinned and began laughing like a maniac at the wild and lucrative
federal Micronesian study that was somehow connected to his
office. And Gustomacho was overjoyed at the strange opportunity
to score some big federal bucks, and he also realized that this was
his chance to teach at least one statesider on Saipan a good lesson
for not following his orders to wear skimpy Saipanese loin wraps.
Furthermore, he concluded that two years on some isolated atoll in
the Caroline Islands would definitely force one dumbass statesider to
better appreciate the ancient Micronesian ways.

He immediately called his chief administrative officer to
arrange a special news conference and gleefully went over a mental
list of potential candidates for the NASA study. The governor finally
picked a candidate and a location and quickly replied to NASA to get
his major funding ASAP!

Two hours later, the governor's CAO joined Gustomacho
at the outdoor press podium and the CAO was now aware of the
special announcement. A restless news media looked at a ginning
Gustomacho, then at the grinning face of the CAO, then back to the
grinning governor.

Finally, one reporter asked, "What gives, governor? The C.A.O. said this was some kind of special announcement."

"It is special, it is!" The governor gloated as he looked across the small crowd of reporters and onlookers. "I'm pleased to announce that NASA has decided to pick our lovely Micronesian islands as a joint site for the first, uh...," he looked at a paper in his hand and announced his own version of the message, "for... the first Micronesian...uh, Spaceman Study."

There was a collective "huh" from the entire group of media and onlookers. Puzo, who wasn't handling the special press conference, had come anyway, and now he couldn't believe it. Was it really true? Was it time to pack his bags for Washington and join the boys at NASA?

"And I am also pleased," the governor continued with a grotesque grin, "that our own Mister Paddy Puzo has been selected to spend two years on Olato Atoll to personally partake in this wonderful NASA project."

Aaaaaaaaaaaaaaarrrrrgggghhhhhhhhh!!!

Puzo immediately closed his eyes and tried to rewind the last portion of this unbelievable announcement. He didn't believe what he had just heard, until he was quickly asked to step forward and make a comment about being selected to spend two years on a small isolated atoll, with the only other inhabitants being three Micronesian sex offenders and their Peace Corps social worker, who had a penchant for perverted case work. And where the hell was Olato?!

After walking to the podium in a daze, he tried to speak, but nothing came out. He just stared into space and then softly cried out, "O Lord, please forgive me for wanting to pee on the Lincoln Memorial"

The press figured he was already mentally prepared for his ordeal by the way he kept mumbling while looking upwards.

The governor then presented him a Saipanese loin wrap. "I want also to present this traditional loin wrap to Mister Puzo," he happily announced, "to wear during the dry season on Olato," adding, "which gets very hot and will always remind him of paradise here in Micronesia."

Aaaaaaaaarrrrrrrrgggghhh!!! Puzo fainted.

After being finally revived, Puzo slowly walked back to his office in a zombie-like trance. He silently walked past his grinning secretary--the news was spreading fast about his demise--and went into his office and locked the door.

He sat down and talked to a NASA photograph hanging on the wall of Neil Armstrong who was standing on the moon. "Well, Neil, they finally got me. The whole free-flying and fucking world of Minorities, Incorporated has finally placed the big ball peen hammer right over my chalk dick and wham-o!"

Later that week, his departure for Olato, which was somewhere between Yap and Palau islands, was officially set for January fifteenth.

Aaaaaaaaarrrrggggghhh!!!

30

OLATO

Early the next morning the phone rang in Puzo's office and he was soon listening to the governor babbling in his left ear.

"Puzo, I want you out of your office by tomorrow. My nephew is returning in a month and we need to remodel your office for his special needs. There's an old tin storage shack behind the parking lot you can use while you're still here."

"Sure, governor," he replied, half-heartedly. "I'm glad your nephew has recovered from his unfortunate accident."

"Not yet," the governor said. "He still has trouble moving around with his fake balls not working right that are hanging between his legs, and he always talks in a funny voice."

"That's too bad." Puzo feigned sympathy. "Uh, excuse me, governor, will I remain your official P.I.O. until I leave next month?"

"Yes, and you can get anything you need for your Olato trip." The governor chuckled, adding, "NASA has been very generous to us, so feel free to get whatever it takes to make your little project successful. Because whatever you personally spend we'll get reimbursed with extra funding, too." The governor sounded overly pleased with Puzo's future predicament.

Having guessed that the governor had gone overboard with his Valium again, Puzo ventured to ask, "Would it be all right to request for a stateside psychologist to check me out before I leave? Just to make sure I'm okay for the project?"

As Puzo talked he was quickly formulating a possible plan of justifiable revenge.

"No problem," the governor snidely replied, "get whoever you need, the U.S. is paying for all of it!"

"Thanks, I'll probably contact someone in the Los Angeles area," Puzo continued, "and governor, there's a good chance the psychologist will bring a whole suitcase of special drugs, if you know what I mean."

"You mean special drugs that I could use, too?" the governor inquired.

"You bet. The latest and the greatest." Puzo continued to bait the governor.

"In that case, I'll personally guarantee whatever you want will be approved immediately. Just make sure I get a special appointment when that psycho-doctor person arrives."

The governor was now delirious about the whole situation, especially with a new source of drugs coming his way.

"Don't worry, governor, you'll get whatever you need, and could I get my final payday in advance by January sixth? I have to pay some bills before I leave."

"No problem, the governor chortled. He then slammed down the phone in Puzo's ear.

A couple of days later, Puzo was formulating his plan of revenge and pondering about his Olato fate.

There was a potential positive to his small island banishment, for he would ironically receive a GS-14 pay rating during his study, and he figured that if he could survive long enough on Olato, he could someday flee the island with a substantial monetary stake in his pocket since there was nowhere on Olato to spend any money.

The GS-Fourteen rating was his prior dream, but, alas, there was no Spats on Olato, and he doubted that he could impress anyone with his GS-14 on the tiny atoll.

He was also beginning to get more irritated at the idea of being pushed out of his office for the governor's idiot nephew. His being reassigned to the outer reaches of the parking lot in a tin shack had clinched his decision to implement a special plan of retaliation against the governor, who he knew had something major to do with his selection for the Olato horror show.

Having his plan mostly formulated, he acted swiftly to possibly get the last laugh on Saipan and Gustomacho. The first priority was checking out the new communication system that the governor had recently installed in his office.

Due to the governor's illicit drug dealings on and off the island, which were attracting public attention, Puzo had discovered that Gustomacho was growing increasingly paranoid about any FBI and CIA spooks interfering with his quest for Valium Valhalla.

As a result of his paranoia, Gustomacho installed a confidential private phone in his office with an anti-bugging device. He also added a private telex machine to prevent any leaks about his illegal drug contacts with Thailand, Mexico and South American pharmaceutical suppliers.

Eventually, Puzo learned Gustomacho's private telex number by secretly rummaging through the governor's trash, and he was now ready to begin his plan of revenge.

He quickly contacted Tak Vierra, who had been recently paroled for promising to build new houses for the entire Parole Board, and he asked to use Vierra's telex machine to play a confidential joke on the governor's office.

Vierra just grinned at the request, and then said, "Go right ahead. But please make it a big joke on that jackass governor."

Puzo proceeded to draft a telex and sent it to Gustomacho with a fake Brirish return address that would be sent back to Vierra's telex machine. The telex would test the waters for the governor's behavior, concerning incoming messages on his private telex machine.

Fortunately for Puzo, Gustomacho didn't trust anyone else and operated his machine all by himself. Puzo was banking on this and the governor's accelerating incoherence, plus his previous fishing for another country to financially support the Commonwealth. Puzo figured this would guarantee the governor's overlooking any unusual circumstances involving Puzo's bogus message.

WWU GOVPOT 164811702"+
788 CONCOM 01268456711 22 12/20/83
702 STC UK LONDON TRAFFIC 2:50 PM SLT

TO: GOVERNOR OF THE COMMONWEALTH OF THE NORTHERN MARIANA ISLANDS
FROM: THE SECRETARY FOR THE PRIME MINISTER, LONDON, ENGLAND

DEAR GOVERNOR GUSTOMACHO:

OUR MINISTER OF FOREIGN AFFAIRS IN HONG KONG HAS INFORMED OUR PRIME MINISTER THAT YOUR GOVERNMENT IS ENTERTAINING NEW POLITICAL RELATIONSHIPS WITH OTHER COUNTRIES. IT IS ALSO UNDERSTOOD THAT YOUR COVENANT WITH THE UNITED STATES IS TO BE TERMINATED NEXT YEAR IF YOU DON'T COME TO A SATISFACTORY AGREEMENT. THEREFORE, THE PRIME MINISTER WOULD LIKE TO MEET WITH YOU JANUARY 9TH ON SAIPAN FOR DISCUSSIONS ON A MUTUAL PACT BETWEEN YOUR ISLANDS AND THE UNITED KINGDOM OF GREAT BRITAIN AND NORTHERN IRELAND. WE WOULD NATURALLY OFFER YOU A VERY LUCRATIVE FINANCIAL PACKAGE FOR THIS MUTUAL AGREEMENT. IF THIS IS A

SATISFACTORY PROPOSAL AND YOU ARE INTERESTED IN OUR MEETING TOGETHER, PLEASE DON'T RESPOND TO THIS MESSAGE WITHIN THE NEXT TWENTY-FOUR HOURS AND WE WILL ACCEPT THIS AS YOUR POSITIVE REPLY. WE WILL CONTACT YOU LATER TO TAKE CARE OF ALL ARRANGEMENTS FOR THE MEETING AND WE DESIRE STRICT CONFIDENTIALITY AT THIS TIME.

REGARDS,

BENTLEY R. ROYCE
SECRETARY TO THE PRIME MINISTER

Gustomacho kept looking at the telex, twitched, and wondered about the contents.

He finally assumed, after swallowing a few more Valiums and several large Darvon capsules, that his banana-brain director of finance had somehow drummed up some business with the British in Hong Kong and they, in turn, got the attention of their superiors in England.

Well, if nothing else, the meeting with the British could eventually be used to brag to those stingy bastards in Washington that other countries were interested in his islands, and that the U.S. wasn't dealing with a coconut brain governor on Saipan anymore.

He read the telex again and began laughing like a deranged hyena until he passed out in a heap of over relaxed muscles.

The following afternoon Puzo kept a vigil next to Vierra's telex machine. It was already past the twenty-four-hour deadline, and he was just waiting a little longer to make sure of his initial success with the bogus telex to Gustomacho.

Finally, in the early evening, Vierra tapped Puzo on the shoulder and woke him from a drowsy nap, which he was taking on the floor next to the telex machine.

Vierra said to him, "Time to lock up, Paddy. Let's go have a beer and shoot some pool."

Puzo yawned and muttered, "I quit drinking, Tak. There's no drinking on Olato due to the perverted loonies living there, and I somehow need to prepare for life without booze." He then noticed that there were still no messages from the governor. "I really think the governor fell for the phony telex."

"Probably," Vierra grunted, helping Puzo to his feet.

"Thanks, Tak, for the use of your machine. I'll see you later."

Puzo left Vierra's office and went home to get a good sleep that night in order to be ready for a full schedule the following day.

After a good night's rest, and without any rain pouring through the holes in his tin roof, he sneaked into his old PIO office an hour early to make a clandestine, long distance phone call to the information operator in Los Angeles, California.

He was eventually connected to a Hollywood talent agency that couldn't help him with any impersonators, but did give him a few numbers of other agencies that specialized in celebrity look-alikes.

Following a couple of calls with no success, he finally got lucky and struck pay dirt by contacting an agency that booked exceptionally talented look-alikes and impersonators, including Jimmy Carter, Barbra Streisand, Ronald Reagan, the Pope, Attila the Hun, and the planned choice for his caper: The Prime Minister of England, Margaret Thatcher.

After being quoted the performance fees and traveling expenses, which were quite high, he quickly calculated that the expenses and airline tickets could all be easily covered by the generous travel authorization that had already been approved by a less than coherent governor.

Next, he partly explained to the talent agent that he needed the Prime Minister of England character to portray a concerned government leader who wants to help the local governor on Saipan with his financial problems during an island festival skit. The agent didn't care what or who she had to portray, as long as she didn't break any laws and the fees were paid in advance.

Puzo guaranteed that nobody would get into trouble and that he would, indeed, pay in advance.

The agent then asked, "Where the hell is Saipan?"

Puzo explained, "Southeast of Japan about twelve hundred miles."

The agent did a back flip over the phone. "Where in the hell did you say you were calling from?!"

"Saipan. It's north of Guam about one hundred miles." He tried a different directional reference.

"Great. Now where in the hell is Guam?" the agent impatiently asked.

"Well, about four thousand miles due west of Hawaii," Puzo said, adding, "and we have regular flights here from Hawaii."

"How regular?"

"She can arrive here, do her act, and be back within three days."

The agent sighed over the phone, then gruffly said, "You pay for every day of expenses and fees in advance, and she can perform on the moon for all I care."

"You got a deal."

"Remember, it's payment in advance," the agent repeated.

"No problem. I'll mail you the money tomorrow." Puzo hung up and smiled.

He then spent the rest of the day preparing a travel authorization for a Miss Lulu Patterson, a.k.a. Prime Minister Margaret Thatcher.

The authorization was worded in such a way to make her appear as a psychologist from Los Angeles. He also typed several advance monetary requests for consultation fees, extra expenses, and several "medicinal" items, which would cover the advance payment to Hollywood and any other necessary expenditures. Furthermore, he did everything himself to prevent his secretary from getting to curious and possible exposing his plan prematurely, although he doubted very much if his temperamental secretary would have typed anything of his anyway.

The way he had it planned, he wanted to be long gone to Olato before the governor discovered what he had done and declared him shark bait.

Before leaving work that day and due to his perverse curiosity, Puzo climbed up on the roof of the civic center to visit the governor's legal counsel Fishblatt, who had decided to continuously clean and guard the statue of Gustomacho.

By guarding and cleaning the bird shit off the statue, Fishblatt was hoping that the governor would cast some favor upon him, and not hold him hostage until Uncle Sam was forced into giving Gustomacho several million in extra federal aid.

"How'ya doing, Fishblatt?" Puzo called out, after getting near to the base of the large statue, which depicted the governor in a Saipanese loin wrap with a crown on his head.

Fishblatt didn't answer him. He was on a tall ladder and just kept scrubbing the right ear of Gustomacho's statue with a toothbrush.

"I said, how'ya going, Mister Legal Counsel?" Puzo called out again.

Fishblatt finally screamed in frustration: "The ears are the most difficult to clean!"

"Is that so?" Puzo retorted.

"Of course they're difficult! What would you ever know about an attorney's work, anyway?"

Fishblatt continued poking and cleaning the statue's ear. He was wearing only a Saipanese loin wrap made out of wilted breadfruit leaves, and he was sporting a monumental sunburn thanks to the hot, tropical sun.

"Don't you think you'd better stay in the shade for a few hours?" Puzo asked, while wincing at the sight of Fishblatt's glowing sunburn.

Fishblatt looked upwards and yelled to the sky, "Can't you see that I'm busy?! Nobody knows what I have to do to be a successful attorney!" He began scrubbing even more intensely.

Puzo backed away, shaking his head. "I'll check you later, Barry, and don't forget the governor's nose"

Puzo then climbed down from the roof and headed for home, thinking maybe his departure from Saipan would be just in time before he joined Fishblatt's world of delirium, too.

The following day Puzo was doing paperwork in the old storage shack behind the governor's parking lot, and he stopped to read a short memo about the governor's nephew with the bionic balls.

The governor's nephew was back on Saipan and he was being groomed to be the new PIO. However, they were having a problem finding the jerk, who decided to become a hermit and live in the jungle caves made by the Japanese during World War II.

Puzo didn't have time to argue why he couldn't return to his old office until they found the little bastard, because he was busily assembling the necessary documents for the prime minister's trip to Saipan. He also received his much needed cash advances from the treasury office and bought a cashier's check.

Everything was ready to mail, so he crammed one round-trip airline ticket from Los Angeles to Saipan and the cashier's check for advanced fees into a large manila envelope, along with an itinerary and a list of instructions. He also added some unusual items for a special photo to be taken in Hollywood. Finally, he addressed the large envelope to "Stars Anonymous" in Hollywood, California, and left his PIO shack for the post office, hoping his grinning and drooling wouldn't give him away.

He arrived at the post office and mailed his clandestine package Special Delivery with his own money, avoiding the use of the nosey government mailroom at the governor's office.

Now it was out of his hands. If it didn't arrive on time, maybe it was a sign for him to leave Saipan quietly and let the gods decide what they wanted to do with Gustomacho and the rest of Saipan.

After mailing the package to Hollywood, he continued his plan of operation and visited the airport. There he asked Clancy Moore to reserve his scenic tour helicopter for the morning of January ninth, and he gave Moore an open purchase order and told him to bill the government whatever he wanted after the flight.

Puzo also gave Moore a hint that he was going to jerk Gustomacho's chain a little and asked him to keep it under wraps until after he had left Saipan.

Moore winked, "Hell, boy, the F.B.I. and the Russian K.G.B. couldn't drag it out of me. It's about time you had some fun with the royalty around here. Say, when you gonna cheat death and go flying again?"

Puzo scratched the top of his head. "I might take a short spin around the island on the night of the ninth."

Moore smiled. "Sounds like some sort of James Bond operation, Paddy. Whatever you do, I'll add it to the bill. The keys will be under the seat."

"Thanks, Clancy. I just hope it doesn't turn into a Woody Allen operation by the time I'm through. I'll talk to you later."

Puzo left the airport and drove back to his PIO shack.

Upon his arrival at the old shack, he decided it was time to relax. So he dug out of his storage an old hammock that he had painted to look like the American flag. He then hung it between two coconut trees next to the parking lot, in plain view of the rear window of the governor's office.

Following a quick test of the hammock's safe attachment to the trees, he gingerly climbed in and stretched out. He leaned over and noticed that Gustomacho was peering out the rear window in his direction. He waved at the governor and gave him the thumbs-up sign. He then saw the governor shake his head and throw some small objects into his mouth.

Puzo waved again, and then watched Gustomacho angrily walk away from the window.

Puzo guessed that some people just can't take a joke. Anyway, it was time to relax and call a cease fire in his plan until after the Christmas holidays.

Even a guy like Gustomacho deserved that.

31

SCREW WASHINGTON

Christmas and New Year's came and went, with the holidays keeping the members of the governor's office in a jingle bell frame of mind until early January.

Then it was back to the business of running the administration, "island style," featuring another strange Cabinet meeting in the governor's conference room.

During the meeting Gustomacho was in a very animated mood, and he looked about the room with an unusual glint emanating from his perpetual glassy eyes. His overall state of euphoria was the result of an earlier phone call he had received from his continuously drunk director of finance in Hong Kong, who had earlier convinced the governor he needed extra travel expenses to stay drunk because he had made important political progress in a stripper bar by buying drinks and lap dances for two alcoholic British guys in Hong Kong, who said they were undercover British secret service agents who could get him a personal visit with the Queen of England.

This bizarre and booze-induced information, especially about the Queen of England, had naturally fueled the governor's drug-induced mental incapacity to embrace any truth about the sheer lunacy of the Queen of England entertaining his imbecilic director of finance or about the fake telex that Puzo had sent, and Gustomacho was gullible as ever about the possible meeting with the British Prime Minister.

Naturally, the governor was already waving a British flag in his mind, when he was asked by a Cabinet member about the future financial negotiations with the United States. He brushed off the question by saying, "Who cares about those bastards in Washington." He started giggling uncontrollably. "I got other plans if the U.S. don't give me what I deserve."

Everyone in the Cabinet meeting considered the remarks made by the governor as the meanderings of a less than lucid mind, and Gustomacho could sense their growing doubt about his leadership capabilities. He just grinned at them with a 'wait and you'll see' expression.

Meanwhile, Puzo kept holding his breath and prayed that the governor continued to keep his glee under control and not mention the prime minister's meeting to anyone.

As the short meeting adjourned without any mention of the British or the prime minister, there was a final report from the hospital director that Fishblatt was now in the intensive care unit with his monumental sunburn. Everyone was asked to donate some money for Fishblatt's trip to the states for further medical treatment. But only nine dollars were collected and the CAO pocketed the money after the meeting for his personal beer expenses.

The rest of the week limped slowly by with Puzo nervously awaiting his return packet from Stars Anonymous.

Finally, he received his important delivery from Hollywood. He quickly ripped open the envelope right outside the post office and read a letter stating that the prime minister was scheduled to arrive the following Monday morning, January ninth at 8:00 a.m., which was ironically Commonwealth Day.

He sighed with relief, and then he inspected the photograph that was included in the large envelope. It was exactly what he had requested, and he felt the gods had truly blessed his remaining days on Saipan.

He immediately left for Vierra's office to send another telex to Gustomacho, which would advise the governor of the very confidential arrival of Prime Minister Thatcher on the following Monday. The telex would further advise Gustomacho that he would be called early Monday morning prior to the exact time of the meeting, and that he should still keep the meeting very top secret, so the American government wouldn't get involved and screw everything up.

After sending the telex, Puzo went to see a stateside friend from his newspaper days, who did professional printing at his home.

He gave the friend the final draft copy of a fake special proclamation he wanted printed into two official-looking identical documents. He also gave the printer the photograph he had received from Hollywood, which was to be printed into a special bulk order job. He asked his friend to keep the work a secret until the following Tuesday. The printer said his lips were sealed and the job would be completed by Sunday.

Puzo then shook his hand and said, "Great, I'll even throw in a case of cold beer for a number one job."

"Nothing but the best," bragged the printer. "See you and my cold beer on Sunday."

Before leaving, Puzo gave the printer a generous cash deposit from his office representation money and then left for lunch.

Having refused to eat spamburgers ever again, he settled for an expensive plate of cold chicken sold by an old Chamorro lady outside Gustomacho's office. The nice lady, an auntie of the governor, had decent meals but high prices because the governor always got a cut of the profits.

Puzo finished his lunch and slipped into the lobby of the governor's office, to see if any prime minister information leaked out. If it had, Guadalupe, the governor's niece and very talkative secretary, would be blabbing in high gear.

After spending some time in the governor's lobby, nothing seemed to indicate that Gustomacho had released any details about the upcoming prime minister visit, excepting a memo to all departments and media outlets that mentioned the planned Commonwealth Day activities.

The memo briefly alluded to a special announcement to be made that day concerning the Commonwealth's future due to Gustomacho's glorious leadership in the Northern Mariana Islands.

Puzo read the memo and asked Guadalupe if she knew anything about the special announcement.

"Who knows what he'll announce." she answered flippantly. "He's been giggling and laughing like an idiot all day."

"It must be the pressures of the office," Puzo said, adding, "uh, Guadalupe, could you do me a favor? Inform the governor that the stateside psychologist is due to arrive early next week for my mental evaluation for the Olato project."

"Your mental evaluation?" Guadalupe scoffed. "What about the governor's?"

"Don't worry, she plans to see the governor, too." He answered with a big smile. "I'll see you later, Guadalupe. I need to take my afternoon nap."

"Don't sleep too good," Guadalupe warned, "I think the governor plans to burn your American flag hammock, and maybe with you in it."

Puzo frowned. "Why don't you people barbeque steaks and hot dogs around here like civilized people? Someone's always threatening to barbeque me."

He then left for his parking lot office to take a wary nap in his customized stars and stripes hammock.

Later, he was getting close to being nice and comfortable in his hammock, with his mosquito netting preventing the intrusion of any flying pests. But complete relaxation eluded him. Everything about his fast approaching departure from Saipan was beginning to take its toll on his tropically-frayed nerves.

He even began to wonder if he would somehow miss the place. Furthermore, his bon voyage caper was giving him mixed emotions because for one reason, the British impersonator could be exposed during the Gustomacho meeting, and his whole plan might result in his going to jail for a long time and he didn't have any money to build houses for the Parole Board's relatives, and for the second reason, the damn plan might work and he could be shot by either the British Secret Service, or the Saipanese local police for embarrassing their respective leaders.

He thought maybe he should call off the whole affair and leave a message in Guam for the impersonator to return to Los Angeles, then he would head for Olato with his loin wrapped tail between his legs. He needed a sign.

"Excuse me, Mister Puzo?" a loud female islander voice suddenly startled him in his hammock.

"Yes." He pulled back the mosquito netting and eyeballed a large local lady from the personnel office who was holding an envelope for him. He also checked to see if she had a gasoline container with a lighter in her other hand.

"This is your lump sum payment for accrued annual leave and final pay period." She handed him an envelope and abruptly walked away.

He eagerly opened the envelope and gasped, "Holy shit! The bastards nailed me for party donations again!!"

His greatly reduced paycheck left him less than three hundred dollars out of a gross of over twenty-eight hundred.

This was definitely a sign for which course for him to take.

First, he had to quickly cash his payroll check before they put a stop-payment on it, and second, he would officially declare war on paradise.

After a restless night he woke up on Saturday morning and contemplated his final departure plans in bed.

Initially, he would call Moore to verify the Monday morning rental of his helicopter, then he would check his printer friend on the progress of his print job. After that, he wanted to check a young British stripper on island and ask her if she would make a certain early phone call for him on Monday.

The British girl was a real character, and loved to do anything for a good tip whether at work as a stripper or after hours in someone's car.

Puzo was confident that she would make the phone call, especially for a generous monetary inducement of say fifty dollars, and without having to even give Puzo a blow job, although he could use one. He had lost contact with sexy Betty Jo Hunter and he only called her on occasion to share updates on their adventures in paradise. He really missed Betty Jo, but he was doomed to a one-way ticket to Olato.

Completing his check list of things to do that Saturday, he took a partial shower under a drizzle of rusty water and left to accomplish his chores for the day.

Before he knew it, it was Sunday evening and he was sitting at his kitchen table, looking over the two official-looking proclamations that he had picked up from the printer. They were beautiful.

The two proclamations spelled out the new political agreement to be signed between the Northern Mariana Islands and England. They were so official-looking, with their fancy borders and flowing script, that Puzo almost started believing they were the real thing. His printer friend had outdone himself and rightfully earned two cases of cold beer. Moreover, the other bulk job of five thousand printed copies of a different sort of proclamation was a classic work of art, too.

Well, whether he would be locked up in the local jail, or be shot by the British Secret Service for his upcoming caper, he still felt good that everything was on schedule--even the British stripper was ready and willing to join his covert team.

His only major worry now was the arrival time of his prime minister impersonator, and he began having a major anxiety attack. So, he took two Contac capsules and washed them down with some Nyquil and was soon passed out on his couch.

Later, a short rain shower poured through his roof and got him soaking wet, but it didn't even arouse him that night. Everything he had planned now rested on the after effects of a colossal antihistamine overdose.

Luckily, a scrawny rooster that had perched on his indoor coconut tree eventually woke him the following Monday morning with a loud and lousy rendition of cock-a-doodle-doo. He was awake but already late for his morning of historical or hysterical scheduled events.

It was past seven o'clock and the prime minister's flight was scheduled to arrive at eight.

He had forty-five minutes to get ready, make a few calls, and greet the flight. He hurriedly threw everything he owned, plus his two "official" proclamations and the large box of the other printed documents in the back of his PIO pickup. He took one last look at his old shack and while wearing the same clothes he slept in, he quickly drove over to the British girl's house as fast as he could. One good thing about Saipan was that it was a small island and it didn't take very long to get anywhere.

After speeding and bouncing along the coral roadways, he was soon pounding on the British girl's front door until a sleepy-eyed, overworked stripper dressed only in a skimpy thong opened the door.

"Yes, luv," she answered in her thick British accent.

"Remember the call you're going to make this morning?" Puzo blurted out, while trying not to stare at her lovely but lop-sided tits.

"Yes, but I don't have a phone here."

"Son of a bitch." Puzo moaned. "Quick, I'll drive you over to the store down the road. You can call from there."

"You got me fifty dollars cash?" the girl asked.

Puzo blurted out: "Right in my pocket. You get it after the call."

"Okay. Give a minute to get me clothes on." She closed the door and Puzo nervously waited for her return.

A few minutes passed, which seemed like an eternity, and he could hear arguing going on in the house.

The door suddenly opened and an older Filipino contract worker stood in his underwear next to the girl, and the girl said to Puzo, "Bong Bong doesn't trust you Americans and wants the money now, and make it sixty instead of fifty." She nonchalantly pointed at her Filipino boyfriend.

"Sure, sure. Let's go!" Puzo handed over the money to Bong Bong, grabbed the girl's hand, and headed for his truck.

They were in the store in a flash, with Puzo explaining what to say to the governor on the way. He told her he was playing a secret joke on the governor and for her to imitate a British staffer and advise the governor of an important eight-thirty morning meeting with the Prime Minister of England in his office.

The stripper soon got through to the governor and told him about the special meeting with the prime minister. She nodded a few times, then hung up.

"What did he say?!" Puzo was in a slight panic.

"He said he would be anxiously waiting in his office for her highness. Now could you drive me back home before Bong Bong leaves and mails me money to his wife in the Philippines?"

It didn't take long to drop the stripper off at her house, but before she got out of the truck Puzo had thankfully kissed her and then had his truck attacked by a jealous Bong Bong who was waving a large machete. Puzo quickly stomped on the gas pedal and as he drove off his poor truck was being pelted by large rocks thrown by Bong Bong, who should have been playing professional baseball in the Philippines. Puzo was soon back at the store to make a final phone call to Gustomacho at his office.

"Good morning, governor. "Anything going on today?" Puzo checked his watch and winced at the time.

"Where in the hell are you, Puzo?! I just had the police check your house and they say it's deserted!"

"I'll be leaving Saipan soon," Puzo replied, "and Spam said I could stay at his place."

It was eight o'clock and he needed to end the call quickly and dash to the airport.

"I don't care where you stay until you leave!" Gustomacho fumed. "It's just important that you tell me about anything you know about a meeting I'm having in thirty minutes."

Puzo coughed, and played dumb. "I don't know anything, governor."

"Are you sure?" demanded the governor.

"Positive, governor."

"Well, good! Because there's going to be a big surprise for you and the rest of you smartass statesiders later. I want you in my office at eight-thirty sharp this morning, and bring your camera!"

"Sure, governor."

"And don't be late!" The governor screamed.

Puzo hung up while the governor was still screaming and glanced at his watch and ran towards his PIO truck, mumbling, "The bastard must be low on his Valium again." He frantically started his truck after a few attempts to get the lousy old truck to cooperate, and made a mad dash to the airport.

His late arrival at the terminal departure area for arriving passengers left him cold and worried. No one was in sight, and he soon found a barefoot security guard and anxiously asked about the arrival of the eight o'clock commuter flight from Guam.

"Excuse me, did you see a British-looking lady passenger get off the flight from Guam?"

The guard smiled. "Only local people come through here. Maybe she walked somewhere else." He was sitting on a bench in the departure area, dipping a green mango in some salt and eating it.

"Are you sure no one walked through here that looked important and very white?" Puzo was numb, and he didn't know what to say or do.

The guard shook his head and offered Puzo some mango.

"No thanks." Puzo then realized he should check Moore's hangar.

So he drove around to the side of the terminal and reached the gate to the hanger area for small commuter planes and helicopters, hoping he could see Moore's helicopter fired up with his impersonator waiting inside.

After passing through the broken security gate, he reached a deserted area outside the helicopter hangar with a closed sign on the door of Moore's office. He pounded on the truck's broken and silent horn to no avail, and then he realized the immense stupidity of his impulsive and outlandish actions.

Puzo just sat in his PIO truck, feeling real rotten. He let out a deep sigh and then slowly ripped off the sample of the special bulk printed proclamation, which was taped to the top of the large box in his truck and he tore it in half.

Damn.

32

THE PRIME MINISTER'S BIG TITS

"Hey, numb-nuts!"

The loud sarcastic yell startled the hell out of Puzo, who was still sitting forlornly in his truck outside of Moore's hangar, staring at the ripped halves of the printed document in his hands. He immediately looked up and out his side window with a surprised expression on his face.

"Yeah, you!" shouted Moore, who was standing about ten feet away from the driver's side of the truck, hands on his hips.

He was wearing shorts, tank top, old tennis shoes, a cowboy hat, and a big shit-eating grin on his face. He walked over to the side window of the truck, peered in at the ripped document Puzo had in his hand, and grabbed it.

He pieced the two halves back together, gave it a thorough glance, laughed, and gave it back to a speechless Puzo. He then put his hands on the door and leaned forward a bit. "You better check out the prime minister before she meets Governor Goofball."

Puzo lit up. "What are you talking about?! She did make it! She's here!"

Moore scratched his head. "I think it's your prime minister, or Lulu, sitting in my chopper in that hangar over there." He had pointed at his closed hangar, continuing, "You were late, and this dead ringer for Margaret Thatcher came walking by the opened hangar, looking real lost. She asked me if I was a Mister Puzo, and where was the governor's office. Well, bingo, I figure she was your special charter flight and I hustled her into my hangar and closed the doors, you know, to keeps things quiet until you got here. Now, Paddy, I think it's time to kick some Gustomacho ass!"

Puzo numbly asked again, "She's really here?"

Moore laughed, "C'mon, she's ready to go with one of my mechanics dressed as her military escort. He's wearing an old uniform of mine and wants to join in on the fun. He also swore to keep his mouth shut. Anyway, we went over your script that you mailed her and she's going to make Gustomacho think he's going to get a duplicate key to the British Crown Jewels." He then opened Puzo's truck door and continued, "Shall we?"

"You bet your ass, Clancy. She can still make the eight-thirty meeting and be only a few minutes late."

After grabbing the two "official" proclamations, Puzo got out of his truck and followed Moore over to the hangar doors.

Once there they both swung open the two large doors and Puzo stared at Moore's helicopter.

In it was a somewhat tired-looking, but sprightly, gigantic-breasted prime minister, leaning out the side door of Moore's Bell Ranger and waving at him.

"Mister Puzo, I presume." she called out.

He swiftly walked towards her, gushing, "Yes, Miss Patterson, but now madam prime minister. Are you ready to meet our governor and give him the royal treatment?"

"Piece of cake, ducky. I'll make him believe he'll be the next King of England." She shook Puzo's hand while the helicopter jerked forward.

Moore was already pulling out the helicopter with the help of his mechanic, as Puzo walked along the side of the moving craft. Puzo kept talking about the script to the impersonator: "You'll be dropped off in the governor's back parking lot and the governor will let you in the back door for your meeting." He handed her the two proclamations that he had stuck in a fancy folder and continued, "You and the governor sign these and take one with you when you leave. Give it to Clancy and ask him to leave it for me in his airplane." She kept nodding her head, as Puzo added, "Have a quick meeting, then Clancy will fly you to Guam and you'll be gone before anyone else realizes that Gustomacho just sold these islands to a nice lady from Hollywood."

The helicopter was now in position and the dressed-up military mechanic joined the prime minister in the rear compartment.

Moore prepared for take-off and Puzo closed the door on the prime minister's side. He then moved up to where he could speak to Moore through a side window. "Drop these guys off in the governor's rear parking lot and have your mechanic escort her to the back door and wait outside. After she's finished with her meeting, you fly her over to Guam. I don't want Gustomacho to find out about my little joke until I'm halfway to Olato, okay?"

"Gotcha!" Moore shouted over the starting whine of his engine. "Now move your ass so we can get this show on the road."

Puzo bent over and began backing away from the helicopter as Moore shouted right before lifting off, "And close my hangar doors after we leave, por favor!"

Puzo nodded yes and waved at everyone, and then the helicopter nosed down a little and headed straight for Gustomacho's office.

It was just after eight-thirty in the morning and sitting anxiously in his office, Gustomacho chewed on his finger nails and stared at a large bottle of Darvon tranquilizers that he had just received from the prison supervisor that morning.

Suddenly, a loud commotion brought the governor to his feet and he stumbled over to his rear window.

Moore's helicopter had made a perfect landing in an empty parking area behind the governor's office, and the governor finally caught a glimpse of the Prime Minister of England inside the helicopter, waving and smiling in his direction.

Moore's mechanic scrambled around the helicopter and the governor watched him in his official looking uniform standing at attention in front of the prime minister's helicopter door. The helicopter's blade wash then blew the mechanic's army hat into the boonies and the mechanic just shrugged.

Meanwhile, the CAO rushed into the governor's office to look at the sight outside the window with the governor.

Everyone else in the governor's office had the day off and they were planning to enjoy Commonwealth Day, but Gustomacho had asked the CAO to stand by in his office for an important meeting.

"This is a big important meeting that I want kept a big secret for now," boasted the governor to the CAO, adding, "Quick, Roque, go open the back door for my special guest, the Prime Minister Margie Thatchy of England." The drug-impaired governor had butchered the real name for Prime Minister Margaret Thatcher.

The CAO hurriedly opened the rear door and watched the prime minister climb out of the helicopter, which was not that far away. Because of the blade wash, she held onto her hat and was assisted out of the helicopter by the hatless military escort.

Not to arouse suspicion over the mechanic's U.S. army uniform, she asked the mechanic to wait by the helicopter and she proceeded alone, walking briskly by a speechless and dazed CAO, who couldn't have distinguished the difference between a U.S. military uniform and a L.A. Laker's cheerleader's outfit at the time.

The CAO stayed at the opened door in a continued daze, even after the prime minister was inside the door of the governor's office, clutching a folder with official documents inside. The CAO numbly watched her while paper trash and various pieces of debris blew in because of Moore's whirling helicopter blades, which were starting to shut down.

"Close the damn door!" Gustomacho screamed, and then he switched moods, saying in sugary tones to the prime minister with outstretched arms, "Welcome, welcome! Welcome to our beautiful and friendly islands, Miss Prime Minister Margie Thatchy!"

The CAO finally stepped inside and closed the door behind him while continually gawking at the prime minister, who was standing just inside the door.

The prime minister had finally let go of her hat after the door was closed, and humorously ignored being called Prime Minister Margie Thatchy, since she really didn't care what she was called as long as the proclamation caper was a success. She then spoke in a perfect British accent. "Why thank you, governor, for your kind greeting. It's a supreme pleasure to visit your quaint little island."

The governor nervously motioned for his stupefied CAO to get a chair for the prime minister, while the CAO kept leering at her big tits.

"Please relax, Miss Prime Minister Margie Thatchy," the governor insisted, as the CAO awkwardly placed a chair right behind where she was standing near the door.

"No, stupid! Over here by my desk!" Gustomacho shouted.

The governor noticed that the prime minister thought she was the target of his latest outburst, and he said, "Excuse me, Miss Prime Minister Margie Thatchy, I didn't mean you."

She smiled and walked over to where the CAO had moved the chair by the governor's desk, and sat down saying, "Why thank you, governor."

The governor then naively asked, "Is it okay I call you just Margie, and can we start discussing the money, I mean, the proclamation agreement about our partnership and of course the money?"

The prime minister chuckled, saying, "Fine, fine," and began her speech about a generous financial aid package with the signing of a special proclamation signifying their new political and economic relationship.

During her convincing speech, Gustomacho began leaping in mental reverie. He then noticed the CAO's continued weird behavior and the governor suddenly remembered that he wanted Puzo and his camera. So, Gustomacho ordered the CAO to find Puzo and get him here immediately, in order to witness the historical prime minister's visit and the millions and millions Gustomacho would soon receive.

The CAO left and found Puzo bursting into the lobby after he had rushed from the airport. The CAO grabbed Puzo and whispered in a frenzied voice in his ear: "The governor wants some prime Margie pictures right away and keep this big secret."

Puzo nodded and rushed over to his PIO shack for his camera and within minutes he was in the governor's office and saw Gustomacho eagerly shaking hands with the prime minister and then hugging her against her enormous tits, while she was trying to break free of his maniacal grip.

"Hurry, get some damn pictures!" Gustomacho shouted in the near proximity of the prime minister's left ear. He then smiled meekly at the prime minister. "Excuse me, Margie, I didn't mean to yell again."

"That's quite alright, governor," she replied with her ear still ringing. "But please, let's sign our proclamations because I'm on a very tight schedule."

"Of course, of course!" agreed the governor with a crazed smile, as the prime minister opened her folder and placed the two proclamations on his desk.

They signed the documents, each keeping one, and had their picture taken several times by Puzo, who murmured to himself, "Margie?"

"Please, governor," she finally said after several more pictures, "I must be going. And remember to keep our new agreement confidential for one more day, so I may properly notify my Queen in England."

"Of course, of course!" the governor slurred, after he had earlier popped a handful of Darvon in his mouth while the prime minister was busy signing the two proclamations.

The governor was so drugged now that he couldn't tell the difference between his current meeting with "Margie" and an official visit by the Royal Queen Mother of Mars.

After the prime minister shook everyone's hand, including a grinning Puzo who whispered to her: "Margie?" The prime minister quickly stifled a laugh and made a hasty exit out the rear door, with the CAO attending the door and saluting her several times. Her military escort quickly threw his can of beer into the bushes and helped her into the helicopter.

Moore had already begun his take-off sequence and they were soon up and away. And as Moore's old Bell Ranger did a little dipsy-do and headed south for Guam, Puzo stood gazing out the governor's rear window and mumbled out loud, "Damn, I don't believe it really happened."

"You better believe it!" Gustomacho shouted with glee. "And shut that stupid door!" He screamed at his CAO, as the debris kept swirling around the governor's office from Moore's accelerated departure.

The CAO closed the door and stood with his mouth open with bugged-out eyes, while the delirious Gustomacho instructed the CAO to organize a big press conference for the next day at lunch time, and not to tell anyone what the conference would be all about.

The CAO just kept nodding and the governor added, "Invite the stupid U.S. State Department, too, so I can give them a thousand copies of the proclamation I just signed." He took a deep breath, nearly fainted, and turned to Puzo. "I want you to keep quiet, too, so no one messes up my big deal."

"Sure, governor, my lips are sealed, and governor, you think it's wise to have the press conference during lunch again?" Puzo further asked, "And do you mind if I leave for my trip to Olato earlier than I planned?"

"You can leave right now for all I care," the governor snorted, continuing, "I just wanted you to see how we islanders can make deals without you stupid Americans being involved, and I'm ordering all statesiders and the media can't eat lunch anymore, so there!"

The governor looked proudly at the proclamation in his hand. "Puzo, one more thing before you go, when's that psychologist coming with the special medical surprises for me?"

Puzo was nodding his head and quipped, "Early tomorrow morning, I think."

"Good, good. That's all, Puzo. Have a nice stay on Olato."

The stunned CAO was still standing and looking out the rear window while scratching his ass. The governor went over to shake the CAO out of his stupor, 'What's wrong with you, Roque, you never acted this crazy before!"

As for Puzo, he quickly walked to the front door of the office, turned, and loudly said, "So long, Reggie."

The governor angrily looked around, but Puzo had already left his office. The governor's face then began to twitch uncontrollably, and he immediately grabbed his bottle of Darvon pills while kicking a trash can towards Puzo's departing direction.

After pocketing the film for later laughs and tossing his camera into his old PIO office, Puzo went back to the governor's office and called Spam on the secretary's phone and asked if Spam could pick him up at the civic center.

Spam said no problem, and thirty minutes later they had packed Puzo's meager belongings in a well-oiled 1964 Cadillac and were headed for Spam's Bar.

"I thought you were supposed to work until Friday?" Spam asked as they drove along Beach Road.

"Gustomacho gave me an early release and I'm leaving for Olato on the midnight connecting flight before all hell breaks loose on my head," Puzo answered.

Spam smiled at Puzo. "In that case, you might as well spend your last day at my place, and you can later spend your last payday in my bar. And what hell will be breaking loose on your head?"

Puzo just nodded at Spam and smiled.

Spam's Bar was real busy that night with the hot topic of discussion being the wild remarks Governor Gustomacho had earlier made during his Commonwealth Day speech in the late afternoon. The governor had taken another healthy dose of Darvon plus a Valium chaser and despite promising the "prime minister" to not reveal the proclamation agreement until the following day, he gave a rambling and incoherent speech about a newly-proclaimed and officially signed agreement that he finally announced, screaming: "SPECIAL NO MORE U.S. COMMONWEALTH OF THE NORTHERN MARIANA ISLANDS!!" He then proceeded to issue executive orders that all U.S. statesiders are now foreigners on Saipan and to leave his islands immediately. The governor finally started laughing hysterically and then passed out and fell from the podium and on top of a seated and still recuperating Lt. Governor Flores, who screamed again for more morphine.

The bar patrons were mostly in humorous disbelief of the governor's earlier ramblings but slightly worried that maybe crazy Gustomacho might have just pulled off an agreement ending the U.S. partnership with the Northern Mariana Islands. Puzo remained quiet during the debate, not wanting to reveal anything until he was safe on Olato and far away from the drug-fueled revenge and possible homicidal intentions of the Honorable Regino J. Gustomacho.

At half-past ten that night, Puzo finally asked Spam if he could drop him off at the airport. He was eager to leave as some bar patrons were getting real drunk and rowdy about the Gustomacho rumors flying around and some stateside people were even joking about making phone calls to Washington, D.C.!

So, after serving another round of drinks and getting Rosey to cover for him, Spam grabbed his car keys and headed out the door with Puzo.

Twenty minutes later, Puzo was retrieving his belongings and the large box from the trunk of Spam's car at the airport. He placed his stuff in a luggage cart and went around to the driver's side of the car to shake Spam's hand goodbye.

"Well, so long, Spam. It's been interesting to say the least. And say goodbye to Betty Jo for me and tell Rosey thanks for covering the bar for you."

"Will do, and Paddy, I think you've done okay here."

"I don't know," Puzo replied. "Look at me. I've been lost in paradise and now I'm headed to a tiny atoll for two long years that has four certified crazies running around naked all day!"

"I know, Paddy. But later you got big plans with NASA, right?"

"I guess so. Yeah, I'll see you on the moon someday." Puzo gave Spam another handshake and began walking towards his luggage cart.

"Hey, Mister Puzo!" Spam called out.

Puzo turned around.

"We're already on the moon!" Spam let out a Confederate war whoop and then drove away.

Puzo just stood still, watching down the airport road where Spam and his Caddy had eventually disappeared. He finally sighed, and started pushing his luggage cart to the airport ticket counter.

Once there he checked in his two small bags, leaving the large box in the cart. He had a little over an hour before his flight and he anxiously looked forward to his last farewell gesture concerning his stay on Saipan.

Without deliberating on any last minute indecisions about his farewell gesture, he grabbed the luggage cart and headed for Moore's Cessna 172.

It didn't take too long to load the big box into the front seat of the Cessna and do his pre-flight, after which he got clearance from a sleepy controller in the airport control center, and then he proceeded to taxi out to the runway.

He soon made a short take-off run, gained altitude, and immediately set a course for the governor's office. Along the way, he grinned at the signed "official" proclamation, which Moore had left in the plane for his Saipan scrapbook, and then Puzo gazed at the other unfolded proclamation that he had scotch-taped back together and had earlier stuck in his pants pocket.

Within a few minutes, he realized he needed to drop his altitude and lower his flaps for a very slow, low-level bombing run. He was nearing the target area and he secured the passenger door into an opened position. Next, he pulled off the top of the box and he was slightly buffeted by some wind blowing into the cockpit as he positioned the box right next to the door opening.

It was time.

Suddenly the hot and humid Saipan night was filled with the flapping and swirling of thousands of pieces of nicely printed documents.

At twenty minutes past midnight, Puzo was flying to Guam aboard a commercial flight that would connect him on an early morning flight to Yap Island. After which, he would be stuck on a long boat ride to isolated Olato, all compliments of NASA.

Saipan was history. And all he had to currently show for his chaotic stay on Saipan was a few dollars in his pockets, although NASA was providing him with free "room and board" on Olato. But the bastard feds were keeping his pay until he completed his two-year study and reported his confidential findings. He also had two documents resting in his hands.

Puzo just stared at the documents with a wry smile on his face. One document was the "official" proclamation that the Prime Minister had previously signed with the governor. The second document was the taped together sample of the "unofficial" proclamation that had been earlier printed into five thousand copies, which were now quietly resting around the governor's office in the middle of the night.

Later that morning, Gustomacho was seen frantically running around and ripping up all the copies of an "unofficial" proclamation that had been deposited all over the governor's office complex. He was joined by several other laughing workers and a few snickering statesiders. Gustomacho was attempting to destroy all the evidence of his personal Waterloo, while gobbling Darvon pills like they were cherry gumdrops.

Pictured in the nicely bordered and professionally printed "unofficial" proclamations, which had earlier been ceremoniously dumped all over the governor's office area during a clandestine night raid by a partly deranged former PIO, was the fake Prime Minister of England posing in a Hollywood photo studio. She was in front of some imitation coconut trees and seductively dressed in only a skimpy Saipanese loin wrap. She had her arms outstretched with her big red lips smooched up and lastly, she had a narrow sign hanging onto the very protruding nipples of her gigantic bare tits that read:

---ROYAL PROCLAMATION---
I Love You, Reggie!

EPILOGUE

Dear Ralph,

How's everything on Saipan? You wouldn't believe what's happened to me. After spending a few months on Olato, I burned down the wooden shack that I had shared with a Peace Corps freak and three island loonies because the fire made a much needed DISTRESS signal to a passing Korean freighter. Luckily, the freighter stopped to investigate and I swam out to the ship and finally ended up in the Philippines with the King of Thieves, President Ferdinand Marcos!

After an interesting month in Manila working as a hotel bar helper, my Filipino-American boss told me that both the CIA and NASA had inquired about my whereabouts at his friend's nearby bar. Apparently, the CIA and NASA tracked me down to the Philippines and still want my American top secrets about outer space survival and living with aliens on Olato. Are they fucking serious?!

Anyway, I immediately fled Manila and I'm now hiding out on Mindoro Island. I got a job as a slop handler at a large piggery and I don't think I'll ever eat bacon again after seeing and smelling the way these pigs live. PLEASE don't tell anyone I'm in Mindoro and destroy this letter after you've read it. I know this thing isn't over yet, and whatever you do, don't ever eat Mindoro bacon!!

Paddy

(The following U.S. postal notice was stamped at the bottom of the letter before it was delivered to Ralph Brubaker.)

ATTENTION**ATTENTION
THIS LETTER WAS OPENED FOR REASONS
OF NATIONAL SECURITY AND FOR ONE
VERY DISTURBED U.S. CONGRESSMAN.
HAVE A NICE DAY.
***

---

www.ingramcontent.com/pod-product-compliance
Lightning Source LLC
Chambersburg PA
CBHW022045020426
42335CB00012B/557